Palgrave Macmillan Studies in Banking and Financial Institutions
Series Standing Order ISBN 1–4039–4872–0

You can receive future titles in this series as they are published by placing a standing order. Please contact your bookseller or, in case of difficulty, write to us at the address below with your name and address, the title of the series and the ISBN quoted above.

Customer Services Department, Macmillan Distribution Ltd, Houndmills, Basingstoke, Hampshire RG21 6XS, England

CEOs as Leaders and Strategy Designers

Explaining the Success of Spanish Banks

Kimio Kase
IESE Business School, Spain

and

Tanguy Jacopin
IESE Business School, Spain
CIFF Fundación, Spain

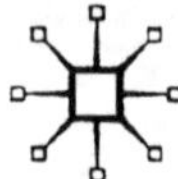

First published in 2008 by
PALGRAVE MACMILLAN
Houndmills, Basingstoke, Hampshire RG21 6XS and
175 Fifth Avenue, New York, N.Y. 10010
Companies and representatives throughout the world.

PALGRAVE MACMILLAN is the global academic imprint of the Palgrave Macmillan division of St. Martin's Press, LLC and of Palgrave Macmillan Ltd. Macmillan® is a registered trademark in the United States, United Kingdom and other countries. Palgrave is a registered trademark in the European Union and other countries.

ISBN-13: 978–0–230–54295–2 hardback
ISBN-10: 0–230–54295–6 hardback

This book is printed on paper suitable for recycling and made from fully managed and sustained forest sources. Logging, pulping and manufacturing processes are expected to conform to the environmental regulations of the country of origin.

A catalogue record for this book is available from the British Library.

A catalog record for this book is available from the Library of Congress.

10 9 8 7 6 5 4 3 2 1
17 16 15 14 13 12 11 10 09 08

Printed and bound in Great Britain by
CPI Antony Rowe, Chippenham and Eastbourne

To Mercedes and my mother, and in loving memory of Gabriel and my father

To Maite and my parents, Josiane and Louis, for their love and support

Contents

List of Tables

List of Figures

Acknowledgements

It was unthinkable twenty or thirty years ago that the benchmark for operational efficiency would be provided by Spanish banks; particularly when Japan and France, the authors' home countries, used to boast some of the world's outstanding financial institutions.

This piqued our interest in the emergence of Spanish banks as world-class competitors and in why they have done so well, especially when compared to the relatively poor achievement of Japanese and French banks. We turned our attention to the speeches of Spanish banks' top executives and were surprised to find that they relentlessly hammered home the need to focus on day-to-day management and cash-flow generation, exhibiting a management approach identified as 'Profit Arithmetic' by one of the authors in his previous study of four excellent CEOs (Chief Executive Officers).

In conducting this research, special thanks are owed to the many bank executives and specialists whose names we are unable to mention here, due to reasons of confidentiality.

We owe our gratitude to a number of top level executives including Juan Arena and Pedro Luis Uriarte (who spent a long working session with us, recounting his management experience and approach as well as taking the time to review our theoretical framework).

Our most heart-felt thanks are especially addressed to Professor Juan Antonio Palacios of IESE Business School whose ideas took shape as Chapter 2 of this book.

Special recognition is also deserved for the support provided by IESE Business School's Anselmo Rubiralta Centre for Globalization and Strategy for carrying out this research.

We are indebted to Katie Carr and Keith Juden, two British communication specialists, who conscientiously reviewed, corrected and marvellously improved our draft. Our thanks likewise go to Dr Pilar García-Lombardía, Carlos Gómez Muñoz, Juan Carlos Gómez, Alfonso Camaño and Antonio Monzón for their input on the Spanish banking industry.

While every effort has been made to ensure the accuracy of the text, any inexactitude should be entirely attributed to the authors.

KIMIO KASE
TANGUY JACOPIN

Foreword

I must confess that writing the prologue to this book is a great pleasure for me. Firstly, I am grateful that professionals as prestigious as the authors consider it appropriate to write a book explaining the great success of the Spanish banking sector. Secondly, I am delighted to be able to lend my support to the theories in this book regarding the reasons for this success.

To summarize these theories, albeit from my own personal viewpoint, the success of Spanish banks is based on three essential factors:

1) An appropriate regulatory framework which promotes and drives competition at the same time as firmly monitoring the solvency and solidity of the banks.
2) Excellent management teams with extensive experience and extraordinary training.
3) A strategy based on the relentless search for short-term, recurring profit as the best means to ensure the long-term, sustainable value creation for shareholders; the future being merely an extension of the day-to-day task of generating results.

The combination of these factors has given rise to a unique banking business model, the traits of which are:

- Continuous emphasis on operational efficiency and cost containment.
- The intensive and strategic use of information technology.
- Client-focus.

Banks have been able simultaneously assess the importance of size and growth in the global economy, as well as incorporate it into their strategy, not as an aim in itself, but rather as a way of meeting profitability and efficiency targets.

I would like to highlight the perfect fit of the strategy and business model with the personality of the leaders and management teams at these banks. Indeed, it could not be any other way because the strategy and business models have been designed and day after day meticulously put into practice by these leaders. This is neither an accident nor the product of academic speculation; rather it is the result of long and extensive experience at the helm of the banks.

I would like to add two further comments.

The authors neatly summarise the historical transition of the Spanish banking system, from one of the most over-regulated and inefficient in Europe in the early 1980s to its current status as one of the most competitive and profitable banking systems in the world. My first comment is on the importance of Spain's accession to the European Economic Community in 1986 and Economic and Monetary Union in 1999 played in this process. Both facts are at the root of the transformation of the financial system's regulatory framework, and the change in the way economic policy is made in our country. The Spanish banks quickly grasped the magnitude of the challenges and opportunities that this created.

My second comment is on the long cycle of prosperity which the Spanish economy has been enjoying since the mid-nineties. Without doubt, this has supported banking activities and constitutes a basic factor in the explanation of the excellent results achieved by the banks. At the same time, it should be highlighted that the efficiency, competitiveness and solidity of the banking system has been equally influential in fostering and maintaining the strength of the economy.

It only remains for me to congratulate, firstly, the authors on their work and, secondly and above all, the readers who have the good fortune of losing themselves inside the pages and reflections of this book.

MIGUEL MARTÍN FERNÁNDEZ
President
Asociación Española de Banca (AEB)

1
Introduction and Overview of Book

Spain's economy, with its nominal 2005 Gross Domestic Product (GDP) estimated at US$1,126 billion, is ranked 9th in the world; dwarfed by the United States at US$12,456 billion, Japan at US$4,567 billion and Germany at US$2,795 billion, according to the International Monetary Fund[1] (IMF).

Despite her relatively small size, Spain now boasts world-class business entities such as Telefónica, the telecoms giant, Endesa, the electricity utility company, and Inditex, the clothes manufacturer responsible for global brands such as Zara. But in the forefront of Spain's multinational companies (MNCs) are Santander and BBVA, both banking giants.

> Spain's Banco Santander Central Hispano and BBVA have become two of the largest banks in Europe. Now larger than German, French and Dutch institutions, the Spanish banks are competing with the powerful institutions of Britain, much like the fleets of Spanish galleons that competed against the English in the sixteenth century. (Universia-Knowledge@Wharton: 2005)

As shown in Table 1.1, in terms of assets Santander, including Banesto, was the 13th largest bank in the world with BBVA at 38th in 2006. They are also outstanding in 'value creation'[2] for their shareholders, as set out in Table 1.2.

In what Fernández and Carabias (2002; 2006; 2007) call 'value created for shareholders', Santander and BBVA are particularly outstanding, though all of the banks showed excellent results where the revaluation of euros invested in these banks in 1991 is concerned (Fernández & Carabias, 2007: 3). As a matter of fact one euro invested in

Table 1.1 *Ranking of world banks in terms of assets*

Current rank	Previous rank	Bank	Assets US$m	+ or 2 (local curr)	Capital US$m	Balance sheet
1	(1)	Barclays PLC, London, UK	*1,586,879	71.76%	2,786.27	31.12.05
2	(2)	UBS AG, ZGrich, Switzerland	*1,563,282	18.60%	660.9	31.12.05
3	(4)	BNP Paribas SA, Paris, France	*1,483,934	38.87%	11,442.56	31.12.05
4	(3)	The Royal Bank of Scotland Group plc, Edinburgh, UK	*1,300,124	29.80%	9,409.44	31.12.05
5	(6)	Crˇdit Agricole SA, Paris, France	*1,251,997	30.19%	20,665.25	31.12.05
6	(5)	Deutsche Bank AG, Frankfurt am Main, Germany	*1,170,277	18.10%	1,674.92	31.12.05
7	(7)	Bank of America NA, Charlotte, USA	*1,082,243	–	2,836.40	31.12.05
8	(8)	ABN AMRO Holding NV, Amsterdam, Netherlands	*1,038,929	21.08%	1,260.91	31.12.05
9	(9)	Credit Suisse Group, Z_rich, Switzerland	*1,016,050	22.91%	473.48	31.12.05
10	(10)	JPMorgan Chase Bank National Association, New York	*1,013,985	4.82%	1,785.00	31.12.05
11	(–)	Sociˇtˇ Gˇnˇrale, Paris La Dˇfense, France	*1,000,728	–	640.48	31.12.05

12	(11)	ING Bank NV, Amsterdam, Netherlands	*983,764	34.51%	619.25	31.12.05
13	(−)	Banco Santander Central Hispano SA, Santander, Spain	*954,361	–	3,688.54	31.12.05
14	(12)	UniCredito Italiano SpA, Milan, Italy	*928,285	–	5,704.46	31.12.05
15	(13)	Sumitomo Mitsui Banking Corporation, Tokyo, Japan	*916,710	−2.37%	6,253.69	31.03.05
16	(14)	The Bank of Tokyo-Mitsubishi UFJ Ltd, Tokyo, Japan	*865,663	8.22%	9,375.77	31.03.05
17	(17)	Caisse Nationale des Caisses d'Epargne et de Prevoy	*739,311	42.88%	8,014.14	31.12.04
18	(18)	Citibank NA, New York, USA	*706,497	1.72%	751	31.12.05
19	(22)	Fortis Bank NV/SA, Brussels, Belgium	*700,515	22.32%	3,670.49	31.12.05
20	(19)	Industrial & Commercial Bank of China Limited, Beijing, China	675,395	6.68%	19,412.07	31.12.04
21	(20)	HSBC Bank plc, London, UK	*663,385	32.12%	1,368.24	31.12.05
22	(21)	Mizuho Bank Ltd, Tokyo, Japan	663,014	0.96%	6,112.76	31.03.05

Continued

Table 1.1 Continued

Current rank	Previous rank	Bank	Assets US$m	+ or 2 (local curr)	Capital US$m	Balance sheet
23	(23)	Rabobank Nederland, Utrecht, Netherlands	*597,115	4.69%	–	31.12.05
24	(32)	Agricultural Bank of China, Beijing, China	*591,190	18.87%	–	31.12.05
25	(24)	Bank of Scotland, Edinburgh, UK	*586,543	25.23%	1,555.00	31.12.04
26	(25)	The Norinchukin Bank, Tokyo, Japan	*582,567	0.47%	11,520.19	31.03.05
27	(26)	Bayerische Hypo-und Vereinsbank AG, Munich, Germany	*582,122	5.59%	2,656.29	31.12.05
28	(–)	Calyon, Paris La D˘fense, France	*567,724	–	7,876.86	31.12.05
29	(27)	Dresdner Bank Group, Frankfurt am Main, Germany	*544,199	–	1,772.82	31.12.05
30	(28)	Lloyds TSB Group plc, London, UK	*531,767	8.91%	2,437.77	31.12.05
31	(29)	Mizuho Corporate Bank Ltd, Tokyo, Japan	526,193	−6.62%	10,071.61	31.03.05
32	(30)	Commerzbank AG, Frankfurt am Main, Germany	*524,724	4.70%	2,011.09	31.12.05

33	(31)	Bank of China Limited, Beijing, China	*515,972	7.30%	22,520.39	31.12.04
34	(37)	Landesbank Baden-Wp rttemberg, Stuttgart, Germany DZ BANK AG Deutsche Zentral-	*477,606	3.66%	5,855.49	31.12.05
35	(33)	Genossenschaftsbank, Frankfurt am Main, Germany	*473,730	12.74%	3,395.85	31.12.05
36	(34)	Wachovia Bank NA, Charlotte, USA	*472,143	–	455	31.12.05
37	(35)	China Construction Bank Corporation, Beijing, China	471,792	9.86%	23,467.65	31.12.04
38	(36)	Banco Bilbao Vizcaya Argentaria SA, Madrid, Spain	*462,833	19.11%	1,959.80	31.12.05
39	(39)	National Westminster Bank Plc, London, UK	*447,387	32.14%	2,880.69	31.12.05
40	(41)	Wells Fargo Bank NA, San Francisco, USA	*403,258	–	520	31.12.05
41	(38)	Bayerische Landesbank, Munich, Germany	*402,046	2.33%	5,775.85	31.12.05
42	(42)	Kreditanstalt fz r Wiederaufbau (KfW), Frankfurt am Main, Germany	401,411	3.81%	3,892.43	31.12.05

Continued

Table 1.1 Continued

Current rank	Previous rank	Bank	Assets US$m	+ or 2 (local curr)	Capital US$m	Balance Sheet
43	(43)	Royal Bank of Canada, Montr˘al, Canada	*398,981	10.16%	6,687.63	31.10.05
44	(44)	Danske Bank A/S, Copenhagen, Denmark	*384,604	18.49%	11,775.60	31.12.05
45	(45)	Nordea Group, Stockholm, Sweden	*383,993	16.24%	1,264.45	31.12.05
46	(49)	Abbey National plc, London, UK	*355,423	12.07%	254.08	31.12.05
47	(46)	Banque F˘d˘rative du Cr˘dit Mutuel, Strasbourg, France	*352,516	15.66%	1,535.74	31.12.05
48	(48)	The Hongkong and Shanghai Banking Corporation Limited, Hong Kong, Hong Kong	*344,687	7.47%	2,901.14	31.12.05
49	(51)	Banca Intesa SpA, Milan, Italy	*322,641	−0.94%	4,241.57	31.12.05
50	(52)	National Australia Bank Ltd, Melbourne, Australia	*320,418	2.01%	8,771.29	30.09.05

* Figures are consolidated: These bank rankings are compiled from balance sheet information included on Bankersalmanac.com available at 26th July 2006.
(*) As of 31st Decemeber 2005.

Source: BankersAlmaac http://www.bankersalmanac.com/addcon/infobank/wldrank.aspx

Table 1.2 Value creation by Grupo Santander, BBVA, Popular and Bankinter

	Market cap increase (*)	Shareholders' value increase (*)	Value created for shareholders (*)
Grupo Santander	85,770	53,575	20,704
BBVA	61,039	47,489	25,442
Banco Popular	14,881	3,866	13,426
Bankínter	17,306	5,131	3,765

(*) In millions of euros between 1991 and 2006.

Source: Fernández and Carabias (2007: 3).

Santander, BBVA, Popular, and Bankinter in 1991 would have been worth €13.16, €15.57, €14.05 and €12.17 in 2006.

Bc that as it may, in this book we centre our attention only on Santander and BBVA, for two main reasons. Firstly, their outstanding value creation for shareholders is a phenomenon meriting close scrutiny. Secondly, they championed the modernization of the Spanish banking system in the 1980s, brought about by three main factors: the pressure of their national environment, Spain's entrance into the EEC (European Economic Community), and finally the necessity to reach critical size (an explanation of the environmental and regulatory development will be further explored in Chapter 2). Therefore, the focus of this book is on how these two banks in particular outperform the Spanish financial system and their European competitors.

Research questions

As an explanation of the successful modernization and globalization of the Spanish banks, we put forward the posit that Spanish banks work on an excellent business model, principally focused on operational efficiency in pursuit of cash flow generation.

The model's characteristics coincide with the Profit Arithmetic or 'PA' approach (Kase, Sáez-Martínez and Riquelme, 2005). In their study of outstanding business leaders, these researchers identified two different strategic models: long-term, corporate culture-biased Proto-image of the Firm ('PIF') and short-term, cash-generation-focused Profit Arithmetic ('PA').

Business model and its historical background

This book attempts to provide data to confirm and information to explain this posit, and to expound on the systemic working of the model predicated on the three components, namely:

1) the bias for growth in retail banking;
2) the development of Information Technology;
3) a constant improvement of operational efficiency.

By combining these components, the two main banks of Spain improved their efficiency ratio in such a proportion that Spanish banks are currently the most efficient banks in Europe.

The model itself (with some variations from one bank to another) is a product of the evolution of the regulatory environment. Accordingly, we will first analyse some of the historical factors that influenced the evolution of the Spanish banking industry.

Historical evolution of regulatory environment

Even though Spanish banks and savings banks (*cajas de ahorros*)[3] were aided by the Bank of Spain to develop their successful banking model, the main players such as Santander and BBVA have still had to cope with some adverse conditions. Accordingly, the Spanish financial system will be analysed from a macro and *meso* (intermediate between macro and micro levels) viewpoint.

The process of bank deregulation in Spain was begun in 1962 with a law liberalizing some interest rates, which was complemented with another law in 1971 lifting the barriers to opening new branches. In 1977 the arrival of foreign banks became possible, and in 1987 all interest rates and commissions were liberalized.

This deregulation led to a bank crisis spanning the period between 1978 and 1985. The first to fail was Banco de Navarra in 1978. In anticipation of further failures the government created the *Fondo de Garantía de Depósitos* (FGD) similar to the US's Federal Deposit Insurance (FDI) in order to be able to rescue and restructure failing banks before selling them.

Out of the seven larger banks, three had serious difficulties (Banesto, Banco Central and Banco Hispano) when they were asked by the monetary authorities to take over and integrate other banks in bankruptcy. For instance, Banesto took charge of three banks between 1977 and

1982: Banco Coca, Banco de Madrid and Banca Garriga Nogués. Partly because of this burden, Banesto faltered and its CEO, Pablo Garnica was forced to resign by Mariano Rubio, the then governor of the Bank of Spain. In the meantime, Banco Hispano had to clean up its finances.

The other four; Banco de Bilbao, Banco de Vizcaya, Banco de Santander and Banco Popular, were financially healthier and able to cope better with the need to expand before Spain's entry into the EEC in 1986. Banco de Bilbao enjoyed a good customer portfolio but at the end of the 1980s felt it necessary to grow in order to gain a greater market share, by accepting a merger with Banco de Vizcaya. Despite the fact that the latter had far fewer customers (ratio 1–6 at this time) this merger took place on an equal basis. The key reason for the merger was Banco de Bilbao's fear that Banco de Vizcaya, Bilbao's dynamic main rival, might overtake them in terms of market share and thus ultimately gain the upper hand.

In this competitive landscape Banco de Santander and Banco Popular seemed to be the best prepared to resist the opening of the Spanish financial market to competition from abroad, despite their being the two smallest banks of the top seven.

Banco de Vizcaya acquired Banca Catalana and the banks of Rumasa Group in 1983. Thus, of the seven large 'national' banks, four in particular fared better than the others during this period – Banco de Vizcaya, Banco de Santander, Banco Popular and Banco de Bilbao. Banco Hispano, one of the other three, saw its CEO resign as a consequence of the bank's poor performance.

The period 1977–1982 was characterized by the difficulties in the larger banks, the impending entry of European banks in Spain and the willingness of the Spanish authorities to foster mergers among Spanish banks for market consolidation.

The consolidation process was given a major boost in September 1989 when Banco de Santander launched the *supercuenta*, a demand deposit with around 20 per cent plus remuneration. The competitors were caught by surprise. Banesto, for example, rose to the challenge launching a similarly high-remuneration current account but its financial health was put in jeopardy because its finances were not strong enough to face the war of attrition that the launch had provoked.

The mergers that took place between 1987 and 1999 contributed to the emergence of two 'national champions' in the form of Santander and BBVA, which rank among the top twenty largest banks in the world, in terms of market capitalization. The former was created by the merger of Santander and Central Hispano (Banesto was acquired by Santander, but has kept its independent status); and the latter comprises the former Banco de Bilbao, Banco de Vizcaya, and Argentaria.

Business model framework

Our empirical research attests to the existence of a specific strategic configuration among the Spanish banks, although some individual variations exist (for example, if one compares Santander and BBVA).

As illustrated in Graphs A, B, and C, the configuration includes:

A. General framework consisting of:

The CEO: The top executive with short-term cash-flow generation-centred Profit Arithmetic (PA) approach (further explained in Chapter 3) enabling simplification of the situation and making sense of it. Rightly or wrongly, the entire organization can thus clearly see in which direction it is, or ought to be, heading. However, the PA approach does not mean that the top executive lacks a long-term vision. The key point is which of the two, in an extreme, trade-off situation, is given priority: cash flow in the short-term, or the long-term vision. As a matter of fact, we believe we can discern

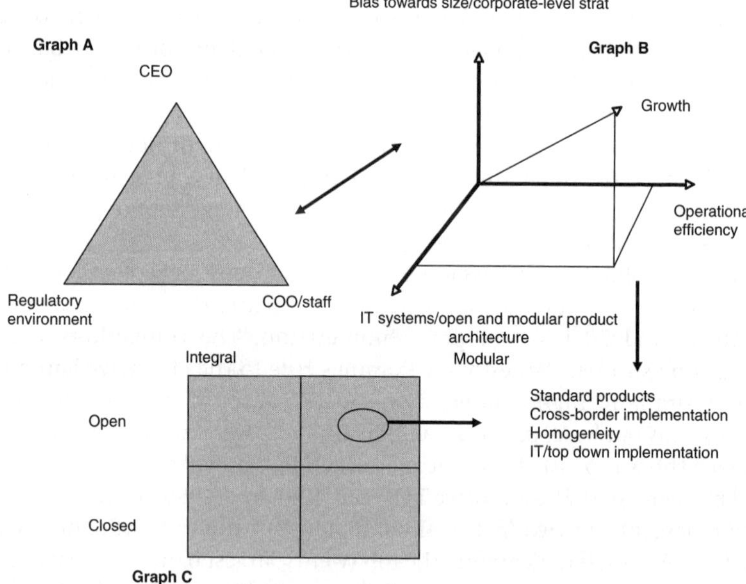

Figure 1.1   Business model framework

a specific direction in Santander and BBVA's strategic orientation, at least judged *ex post facto*.

The CEO's team (COO/staff): The historical pattern betokens the existence of CEO-COO/staff teams in Santander and BBVA which combine very well: Banco de Bilbao-Vizcaya's Ybarra (CEO) and Uriarte (COO), BBVA's González (CEO) and Goirigolzarri (COO), Santander's Botín (Chairman) and Sáenz (CEO) are outstanding examples.

From outside observation we cannot explicitly assert that the CEOs set direction and the COOs implement their superiors' decisions. We conjecture that, more often than not, the role of CEO and COO shifts between these key players.

The regulatory environment: We touched on this point earlier in this Chapter, but we ought to point out that the existence of a demanding regulatory environment favouring competition among the banks is one thing, but it does not explain the different outcomes the banks have achieved. We assume that the varying success of different banks, while facing the same business environment, can only be explained by the existence and influence of a leadership figure.

B. Basic business model comprising:

The bias towards size resulting in focus on the dual strategy levels; business or competitive, and corporate-level strategies.

Discussions on whether size translates to economies of scale still seem to be going on. However, size must be a factor seriously taken into account by the incumbent CEOs. We have heard top executives of large Spanish banks expressing their conviction that growth in search of size has been the driving force behind their success.

Common sense argues in favour of size because it allows for the cost of technology, particularly in the research and development of Information Technology, to be spread among a larger number of operational units.

Be that as it may, the size, or rather the penchant for growth based on the conviction that size ultimately decides the survival of a bank, determines the behavioural pattern of bank management.

The growth of Spanish banks, first in Latin America (in parallel with other Spanish enterprises that entered the Latin American market around the same time), then in Continental Europe and perhaps ultimately in the US market, can only be explained by the inherent penchant for growth among the Spanish banks.

The centring on size and growth for size is something to be pursued at the level of corporate strategy rather than competitive strategy. The difference between these two levels of strategy is that, at the corporate-level, you carry out the selection of business domain, rather than 'navigating' in the same existing domain (which falls to competitive strategy to take care of).

The growth for size was achieved in many cases by the acquisition of other banks, both inside and outside Spain. Decisions such as which banks to acquire, whether to grow organically or by acquisition, what value is created from the corporate centre, and so on, are typical questions answered by the corporate-level strategy.

By itself, a competitive strategy centred on the maximization of profit by pursuing cost leadership (the generic strategy developed by Spanish banks) may not be able to cope with concerns about size or growth. It needs to be complemented by corporate-level strategy.

The pursuit of operational efficiency

The strategic use of an efficiency ratio (expenses as a percentage of revenue, or expenses divided by revenue) as a key performance indicator among a bank's staff and employees helps to harness the organizational energy of a bank.

The shrinking interest spread as the main income source for retail banks has made it essential for them to reduce their costs faster than the fall in the lending rate.[4]

It is true, though, that banks cannot reduce operational costs forever. At a certain point in time the diversification of income sources must necessarily be taken into account.

The efficiency ratio acquires an even deeper significance when combined with IT systems and the entire operational culture of the organization.

The strategic use of IT systems

Spanish banks fundamentally understand that their business relates to customers and the handling of information and data about those customers. IT systems facilitate the flow of this information, the identification of interesting data and trends, the strategic combination of these data in search of competitive advantage, and so on.

Moreover, IT systems enable competitive advantages such as the transfer of financial products, exhaustively tested in Spain, to Latin America or other markets. As key indicators for the handling of these products become known, it is essential to be able to keep track of them, and IT systems can do just that.

The efficiency of payment settlement is also typically a function of time – the faster, the better – and therefore it is essential to have a homogenised IT system network throughout the entire organisation and across borders.

Product architecture orientated towards an open and modular type

Another relevant feature of the transfer and implant of products into other markets is the product architecture.

The pursuit of operational efficiency is predicated on cost leadership, combined with the commercialization of similar products and services throughout the geographical spread, with subsequent savings in research and development expenses and learning-curve effects.

Offering the same or similar financial products and services across markets is facilitated by an open and modular product architecture.

This modular architecture assembles standard 'parts' and 'components' using standard production facilities. The actual interfacing of parts and components with each other and with the total product concept is not essentially important. A typical open and modular type of product is the PC (Personal Computer) for which the competitive advantage comes from finding standard but cost-efficient components and efficiently combining them.

The ability of Spanish retail banks to convert their product architecture into modular and open types allows them to capitalize on IT system advantages such as central management of costs and personnel, and to implement the same products across borders.

Organization of book and reading guide

This book is organized into six chapters and four annexes.

Readers who wish to quickly go through the book to grasp the findings and theoretical framework expounded in this book are recommended to peruse Chapter 3 and Chapter 6.

Chapter 3 combined with Chapters 4 and 5 provides a fairly comprehensive idea of the theoretical framework, which is considered in detail in Chapter 3 and fleshed out and applied in the two later chapters.

This chapter, Chapter 1, gives an introduction and summarizes the framework of the book.

Chapter 2 presents the regulatory evolution of the banking industry in Spain, in the belief that it sets the backdrop to the emergence of Spanish retail banks as world-class competitors.

Chapter 3 describes in more detail the business model, as an 'ideal type' identified in the major Spanish retail banks. The regulatory environment, the existence of leadership figures, their cognitive processes, the use of IT systems, the pursuit of operational efficiency, etc., are explained along the way.

Chapters 4 and 5 detail two variations in the business model we identified in Chapter 3. The two main representative banks show some variations from that generic model, but the essential working is similar. We also look at the influence of other factors such as leadership figures, corporate culture, remuneration systems, internal power structures, strategic positioning (e.g. strategy setter or follower), the process of mutual replication of strategic steps, and so on.

Chapter 6 concludes and discusses our findings. The existence of one generic business model which branched into different variations in each of the competing banks does not guarantee the success of the Spanish banks forever. Since we're dealing with an idiosyncratic combination of leaders and their strategic approaches, and evolution in the regulatory environment, the model itself will necessarily undergo modifications, superficial or radical, in years to come. The existing leaders will be replaced by younger generations. The environment will evolve. Therefore, it will be relevant that further analysis be made of the business model and its modifications over time.

Annex 1 provides statistical validation that a basically similar strategic approach exists among Spanish banks compared to Japanese banks. Content analysis of the speeches by CEOs in large Spanish and Japanese banks is conducted, as is cluster analyses of Spanish and Japanese banks.

Annex 2a presents the behaviour pattern of Japanese banks and shows how they do not share a common approach. We attempt to provide circumstantial evidence that these banks lack a clear-cut strategic approach due to historical reasons, and this places them at a distinct disadvantage compared to Spanish banks.

Annex 2b describes the case of Suruga Bank, a small regional bank in Japan which, unlike other banks in Japan, pursues a strategy remarkably similar to the business model of the leading Spanish retail banks. The existence of a similar strategic approach in a different business environment and regulatory evolution may confirm the validity of the Spanish banks' business model in totally different national culture and business environments.

Annex 3 offers an analysis of the business model used by Banco Sabadell as an example of another Spanish bank validating the generic business model explained in Chapter 3.

Annex 4 provides an explanation of the research process and methodology adopted in conducting this project.

2
The Great Leap of Spanish Banks, 1987–2005: A Profit–Arithmetic (PA) Approach[1,2]

Introduction

In the first chapter we raised the question of why the Spanish banking industry came to the forefront of the international competitive arena, and we undertook to provide an explanation. Our theory is that a common generic business model (albeit with some variations by banks) was adopted by the successful retail banks in Spain, and we believe that this may explain their emergence onto the world-banking stage.

While the business model consists of several key components, perhaps the most important is the historical development of the sector stemming from changes in the regulatory environment.

In order to grasp the drastic transformation which all parts of the sector underwent in such a short space of time, it is fundamental to understand the development of the regulatory environment. Deregulation of the sector, brought about largely due to Spain becoming an EU member state and preparing to join the single market, forced Spanish banks to expand, merge or perish in their home market before contemplating internationalisation in Latin America. The success of their presence in South America was mainly due to the fact that the Spanish executives were able to use the experience gained from modernising the Spanish banks and adapt their successful strategies to the upgrade of the Latin American banks. This international strategy gave Santander and BBVA particularly another dimension that has enabled them to expand into Europe, North America and Asia.

Evolution of the regulatory environment in the Spanish banking

Very few industries in Europe have experienced quite such an overwhelming change as that endured by the banking industry in Spain over the last twenty years. Indeed, this industry had to struggle through a drastic liberalisation process, completed in 1987. A plethora of inefficient players and various banks involved in the oft-repeated story of ill-conceived mergers and acquisitions, orchestrated by the Spanish Government/the Bank of Spain and/or the banks themselves, failed to compete in this new aggressive sector and were gobbled up by their more savvy counterparts.

Despite, or perhaps because of, these adverse factors, Spanish banks have managed to overcome their limitations by adopting similar management approaches: maintaining a strong focus on the generation of cash flow and taking a Profit Arithmetic (PA) approach in an uncertain environment (to be discussed in Chapter 3). Moreover, unlike banks of other nationalities, particularly German ones, Spanish banks were not oblivious to the fact that their strengths were in retail banking, and always remained focussed on increasing their customer base and their efficiency, while also trying to lower their risk management.

The regulations brought in 1941 were still governing the activities of Spanish banks in 1980. These regulations prevented existing banks from opening new branches, and prevented new competitors from entering the market. It also thwarted competition in interest rates, since all bank rates were fixed by the Ministry of Economy. On top of that, banks were required to freeze a substantial part of their assets in illiquid investments, mostly in the public sector.

Overall, these restraints resulted in a fairly inefficient financial system. The public investments made by the banks, granted at very low interest rates, had a crowding-out effect on credit to the private sector, which was comparatively scarce and quite expensive. Holders of savings and demand deposits earned virtually no interest on their accounts, but had no other choice. Under those conditions, no money or debt market could exist, nor was there any reference to what the real market interest rate could be. Only a narrow and inefficient stock market managed to survive, with no pension, mutual funds or other institutional investors that could direct saving flows into it. In the latter years, the inefficiency of the system was partly mitigated when banks managed to side-step regulations to some extent, by covertly offering deposit interest rates above the legal limit to their best customers. The following Table 2.1 compares the different financial regulatory environments in Europe in 1980.

The Spanish banking industry

In the late 1970s, the Spanish banking industry was characterised by a small concentration of leading institutions. Out of more than 120 private

Table 2.1   Banking regulation in Europe in 1980

	L	UK	B	DE	IRL	NL	DK	I	F	GR	E	P
Control over interest rate	●		●	●	●		●	●	●	●	●	●
Control over capitals			●		●		●	●	●	●	●	●
Access to stock markets		●					●	●	●		●	●
Expansion of office network								●	●			●
Entry off oreign banks								●	●	●	●	●
Restrictions on credits							●	●	●	●	●	●
Coefficients of investment						●			●	●	●	●
Restrictions on insurances				●		●	●		●	●	●	●
Leasing										●	●	●

L: Luxemberg, B: Belgium, DE: the Netherlands, DK: Denmark, I: Ireland, F: France, GR: Greece, E: Spain, P: Portugal.

Source: Dermine (2002:40).

banks in existence at the time, not including savings banks and state-owned banks, just seven commercial banks accounted for more than half of the total bank deposits.[3]

Nevertheless, competition was abated in the Spanish financial system because 1) regulations prevented competition, helping larger banks to maintain the status quo and, 2) because banks were allowed to conduct both commercial and investment banking operations unchallenged, on account of the limited liberalisation of the 1962 banking reform, despite the fact that some interest rates were liberalised. The largest seven banks held significant stakes in private firms and other banks, which enabled them to control important industrial groups without maximising the value creation of their industrial portfolio. Banesto and Banco Central, the two leading Spanish banks at this time, were typical examples of this.

In those years SMEs (Small and Medium Enterprises) had no easy access to long-term loans with private banks. This led to the creation of official credit institutions aimed at providing financing on a medium-to long-term basis to firms which had no access to security markets and could not obtain funds from the banks. The market-share of these institutions in this type of funding was small, yet until new markets were developed many years later, they were the only source of medium- to long-term credit for SMEs.[4]

The other group of players, the savings banks, were non-profit institutions whose purpose was to lend to farmers, small businesses and household savers throughout Spain. With the establishment of democracy in 1976, Spain soon opted for a federal regime in deference to regional differences, in particular between the Catalans, Basques and Galicians. This led to an empowerment of the savings banks because they converted themselves quickly into an auxiliary of the regional executive power. As a consequence, by the middle of the 1980s, they represented around 50 per cent of all deposits and loans in Spain.

The long process of deregulation[5]

Despite the relatively minimal success of the 1962 law that liberalised some interest rates,[6] Spain had to wait nine years more, until 1971, for the liberalisation of the rules on the opening of new branches to come into force. It was a fundamental move because the Spanish banks were retail banks, and the capturing of customers was almost impossible without amendments to the regulations. In 1974, a new law opened the door to the creation of new banks and increased the liberalisation of interest rates to some extent. In 1977, foreign banks were allowed to enter Spain, and the operating differences that remained between commercial and saving banks were eliminated. (See Appendix 2.1 *Overview of the deregulation milestones*).

However, this deregulation process suffered some serious setbacks. In 1982, for example, the investment coefficients of the banks (set to finance the public sector) increased from 27 per cent to 52 per cent of their deposits, as a result of soaring public deficits. New legislation passed in 1985 maintained this high coefficient but also brought some initiatives that would help the banks to better face the upcoming European challenge. The initiatives contained in the new legislation brought with them a much improved way of computing capital requirements, made the consolidation of financial accounts compulsory and introduced new information requirements for the sake of customers and shareholders. Although at first opposed by most banks, these measures were crucial in transforming banking in Spain into a more efficient and transparent business.

Finally, in 1987, all interest rates and commission were liberalised, and a programme was put forward to gradually eliminate the investment coefficients, setting them to disappear by 2000. Also, two important measures to protect the customer were enacted. One was a service created by the Bank of Spain to process the complaints filed by the banks' customers. The other required banks to inform their clients of the true rate of interest carried by all their products.[7] For the first time the clients were able to use homogeneous interest rate data to compare competing offers from different institutions, and thus price competition became a basic tool in gaining market-share towards the end of the 1980s, when keen desire for growth through mergers and acquisitions between Spanish banks was unleashed.

Deregulation, new financial markets and new regulatory body, the CNMV

In the late sixties, the only existing financial market in Spain was the Stock Exchange. This was a narrow and quite inefficient market, still working under rules established forty years previously. In 1977, the Government appointed a Commission, which came up with some proposals for modernising this market. These measures were, however, not implemented until ten years later; about the same time as the Paris and London reforms.[8] In 1988, the CNMV (Comisión Nacional del Mercado de Valores or 'National Stock Market Commission') was created to supervise stock market institutions, intermediaries and issuers, with the aim of ensuring transparency, safety and efficiency in stock market transactions.[9]

Perhaps more important than the reform of the Stock Market itself, was the creation of the money market, the fixed income market and the derivatives market.[10] The money market barely existed in the late seventies, with a few commercial banks borrowing from the cash-rich saving banks. Rather than a market, this was more like a network of personal relationships between treasurers of certain banks. The Bank of Spain was eager to develop this fledgling market which would allow it to better implement its monetary policy, but the larger banks remained unresponsive to this initiative.

Despite this, the market began to take off steadily when a group of four banks joined forces and began to operate under the supervision of the Bank of Spain. Some years later the rest of the banks followed suit and in 1978 the arrival of foreign banks, in need of a ready source of funds, greatly helped to further develop the market. In 1985 commercial papers were sold on the wholesale market for the first time.

By the mid-eighties the Government was under pressure to launch a public debt market to finance its huge deficits, which at a certain point stood at over 7 per cent of the GNP. Public debt soared from 12 per cent of the GNP in 1976, to 60 per cent in 1994. During those years the Government forced the banks to finance its deficit at very low rates and when, in the late eighties, this proved insufficient it turned to the Bank of Spain to fulfil its needs at zero cost. This crowded out private credit, which became scarce and expensive.

The initial steps to build the new public debt market were not easy. The Government made a first attempt at the creation of such a market jointly with the Stock Exchange but its proposal was turned down. It then approached the banks for support, only to find them extremely reluctant. Banks feared the effect that the disintermediation process would have on their business, and considered the placement commissions offered by the Treasury to be too low. After a substantial increase in the commissions, the new market was created and began to operate quite efficiently shortly afterwards.

Whereas the launch of the monetary and the public debt market was a Government initiative, the creation of the derivative market was an initiative of a group of banks in 1989. This project gained the support of the monetary authority early on, as the authority was aware of the proposal's potentially valuable contribution to the financial system. Although some of the largest banks declined to participate in the new project, once again, they later joined the group when it proved to be a success.

The development of all these markets brought the Spanish financial system on to a par with the best in continental Europe, in terms of scope and efficiency, thanks to the actions of the Bank of Spain.

Overall, it can be said that the Spanish banks reacted quite suitably to a new situation of greater competition that began eroding their traditionally handsome profit margins. The deregulation was a timely and far-sighted move on the part of the Bank of Spain, which anticipated the forthcoming challenges arising from joining the European Union. Thanks to this deregulation, the Spanish banks were able to withstand foreign competition. This positive effect was also enhanced by the fact that other banking regulators in the rest of Europe were, in general, moving towards liberalising their markets at a desperately slower pace.

The contrast is stark when we compare the situation with that in Japan, where banking has always been guided by monetary and governmental authorities under the so-called Convoy System (*Goso sendan hoshiki*),[11] whereby risk was spread evenly as all banks pursue similar actions under the supervision of the Ministry of Finance. This system is widely believed to have thwarted competition between Japanese banks and suppressed their creativity.

This lack of competition or competitive atmosphere in Japan is exemplified by the conflict between Tokyo Star Bank and the Bank of Tokyo Mitsubishi UFJ, on the use of commission-free cash cards adopted by the former. Asahi.com, the electronic version of Asahi Shimbun, a major daily newspaper in Japan, published an article on 15th September 2006 on the predatory behaviour that some banks (lead by The Bank of Tokyo Mitsubishi UFJ) had exhibited towards Tokyo Star Bank for its policy of making its cash card holders shoulder the commissions paid to other banks for cash withdrawal from their machines. For Lone Star, the owner of Tokyo Star Bank, it was a legitimate commercial weapon, but for others it was seen as a breakaway from the traditional spirit of harmony among peers.

Deregulation leading to an internal reorganisation of the Spanish financial system

The impact of the deregulation process took place in three waves. First, competition induced a crisis amongst the Spanish financial institutions. Second, financial restructuring led to mergers and the modernisation that made it possible for the banks, in the third move, to internationalise themselves in Latin America.

The banking crisis: 1978–1985

At the time that competition was introduced, Spain was a highly regulated market, and the banks and savings banks were inefficient. The banking crisis began in 1978 and was not over until 1985, seriously affecting 55 out of a total of 120 banks, the assets of those 55 representing 20 per cent of total assets held by the banking industry. It was a severe crisis that required several controversial measures to limit its effects.

The first failure was a small local bank, Banco de Navarra, in 1978. Once the Spanish government realised that more failures could be expected, it decided to adopt measures to prevent them from taking place. This was done against the will of the banking industry which knew that it would have to pay for the rescue of failing banks. The prevailing opinion of the banks was that poorly managed banks, similar to poorly managed companies in any other industry, should be left fail if necessary, particularly given the fact that their deposits were insured up to a certain level. This insurance was entrusted to the Fondo de Garantía de Depósitos (FGD), a newly created institution with some similarities to the Federal Deposit Insurance (FDI) of the United States.

Without delay it was decided to use the FGD to buy-out troubled banks. Once they were bought, the FGD was expected to clean them, get rid of all non-performing assets, and then try to resell them to other banks. It was agreed that the Government and the banking industry would share the cost of the rescue scheme equally. Ultimately, this plan worked fairly well and, seven years later, the crisis was over with only two minor bankruptcies.

However, problems had existed since the inception of FGD, inasmuch as the majority of the banks refrained from participating in this rescue scheme. Banco Popular, for instance, flatly refused to buy any bank from the FGD. The widely-held opinion was that troubled banks were grossly overstaffed and highly unlikely to ever become profitable.

Accordingly, Banesto, the biggest Spanish bank at the time, had to acquire three banks between 1977 and 1982. The restructuring of Banco Coca, Banco Madrid and Garriga Nogués led Mariano Rubio, the governor of the Bank of Spain, to force the resignation of Pablo Garnica as CEO of Banesto in 1986 and to replace him with López de Letona, a former governor of the Bank of Spain between 1976 and 1978. Pablo Garnica accepted the resignation but remained at Banesto as Vice President.

By contrast, Banco de Vizcaya, one of the smallest of the *big seven*, took advantage of the rescue scheme and managed to expand through buying failed banks from the FGD. Banco de Vizcaya thus spotted a unique opportunity in the scheme to propel its growth, and felt confident of coping with the risk involved in making these banks profitable again. The bank's strategy proved to be successful and contributed to the consolidation of the image of Vizcaya as an efficient and innovative bank, at the time when it was in the middle of acquiring two banking groups: Banca Catalana and Rumasa, in 1983.[12,13]

In terms of performance during these years, out of the league of the seven largest banks, the successful banks were to be found among the smaller ones: Banco de Vizcaya, Banco de Santander, Banco Popular and, to a lesser extent, Banco de Bilbao.

In stark contrast, Banco Hispano, the third largest Spanish bank at the time, had similar financial and business difficulties to Banesto, suffering from uncertainty about their top management's continuity. Turnover at the top was high. After Luis de Usera passed away in 1982, Alejandro Albert was forced to resign as the bank's CEO in 1984 and was replaced by Claudio Boada, previously the CEO of Banco Coca.

Banco Central, the second bank in Spain with a powerful portfolio in manufacturing industries was considered as bureaucratic and oversized despite the prestige of its CEO, Alfonso Escámez.

This stage was characterised by (1) the larger banks' difficulties, (2) the imminent arrival of European banks in Spain with its entry in EU and, nonetheless, (3) the willingness of the Bank of Spain and the Spanish government to let 'national banking champions' proceed to the second phase of deregulation, i.e., the restructuring of the Spanish banking system through mergers.

Mergers and acquisitions: 1987–1999[14]

At the present time, leading Spanish banks may be considered to be at the forefront of global banking. The mergers and acquisitions between 1987 and 1990 originally conceived by the Spanish Government/Bank of Spain,[15] or devised by the banks themselves, greatly contributed to this position. Amongst the newly created banks born of these mergers and acquisitions were two world-class competitors: Santander and BBVA, which rank among the twenty largest banks in terms of market capitalisation in the world.

In the process of mergers and acquisitions between Spanish banks Santander's launch of a highly-remunerated current account (the '*supercuenta*') made deep inroads into Spain's deposit market and irreversibly influenced the competition landscape. The change brought about by the '*supercuenta*' became known as the 'war of the *supercuentas*'.

The war of the 'supercuentas', in 1989

The introduction and the widespread use of the 'true' rate began to foster competition very effectively. In September 1989, Banco de Santander launched the '*supercuenta*', a demand deposit with a hitherto unimaginably high yield (over 20 per cent per annum). Its competitors were caught by surprise and proved to be very slow in reacting to this move. Finally, after six long months of soaring growth for Santander, the move was countered by Banesto, a troubled bank and ill prepared to pay a higher cost for its funds. Shortly afterwards, the rest of the big banks followed suit, except for Banco Popular. However, by then the early advantage gained by Santander was quite substantial and continued to increase over the following months.

Mergers that took place

Mergers and acquisitions between banks, which resulted in less synergy than originally thought, allowed savings banks to grow faster than the banks themselves.[16] At the end of 2006, savings banks controlled as much as 52 per cent of the total deposits in the banking system, while commercial banks captured only 41 per cent. The market shares of the two largest banks, Santander and BBVA, were 10.2 per cent and 9.3 per cent, respectively, in the same period.

Finally, after 1987 the mergers caused a shift in the way the banks were managed and the cash-flow centred,[17] short-term focused, Profit Arithmetic (PA) approach became more prevalent. Interestingly, this more aggressive competitive approach heralded the end of the traditional group photo taken of the Chairmen of the seven largest banks after their periodic lunch, perhaps marking an end to the harmony once enjoyed in the sector.

Three banks survived this merger process: 1) Santander, resulting from the merger of Bancos Santander, Central and Hispano, with Banesto maintained as a separate firm, 2) BBVA resulting from the merger of Bilbao and Vizcaya Banks first and the formerly state-owned Argentaria afterwards, and 3) Banco Popular, the only one among the so-called *big banks* that did not seek mergers as a means of growth.

The prospects for Spanish banks on 1st January 1986, the day of joining the EEC,[18] were rather Variegated, taking into account the size of Spanish banks compared with potential entrants from this enlarged market. However, opinions were divided. Some banks, such as Bilbao and Vizcaya, took the view that in order to survive the potential onslaught of competition, Spanish banks ought to merge. This was based on a desire to gain a wider customer-base – a key variable for retail banks – and create economies of scale by reducing redundant branches and payroll. Moreover, it was thought that the larger the bank, the better the opportunity for diversification into new products and markets, as well as providing increased protection against hostile takeover bids. This view was contested by Popular and Central, which reportedly believed that good management and profitability were much important than sheer size. Fernández and Carabias (2006) demonstrate in their studies the permanence of this focus.

The Bank of Spain, aware that research on economies of scale in banking was inconclusive,[19] did not lean towards either view. However, at the time, the Government clearly sided in favour of mergers and made this known to the chairmen of the largest banks. This pressure soon paid off and, in September 1987, Banco de Bilbao launched a hostile takeover bid against Banesto, which was only thwarted a few weeks later by pressure from various interest groups. This initiative deeply shocked the banking community, which for many years had behaved as a fairly cohesive group. From that moment onward, things were never to be the same again.

In January 1988, Banesto proposed a merger with Banco Central, but this initiative never went ahead despite being approved by the shareholders of both banks. The first successful merger was that of Bilbao and

Vizcaya in that same month. The new bank, BBV (Banco de Bilbao Vizcaya), became the largest bank in Spain and the 37th in Europe in terms of deposits. It also owned the largest investment portfolio of any Spanish firm. A unique feature of this merger was that the agreement was made in such a way that management of the consolidated bank was to be conducted on a 'between equals' basis. According to this principle, both chairmen, Angel Sánchez Asiaín of Bilbao and Pedro de Toledo of Vizcaya, became co-chairmen of the new bank. This was seen as fair since, although Bilbao was a somewhat larger bank, Vizcaya was growing at a much faster pace. Nevertheless, the agreement did not work well and gave rise to a variety of problems including internal conflicts which continued for many years. The main reason for the conflicts was that the two banks shared the same customer base in the Basque country.

In December 1989 Pedro de Toledo, one of the two co-chairmen, died unexpectedly. The bank was unable to come up with a solution to the issue of his succession. With no prospective solution on the cards, the Bank of Spain intervened to settle the succession issue. They did this by appointing a new Chairman and four new Board members. As a result, Sánchez Asiaín, one of the key players in the merger and the only remaining chairman, stepped down and was replaced as CEO by Emilio Ybarra, a member of one of the traditional shareholding families of Banco de Bilbao, and by Pedro Luis Uriarte as COO. This measure seemed to bring activities back to some sort of normality, although the performance of the merged bank seemed, nevertheless, to be light years away from that of the two banks prior to the merger.

In May 1991, various state-owned or state-influenced banks, (Banco Exterior de España, Caja Postal de Ahorros, Banco Hipotecario, among others) were consolidated into a large single group, Argentaria, under the leadership of Francisco Luzón. The change in government to the conservative *Partido Popular* or 'People's Party' resulted in the replacement of Francisco Luzón by Francisco González as CEO of Argentaria. Luzón was subsequently offered a position by Santander.

A few days later, the merger of Central and Hispano was announced and the resulting bank became the largest financial and industrial group in Spain, surpassing BBV. While the Hispano was restructured by Claudio Boada,[20] the new bank under José María Amusátegui's leadership faced the same difficulties as BBV due to lack of synergies.

In December of 1993, eight years after the banking crisis was assumed to be over, the monetary authorities had to intervene in Banesto, one of the former *big seven* banks, which by then was in deep trouble. Mario Conde, the Chairman of the Board, was later found guilty of fraud and embezzlement during his chairmanship (1987–1993). The Board and the top executives of the bank were dismissed and replaced by a provisional committee responsible for revitalising the bank. This committee was composed of appointees from the five largest banks: BBV, Banco Centro Hispano, Santander, Popular and Argentaria.[21]

The first task of the committee was to appoint a provisional chairman able to turn the bank around. BBV suggested that its Vice President, Alfredo Sáenz take on the job. Sáenz was readily accepted, thanks to his role in the successful turnaround of Banca Catalana. When the time for tenders came, BBV was out-bid by Santander for the control of the bank. This was a serious blow for BBV, until then the undisputed leader of the banking industry. With Banesto under its control, Santander now came close to BBV in size, and what was more, it was able to retain Sáenz (later to become Santander's CEO) and the best part of his team.

This concentration process of big banks came to an end in January 1999 when Santander announced its merger with Central Hispano, and became the largest Spanish bank. Amusátegui and Corcóstegui, both originally from Central Hispano, were dismissed and Emilio Botín took over the reigns.

A few months later, feeling the pressure from the new super-sized Santander, BBV merged with Argentaria to form BBVA. It was a last-chance attempt to keep up the fight for size in both the Spanish and Latin-American markets (Santander and BBV had already begun expanding into Latin America). Once again, and notwithstanding previous experience, the banks decided to attempt a merger on a *'between equals'* basis, despite the fact that Argentaria was less than half the size of BBV in terms of market capitalisation. This new merger proved ill fated and several months later, all former board members of BBV, including its former CEO, Emilio Ybarra, were forced to resign.[22]

A remarkable exception in the race for size was Banco Popular, the smallest of the *big seven* banks. When Rafael Termes was appointed Managing Director of this bank in 1965, he immediately stressed return on equity (ROE) and efficiency as a cornerstone of the bank's strategy, dismissing growth as an objective. Termes also pioneered the improvement of disclosure practices which at that point were regarded as far from relevant in Spain. This effort included the creation of the Spanish Financial Analysts Association in 1970, which served to introduce this profession in Spain and later became one of the two leading associations of its kind in Europe.[23]

This rapid concentration process was reflected in the behaviour of Spanish savings banks, but at a somewhat slower pace. Similarly, inter-bank mergers were also being frequently seen in other European countries (see appendix 2.2 for details). Having said that, most of the mergers completed thus far in the rest of Europe were on a national level. Cross-border mergers faced many barriers created by the national authorities trying to protect their markets from the entry of foreign banks.

Spanish firms rediscover America: 1995–2000

In the early nineties, Spanish banks concerned with size were actively looking for growth opportunities. Although innovation in the financial system provided a good number of them, the banking industry was becoming more mature and competitive and its prospects for growth seemed to be fading. In 1995, this situation led Santander and BBV to begin investing in banks in Latin America. Their first steps were cautious, but soon the pace of acquisitions greatly increased, to the point where this process was fully completed in 2000. By the millennium, Santander had become the largest banking group in Latin America with total assets of over US$85 billion and BBV the second largest with some US$68 billion. Citibank, the former leader, was knocked down to third place, with total assets of some US$60 billion.

Investing in Latin America offered four main advantages for Spanish banks: 1) higher profit margins than those found in Spain, 2) substantial growth potential catering to their Spanish customers going through internationalisation processes, 3) feasible amount of required investment when compared to the size of the Spanish banks, and 4) the ease of working in the same language and a similar culture.

Higher profit margins were possible since the banking in those countries was hitherto less efficient than in Spain, a fact which translated into higher operating costs and a reduced offer of products. In the area of costs there were clear opportunities to introduce new technology and to lower bloated payrolls, both moves that generally led to a much better standard of service.

There seemed to be plenty of commercial opportunities as well, by launching new products and applying marketing innovation previously tested in Spain. The underlying idea was to export the entire know-how and business model, proving so successful in Spain, to those new markets. This was usually done by appointing a new Spanish manager for each bank bought, along with a handful of experienced specialists tasked with helping him implement the model.

Opportunities for growth arose from the low use or accessibility to banking institutions (known as low bancarisation) in those countries, in terms of banks assets, families with a bank account, and population per bank branch (as illustrated in Figures 2.1a, 2.1b and 2.1c). In the mid-1990s, the economic growth of these countries, the improvements made in the regional integration (with the Mercosur and the Andean Group) and the Spanish experience in restructuring and modernising obsolete financial systems, was expected to foster the demand for both new and existing bank products.

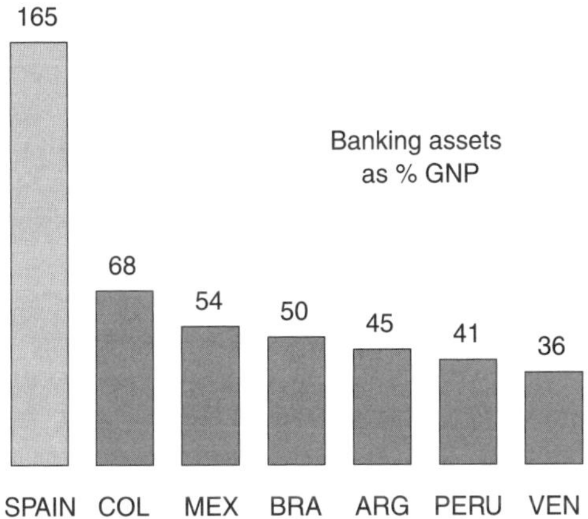

Figure 2.1a   Bank penetration in 2000: Spain vs. Latin America – banking assets
Source: Cited by Palacios (2006).

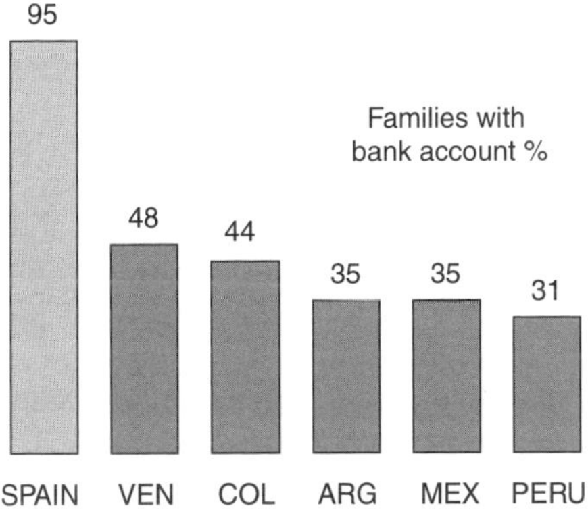

Figure 2.1b   Bank penetration in 2000: Spain vs. Latin America – Families with bank account
Source: Cited by Palacios (2006).

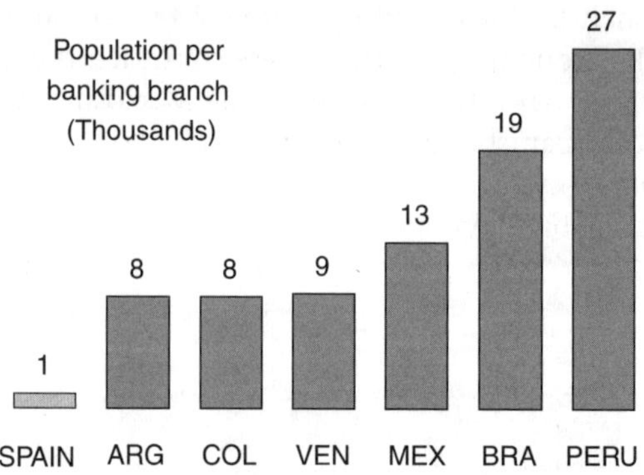

Figure 2.1c   Bank penetration in 2000: Spain vs. Latin America – Population per banking branch

Source: Cited from Palacios JA. 2006. The leap of Spanish banks: 1987-2005. Unpublished manuscript: Madrid.

Overall, the initiative to invest in Latin America seemed well timed. The banking industry in those countries was quite fragmented and seemed to be waiting for its concentration process to commence. This made it easier and more affordable to enter and buy a share of the market. Another crucial factor at that time was that national authorities were keen to liberalise the economy and welcomed foreign investment. Banks seeking to invest in Latin America found local regulators to be competent, well prepared and fairly receptive. The following Table 2.2 compares Santander and BBVA in Latin America.

Santander's and BBV's strategies for Latin America were similar. Both banks were looking for growth and diversification of their sources of revenue and both strove for leadership in all markets they operated in. Firstly, this was done by buying the leading banks in terms of market share and quality of their assets in each market and secondly, by taking over the management of the banks bought with the aim of improving their efficiency and expanding their range of products. There were, however, some differences in the style of these two banks. For example, whereas BBV tried to preserve national brands, Santander chose instead to operate under its own brand, in all countries.

The Spanish drive towards growth in Latin America

Santander and BBV were not alone in their drive to invest in Latin America. On the contrary, they followed their customers abroad. Indeed,

Table 2.2   Acquisitions of the Santander and BBV realized in Latin America

Country	Santander	BBV
Argentina	Banco Rio	Banco Francés
		Banco Argentino
Brazil	Banco Meridional	Banco Excel
	Banco Noroeste	(ceased in 2002)
	Banespa	
Chile	Osorno	Banco HIF
	O´Higgins	Provida
	Banco Santiago	
Colombia	Santander Colombia	Banco Ganadero
México	Serfin	Probursa
		Banco Cremi&Oriente
		Bancomer
Peru		Banco Continental
Puerto Rico	Santander	Poncebank
Uruguay	Banco Litoral	
Venezuela	Banco Caracas	Banco Provincial

Source: Prepared from Santander's and BBVA's websites.

a bank can only grow if its number of customers grows and if the customers earn more under a constant cost-reduction approach. Firms like the telecoms company, Telefónica, electric utilities Endesa and Iberdrola, energy firms Repsol and Gas Natural, and the insurance company Mapfre, all initiated their expansion into Latin America at the beginning of the 1990s, around the same time that Argentina was privatising all its state-owned companies.

Nevertheless, it should be noted that not all the banks entered the race to expansion. Popular, Sabadell and Bankinter were performing very well at that time, yet due either to their size not being optimum for the leap abroad or to their Spain-centric strategy, they did not attempt to enter the Latin American market.

The Latin American experience strengthened the position of both Santander and BBV, and prepared them to compete better in Europe. As mentioned, other Spanish firms followed suit, in trying to take advantage of this opportunity (Kase & Kinoshita, 2001). (See Table 2.3 *The International*

Table 2.3   International expansion of selected Spanish firms at the end of 2006

Firm	Industry	Market Value (€ billions)	Rank in size			Investments in		
			Spain	Latam	Europe	Europe	USA	Asia
Telefónica[1]	Telecoms	78	1	1	2	Yes	No	Yes
Santander[2]	Banking	87	1	1	3	Yes	Yes	No
BBVA[3]	Banking	65	2	2	8	No	Yes	Yes
Endesa[4]	Electrical utility	38	1	1	5	Yes	No	No
Iberdrola[5]	Electrical utility	31	2	3	7	Yes	No	No
Repsol	Oil	33	1			Yes	Yes	Yes
Gas Natural	Gas	14	3	4	8	Yes	No	No
Ferrovial[6]	Construction	1	2	–	2	Yes	Yes	No
Mapfre[7]	Insurance	4	1		22	Yes	Yes	No

[1] Telefónica ranks first or second in 13 Latin American countries. In Europe it owns O2 and Chesky Telecom. In Asia it has a 10 percent stake in China Netcom.

[2] Santander owns eight banks in Latin America. In 2004 it bought Abbey in the UK for € 13.5 billion. It has also significant operations in Germany, Portugal, Norway and Poland. In 2006 it bought 25 percent of Sovereign Bancorp, the 18th bank in the USA, for € 2.3 billion.

[3] BBVA owns six banks in Latin America; its biggest stake is in Bancomer in México. In the USA it owns four banks in Texas. In China it has a 10 percent stake in Citic.

[4] Endesa has operations in five Latin American countries, being the leader firm in four of them. In Europe it has invested over 600 million € in Italy.

[5] Iberdrola operates in five countries in Latin America. Its investments in Europe are over 600 million €. In November 2006 it launched a takeover bid on Scottish Power.

[6] Ferrovial focuses its strategy of international investments in OCDE countries. Its only operations in Latin America are located in Chile. In 2006, it bought BAA in the United Kingdom, for a total investment of £12 billion.

[7] Mapfre has operations in 37 countries.

Source: Palacios (2006).

Expansion Of Spanish Firms.) For example, César Alierta, Chairman of Telefónica, explained the strategy of his company in this way:

> Our move to Latin America transformed Telefónica into an international company, significant in terms of its number of clients and its knowledge of different markets. The good results we achieved gave us external credibility and an appropriate size to face the European challenge with confidence. Some other Spanish firms decided to undertake a move similar to ours and became heavily involved in Latin America. Thanks to this initiative, they are capable today to aim for an important position in the European markets. I think that we have been able, together with those firms, to find new ways to enter into Europe, where we are now much better known. I guess that this effort has helped to pave the way for any Spanish firm willing to follow our steps. Lucas and Palacios (2006)

By 2000, most of these companies had completed their acquisitions in Latin America and begun looking to continue their expansion in Europe. This proved to be more of a challenge, with a plethora of problems never encountered before in Latin America or Spain. Europe was less homogeneous in terms of banking concentration and efficiency. Moreover, European markets were much more mature, more competitive and seemed far less profitable than those in Latin America.

Breaking into the European League

After a necessary restructuring of the Spanish banking system, the two main entities, Santander and BBVA, managed to finance their expansion into Latin America by getting rid of their industrial portfolio to focus on their core business. Their ability to modernise the Latin American banks opened new frontiers for them, but the challenge to outperform their European retail competitors in terms of efficiency and number of customers was far tougher than they had imagined.

The current situation of the European financial system can be summarised as follows. The money market is fully integrated, as is the bond market to a great extent, as well as the derivative market which is based on the first two. The stock exchanges and their derivative markets are not integrated. As for the financial intermediaries, wholesale and investment banking work as a single market, as was the case before European integration. Commercial banking, asset management and insurance are fairly fragmented across countries and still very far from integration.

For these businesses the concept of a single European market does not yet seem to exist.

Four main barriers are associated with the challenge of pan-European banking: 1) language barriers, 2) required investment is much larger than that in Latin America, 3) significant entry barriers created by national authorities to keep foreign competition out of their markets and, 4) highly concentrated markets.[24]

The banking business is much more consolidated in Europe than in Latin America. Figure 2.2 shows the share of assets held by the top five private banks in each country, as a percentage of the total assets of that country's financial system.[25]

Higher consolidation in Europe, coupled with larger and more developed markets than those of Latin America, meant that the investment required to obtain a significant share of the sector was much greater in Europe. This can be seen in Figure 2.3, which shows the market price of a 10 per cent share of the banking sector in different countries. Based on this data, and generally speaking, investment required in Europe to get a similar degree of market penetration was on average about ten times higher than that in Latin America.

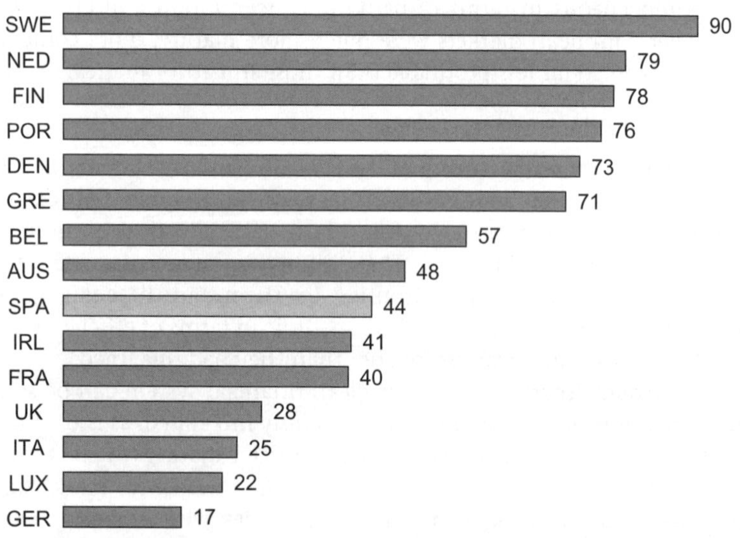

Figure 2.2   Concentration of European banks in 2000 (share of assets in the top five banks as a percentage of the total assets of the financial system)
Source: Cited by Palacios (2006).

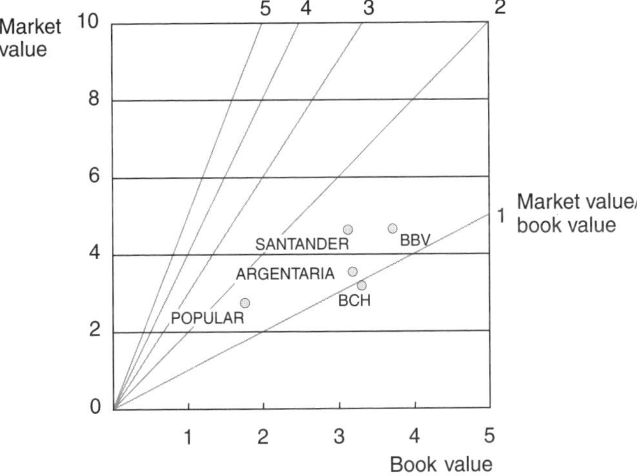

Figure 2.3   Spanish banks: January 1994 (values in billions of euros)
Source: Palacios (2006).

Due to an inefficient and complex regulatory system, Europe still has a long way to go to reach an integrated, competitive financial system. Prominent European central banker, Alexandre Lamfalussy, presented a report in February 2001, stating that:

> the basic legislation for an integrated financial market is not in place. The mosaic of European regulatory structures is well documented – over 10 of them – with different powers and competences. The current regulatory system is simply too slow, too rigid and ill-adapted to the needs of modern financial markets. Even when it does work, which is rare, it often produces texts of legendary ambiguity – along with little or no common effort to transpose the agreed texts consistently – nor enforce their proper application. (Lamfalussy, 2001)

Last, but by no means least, there has been a widespread lack of political will to give up the national champions in the banking system. Many examples of national authorities trying to block acquisitions by foreign banks can be found in Germany,[26] France with CIC, Belgium with Generale de Banque, and Portugal with the Champalimaud group, to name a few. The sole exception to this general stand is the UK, whose regulators seem truly committed to fostering the efficiency of their financial system, as confirmed by the acquisition of Abbey National by Santander.

Despite all these obstacles, a few banks have tried to expand into other European countries. This has been attempted in four different ways: through 1) opening branches or subsidiaries, 2) Internet banking, 3) alliances or cooperation agreements, and 4) mergers and acquisitions.

More often than not, expansion through opening branches has been unsuccessful. For example, BNP Paribas, one of the top banks in Europe, began building a network of branches in Spain in 1980 but decided to sell it in 2000 in view of high costs and a disappointing gain in market share. Several banks, among them Santander, are using the internet to penetrate other European markets. This initiative shows some promise but so far only represents a marginal part of the sector. An interesting experience is that of ING which has been able to make significant inroads by offering high-margin products with an extremely low-cost network. Alliances have been set up by BNP Paribas in Germany, and BCP (Banco Comercial Português) in several countries; but again, this effort does not seem to have accomplished much in global terms.

Mergers and acquisitions are not easy but have proved to be the most direct and effective way to build size and market share, as can be seen from the fact that the larger financial services firms tend to be the result of recent mergers. Despite opposition from national authorities, a handful of banks have been able to expand into Europe in this way. The largest transaction so far has been the acquisition of Abbey National, the UK's 6th largest bank, by Santander for €13.5 billion in 2004. Another important deal was the purchase of Crédit Commercial de France by HSBC for €11 billion in 2000. Other smaller operations were the creation of Fortis in 2001 from a group of banks and insurance companies in the Netherlands, and Nordea in 2002, which merged the Norwegian Christiania, Finnish Merita, Swedish Nordbanken, and Danish Unidanmark.

Thus far the fate of BBVA and Santander in the race for successful cross-border expansion within Europe has been very disparate. By 2000, BBV had built up a stake of 15 per cent in the Italian BNL (Banca Nazionale del Lavoro), and held 3.75 per cent in the French Crédit Lyonnais. However, at the end of 2002, BBVA disclosed that it was selling its shares in Crédit Lyonnais to Crédit Agricole. Later, in March 2005, BBVA announced a takeover bid for 85 per cent of the shares in BNL. However, this operation became entangled with a failed attempt from an Italian group that tried to challenge it. In the end, BBVA was outmanoeuvred by BNP Paribas which launched a more competitive bid in February 2006 and took control of the Italian bank. This left

BBVA with no significant international investment in the rest of Europe.

Santander has probably been the bank most committed to expansion within Europe. Prior to acquiring Abbey National in 2004, in 1999 it took control of Portuguese Totta & Açores, overcoming fierce local opposition. In June of that year Santander announced an agreement to buy the Champalimaud group. This group was a holding company comprising, among others, the banks Totta & Açores, Pinto e Soto Mayor, Crédito Predial Português, and the insurance company Mundial Confiança. The deal was immediately opposed by the national authorities who backed an already-prepared takeover bid from BCP, the largest Portuguese bank.

The conflict escalated greatly in the following months and Santander took the case to the European Court of Justice in Luxemburg. Finally, Totta & Açores and Predial were assigned to Santander. Pinto e Soto Mayor was later bought by BCP. Santander began applying its retail banking model to its new acquisitions and their results began to improve steadily year on year. Today Totta & Açores is the 3rd largest bank in Portugal.

Santander has also made inroads into Europe through Santander Consumer, a network of more than 200 branches specialising in selected services, such as car financing. Santander claimed to have 8 million customers spread over 12 European countries in 2005. Santander Consumer is a retail initiative that enables Santander to gain presence in European countries, without incurring such high fixed costs as those linked with opening branches.[27] All these initiatives have converted Santander into the number one bank in the Euro-zone and the 4th largest bank in Europe in terms of market value.

While the process of consolidation in Europe is being hindered by politicians and regulators, banks in United States and Asia are merging and enjoying rapid growth. This poses a serious threat for the leading banks in Europe which are all too aware of how they are losing ground in the global banking race. Romano Prodi, then President of the European Commission, voiced his concern on the attitude of political leaders:

> Member states do not seem to realise that … we are going to miss our mid-term targets. This should be a strong enough message to serve as a wake-up call to governments. At European level we have advanced steadily in setting the right priorities but Member States have not demonstrated enough 'ownership'. For 2004 we set three priorities: more investment in networks and knowledge, the reinforcement of

industrial competitiveness and more measures to increase labour market participation. We ask governments to react on all three fronts swiftly. We have to take advantage of the economic recovery in order to make up lost ground. Europe deserves to do better. European Commission (2004).

A few European banks have reacted to this situation by looking for investments elsewhere. This is the case, for example, with The Royal Bank of Scotland, whose Chairman, Fred Goodwin, is reported have said recently: *'there are plenty of interesting opportunities to buy banks in the United States, against almost none in Europe.'*

Both Santander and BBVA have joined the move. In October 2005, Santander announced the acquisition of 20 per cent of Sovereign Bancorp, the US's 18th largest bank in terms of assets, for US$2.4 billion. In 2006, BBVA decided to buy two banks in Texas for total joint investment of US$2.6 billion, having acquired another bank in the same state for US$900 million in 2004. In November 2006, BBVA also announced that it was buying 5 per cent of China International Trust and Investment Company (CITIC), a state-owned investment company and the 7th largest bank in China, for €500 million, with an option to buy an additional 5 per cent the following year.

Progress in new areas

This section illustrates the progress of Spanish banks in a few areas, from 1994 to 2004. Figure 2.3 presents the situation of the leading Spanish banks in January 1994, seven years after deregulation was completed but just before expansion in Latin America began. The horizontal axis measures the book-value of each bank while the vertical axis gives its market-value, (i.e. the market capitalisation on the stock exchange). The units used in both axes are billions of euros. The book-value is a good measure of the size of the bank, while the market-value reflects not only size but also a measure of the performance of the bank as seen by the market. The slanted lines represent different levels of the ratio of market to the book-value, a widely used measure of relative value.

This Figure may be useful to quickly size up the prospects of consolidation between different banks. For example, banks located in the low right-hand corner of the graph are large banks but low performers, as compared to others banks in higher-up locations. Their main strength is sheer size.

In contrast, banks in the upper left-hand corner are not the biggest banks but the ones that perform best in terms of profit and growth, translating into high market-value. Their strength is based on results, not size.

Overall these two groups have partial control of the situation when faced with a process of consolidation. In the former case this is based on sheer size and in the latter on performance.

Banks in the upper right-hand corner can be considered the ones in the best position to deal with a changing situation, based on their large size coupled with their good performance.

Finally, the banks in the lower right-hand corner have limited options due to their small size, no matter what their results may be.

Going back to the situation of January 1994 depicted in Figure 2.4, we can observe important differences in book-value between this group of banks; for instance, Popular was about half the size of BBV. The market value of all these banks lay between one and two times their book value. BBV had the highest market value, however in relative terms Popular and Santander where better valued than BBV, as measured by the ratio of market to book value.

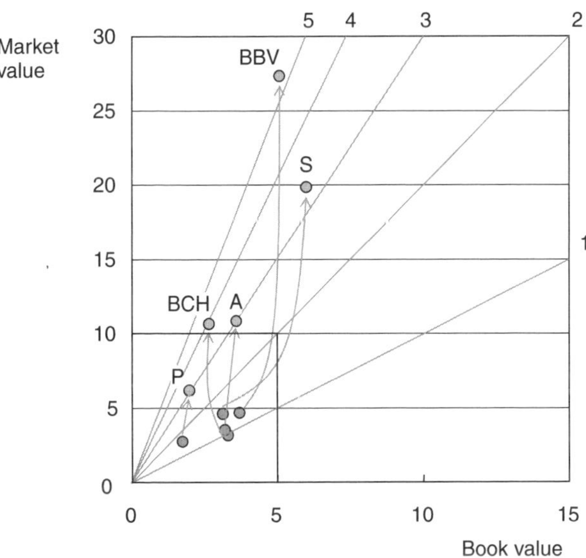

Figure 2.4   Spanish banks: January 1999 (values in billions of €)
Source: Palacios (2006).

Figure 2.4 shows the dramatic changes that took place over the next five years. The scale of this figure has been adjusted to allow for a threefold increase in the values shown. By January 1999, Santander had doubled its size and was the largest bank, pushing BBVA down to the second place. BBV had increased its market value seven times, and was the bank best valued by the market, after BCH, which had experienced a positive upturn since its difficult situation five years previously. Popular was left somewhat behind by a bourgeoning stock market that seemed to punish its strategy focused on profits and organic growth, ruling out any significant acquisition.

Figure 2.5 shows the situation one year later, just after the consolidation process was over. The mergers of the two biggest banks had brought their size to about 10 billion euros and Popular was left far behind. The market continued to value growth through mergers and consequently assigned high market to book value ratios to both banks.

To get a broader picture it may be useful to consider the same graph, including the leading European banks. Figure 2.6 shows this information corresponding to January 1999. In this figure we can see that the two leading Spanish banks, BBV and Santander, were relatively small in

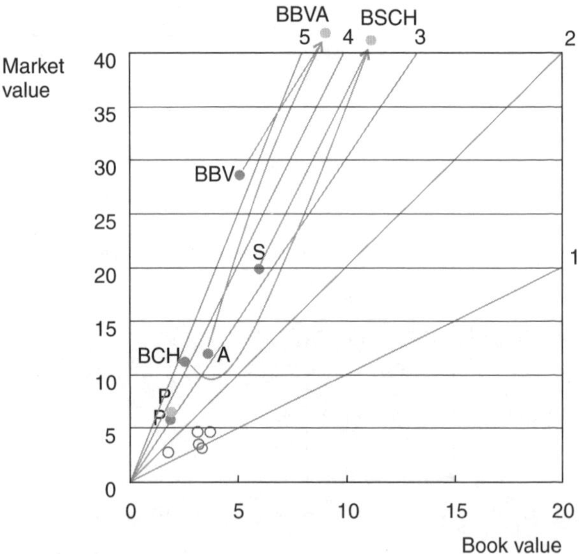

Figure 2.5   Spanish banks: January 2000 (in billions of €)
Source: Palacios (2006).

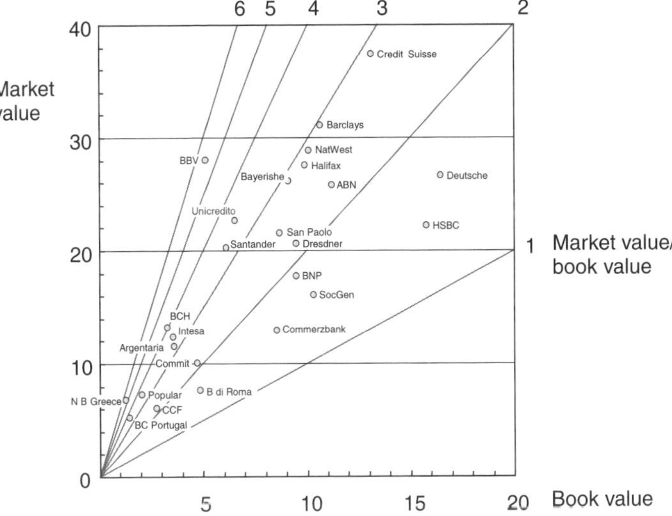

Figure 2.6   European banks: January 1999 (in billions of €)
Source: Palacios (2006).

size when compared to their European peers. On the other hand, they faired quite well in terms of market value.

BBV, for example, had twice the market value of BNP or Societé Generale, banks that were double BBV in size. BBV's market value was even higher than that of Deutsche bank, the largest European bank at that time. The smaller size of the Spanish banks was more than compensated by their better performance, in terms of growth and profitability, when compared to their European competitors. However, as we have commented above, European regulators prevented any possible move to capitalise on these advantages.

Figure 2.7 presents the situation of a selected group of financial institutions including banks and insurance companies in June 2000. As we can see, at that time most financial firms were valued at more than three times their book value; and five of them were considered to be worth over six times their book value.

The Spanish banks ranked second and third in terms of value among their group. However, their position was dwarfed by the higher values commanded by the insurance companies which seemed to have control of the European financial industry. To get a more complete perspective, a mark appears in the figure showing the position of Citibank that gives

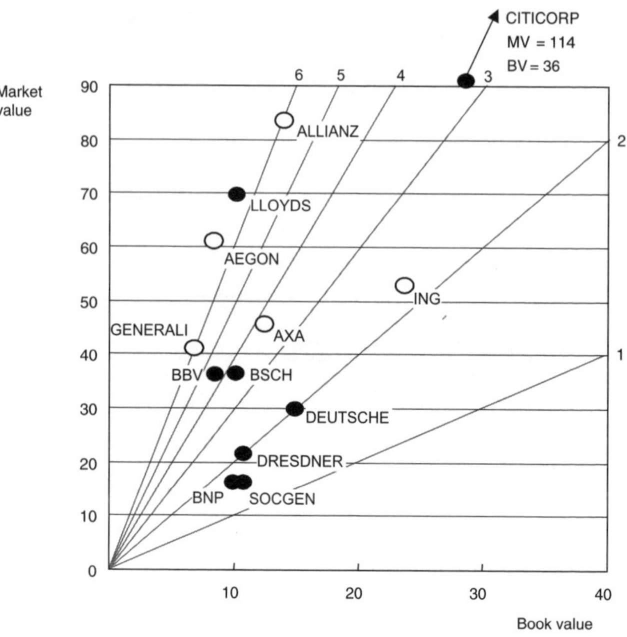

Figure 2.7   Selected banks and insurance companies: June 2000 (in billions of €)
Source: Palacios (2006).

a sense of the small size of the European institutions compared with those of the United States.

Finally, Figure 2.8 brings the situation closer to June 2004. It is impressive how the insurance industry has changed in those four years. Their positions on the graph are now mixed with those of the banks. Almost all institutions now have ratios of market to book value of between 1 and 2, a sharp drop from those reached four years earlier. Meanwhile Citibank, similar to the majority of American and Asian banks, has continued to grow quickly and its position is now much further away from Europe.

Conclusions

Within the context of the Spanish business model we identified in Chapter 1, this chapter has elaborated on the regulatory environment that has surrounded the banking industry in Spain for the last thirty years.

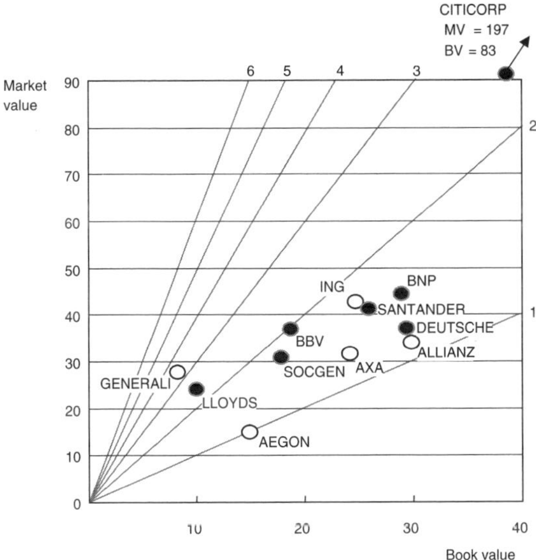

Figure 2.8   Selected banks and insurance companies: June 2004 (values in billions of €)

Source: Palacios (2006).

Our theory is that the development of Spanish retail banks, and their emergence in the world competition arena over the last decade, has much to do with the favourable conditions offered by the regulatory environment, aimed at fostering the creation of a world-class business model.

Of course, the existence of the favourable environment does not explain why there are variations in the speed with which banks adapted to situations or the success of the business models of some banks above others.

The latter can be called the sufficient condition and the environment the necessary condition. The necessary condition has been dealt with in this chapter and we will go on to explain the sufficient condition in Chapter 3. We will provide more detailed analysis of the business model including the three main axes upon which the model is based – the strategic use of IT systems, bias towards the size, and the pursuit of operational excellence.

Appendix 2.1   Major event in the modernization of the Spanish banking industry (1983–1996)

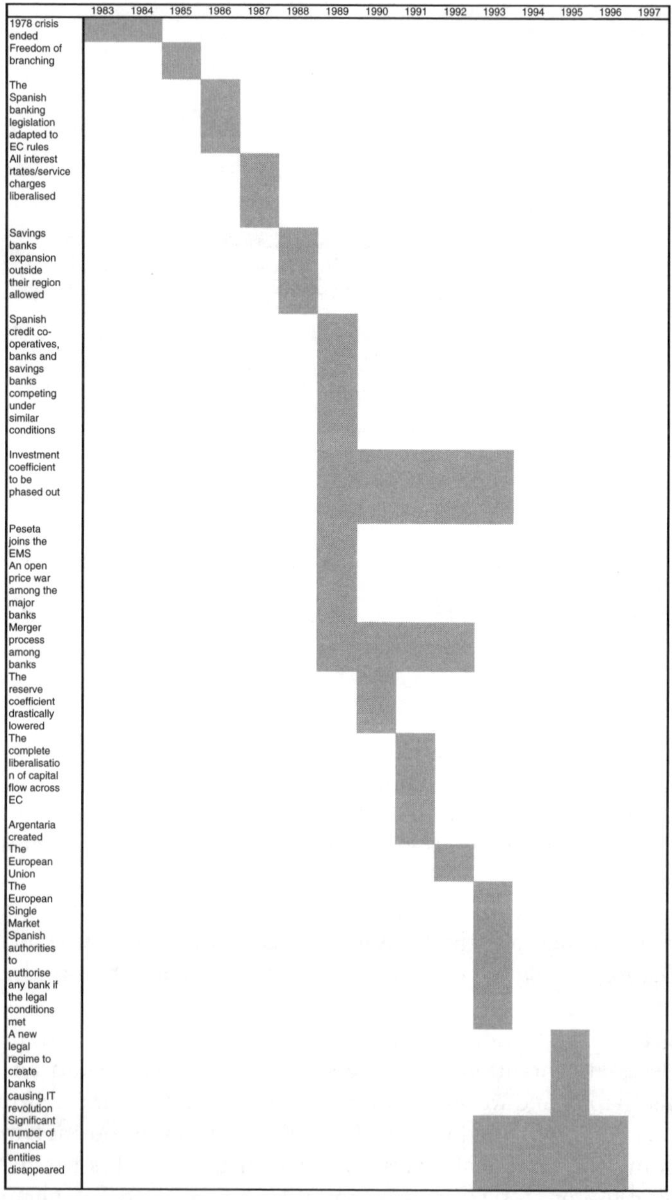

Source: Adapted from Zúñiga-Vicente, de la Fuente-Sabaté, and Rodríguez-Puerta (2004).

Appendix 2.2   Bank mergers and acquisitions in Europe: 1990–2005

A. Selected national mergers and acquisitions

Belgium	1992	CGER – AG (Fortis)
	1995	Fortis – SNCI
	1995	KB – Bank van Roeselaere
	1997	BACOB – Paribas Belgium
		CERA – Indosuez Belgium
	1998	KBC (KB – CERA – ABB)
	2001	Dexia – BACOB
Denmark	1990	Den Danske Bank
		Unibank (Privatbanken, Sparekassen, Andelsbanken)
	1999	Unibank – TrygBaltica
	2000	Danske Bank – RealDanmark
Finland	1995	Merita Bank (KOP – Union Bank of Finland)
France	1996	Crédit Agricole – Indosuez
	1999	BNP – Paribas
Germany	1997	Bayerische Vereinsbank – Hypo Bank (HBV)
	2001	Allianz – Dresdner
Italy	1992	Banca di Roma (Banco di Roma, Cassa di Risparmio di Roma, Banco di Santo Spirito)
		San Paolo – Crediop
	1995	Credito Romagnolo (Rolo) – Credito Italiano (UniCredito)
	1997	Ambroveneto – Cariplo (Intesa)
	1999	San Paolo – IMI
		Intesa – BCI
		SanPaolo IMI – Banca di Napoli
	2000	Banca di Roma – Bipop (Capitalia)
Netherlands	1990	ABN – AMRO
	1991	NMB – PostBank – ING
Portugal	1995	BCP – BPA
	2000	BCP – BPSM
Spain	1988	BBV (Banco de Bilbao – Banco de Vizcaya)

Appendix 2.2   Continued

	1989	La Caixa – Caja de Barcelona
	1992	Banco Central – Banco Hispano
	1994	Santander – Banesto
	1999	Santander – BCH
	1999	BBVA (BBV – Argentaria)
Sweden	1993	Nordbanken – Gota Bank
Switzerland	1993	CS – Volksbank – Winterthur
	1997	SBC – UBS
United Kingdom	1995	Lloyds – C&G – TSB
	2000	RBS – NatWest
	2000	Barclays – Woolwich
	2000	Abbey Nat. – Scottish Provident
	2001	Halifax – Bank of Scotland (HBOS)

B. Selected international acquisitions of commercial banks

Acquiring company	Target
Dexia (B, F)	Crédit Communal (B), Crédit Local (F), BIL (L),Crediop (I), BACOB (B)
BACOB (B)	Paribas (NL)
ING (NL)	BBL (B), BHF (D)
Generale de Banque (B)	Crédit Lyonnais (NL), Hambros (RU, corporate)
Fortis (B, NL)	AMEV + Mees Pierson (NL) / CGER/ SNCI (B) / Generale de Banque (B)
Nordbanken (S)	Merita (FIN), Unidanmark (DK), Christiania (N)
Santander (E)	Champalimaud (P)
HSBC (UK)	CCF (F)
Hypovereinsbank (D)	Bank Austria – Creditanstalt(A)
Santander (E)	Abbey

C. Selected international acquisitions of investment banks

Acquiring company	Target
Deutsche Bank	Morgan Grenfell
ING	Barings
Swiss Bank Corp	Warburg, O'Connor, Brinson, Dillon Read
Dresdner	Kleinwort Benson
ABN – AMRO	Hoare Govett
UNIBANK	ABB Aros
Merrill Lynch	Smith New Court
	FG (España), MAM
Morgan Stanley Dean Witter	AB Asesores
CSFB	BZW
Société Générale	Hambros
Citigroup	Schroder
Chase	Robert Fleming
ING	Chaterhouse Securities

Source: Dermine [2002] and own elaboration.

3
Generic Business Model in Spanish Retail Banks

In the introduction and overview to this book we touched on the generic business model identified between Spanish banks, in this Chapter we will consider this in more detail.

As a construct or ideal type,[1,2] the model comprises three key components, (1) a regulatory environment favouring Spanish banks becoming world-players, (2) excellent CEO's leading those banks, and (3) competent COOs (Chief Operations Officers) and management teams within the banks.

Considering the first point as being of utmost importance, we dedicated the previous chapter to reviewing the historical background and regulatory environment of the banking industry in Spain.

However the mere existence of a favourable regulatory environment does not automatically lead to the emergence of world-class banks, as this would fail to explain the differences between the development of the various banks. Rather, our attention must be focused on the conditions necessary for Spanish banks to stage their entrance to the world banking arena. For this, the leaders of such companies are pivotal to their success.

Therefore, we will first look in detail at the generic business model[3] commonly exhibited by Spanish retail banks and then go on to consider the success of Spanish banks in terms of value creation.[4] We will look particularly at Santander and BBVA (Banco Bilbao Vizcaya Argentaria).

Strategic configuration: outline

Our research shows that Spanish banks share a common strategic configuration. However, some variations to this can be observed by comparing Santander and BBVA, for example. As illustrated in Figure 3.1 the configuration (Graphs A, B, and C) includes:

A. The general framework consisting of
   1. the CEO,
   2. his team (COO/staff), and
   3. the regulatory environment, and
B. The basic business model comprising
   a. bias towards size resulting in focus on dual strategy levels – business or competitive, and corporate-level strategies,
   b. the pursuit of operational efficiency
   c. the strategic use of IT systems.
C. The product architecture oriented to the open and modular type.

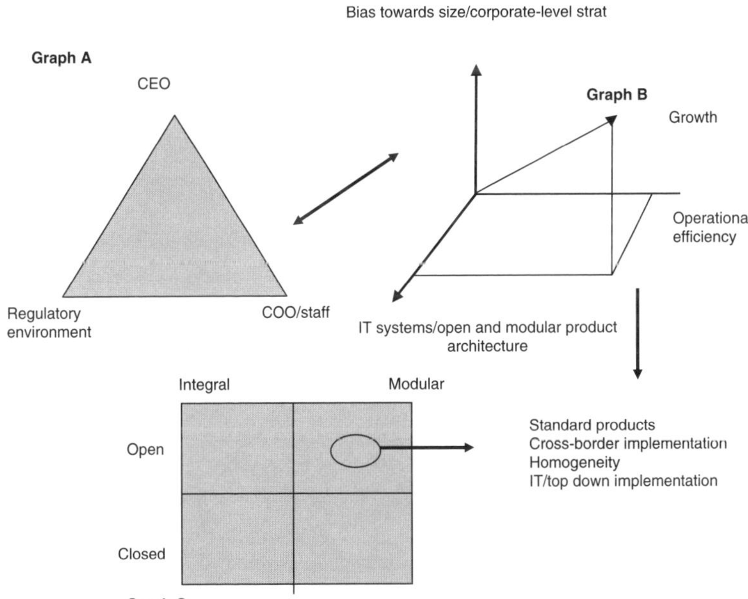

This chapter will first present an overall description of the Spanish banks' business model and then consider the importance of the thought processes of the leaders of these institutions, including a detailed description of Proto-Image of the Firm (PIF) and Profit-Arithmetic (PA) cognitive models.

The strategic configuration: overview

Triangle: The CEO, COO/staff, and the regulatory environment

The first element of the strategic configuration, illustrated in Figure A, is shown by a triangle, the corners of which correspond to the three components; the regulatory environment, the CEO, and the COO or staff. (See Figure 3.1.1: General framework: the triangle.)

(1) A legal and regulatory framework fostering a series of actions leading to increased competitiveness between Spanish banks.
(2) The prominent role played by CEOs with a specific and distinctive cognitive process.
(3) The existence of COOs and middle management who excel in OE (operational efficiency).[5]

These three components will be described and analysed in turn, particularly considering their roles in the Spanish banks' success in the international arena and the relationships between the banks.

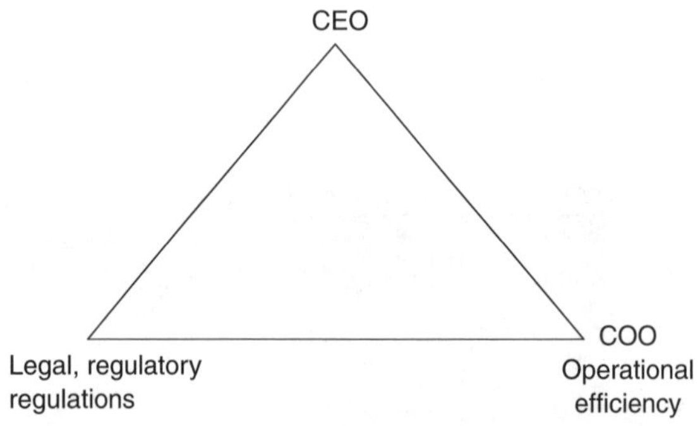

Figure 3.1.1   Graph A

Regulatory and legal framework in historical perspective

Deregulation of the Spanish banking sector started in 1962 with the *'Ley de Bases de Ordenación del Crédito y de la Banca'* (Law on credit and banking arrangements). This liberalisation was further propelled by a reform during the time of Minister Fuentes Quintana in 1977, which opened the door, allowing foreign banks into Spain and removed many of the distinctions hitherto made between banks and savings banks (*cajas de ahorros*). In 1987 the government liberalised all interest rates and commissions, and decided to reduce the percentage of obligatory investments, gradually eliminating them by the year 2000.[6]

The implementation of a series of measures to protect the banks' clients also became important for the development of the industry, insofar as it encouraged competition between the banks. The so-called, *'Guerra de supercuentas'* or 'War of Interest-bearing Current Accounts' in 1989 instigated by the then light-weight contender, Santander, heralded competition between Spanish banks on the basis of price.

A major spurt in rate of change came about from 1971 when branch opening restrictions were lifted, which ultimately drastically influenced in Spain's banking industry. Table 3.1 shows (1) a radical difference in the percentage of market share held by the banks; some like Santander moving up, while others such as Banesto disappear as independent entities (in this case absorbed by Santander), (2) the concentration of the

Table 3.1　Marketshare change of the seven largest banks (%)

	1985 (*)		2005 (*)
Central	9.57	Santander	40.25
Banesto	8.88	BBVA	29.72
Bilbao	7.51	Popular	8.34
Hispanoamericano	7.51	Sabadell	5.61
Vizcaya	6.30	Bankinter	3.98
Santander	5.35	Barclays	1.99
Popular	3.55	Pastor	1.87
Sum	48.68	Sum	91.72

(*) The market-share in the total assets in Spain's financial system.

Source: Planellas (2006: 20).

market-share held by the ten largest banks increased from 49 per cent to 92 per cent, and especially (3) the concentration of the market-share held by the two largest banks which by 2005 controlled as much as 70 per cent of the Spanish market.

During the aftermath of the crisis in the 1980s some of the most significant players disappeared, while others managed to position themselves amongst leading global banks in terms of market capitalisation. Due to active merger and acquisition polices, out of the large banks formerly known as the 'Seven Big Players', Banesto (originally the largest bank), Banco Central, and Banco Hispanoamericano disappeared as independent entities, whereas those that had held a lower market-share originally, in particular, Santander, Bilbao, and Vizcaya, began to figure as leading banks thanks to their clear, successful belief in innovation and the search for profitability and operational efficiency. (See Table 3.2 *Timeline Of Deregulation And Changes To The Financial Market In Spain*.)

Throughout this process leader figures played a key role in their respective entities: Rafael Termes, president of the Spanish Banking Association 'Asociación Española de Banca' (AEB) between 1977 and 1990, Pedro de Toledo, Banco de Vizcaya's CEO and architect of the bank's merger with Banco de Bilbao together with Angel Sánchez-Asiaín, his counterpart at Banco de Bilbao, and Emilio Botín, president of Santander.

Thanks to a change of tide that took place after a series of dynamic regulatory measures,[7] the Spanish banking sector developed from inefficient and backwards to a European leader in the sector.[8] Spanish banks benefited from the new international banking regulations, Basel II,[9] Solvency II and IAS.[10,11] This aside, some prudential measures, such as the banks' obligation to cover credit at a higher percentage than their competitors and the unequal treatment of banks and savings banks, were to constitute barriers to the development of Spanish banks. (See Chapter 2 on the deregulation of the sector in its historical framework).

CEOs and COOs

The deregulation of the sector nurtured competition between the banks, which gave rise to a significant improvement in efficiency and profitability. (González, n.d.; Palacios, 2004; Salas & Saurina, 2003; Termes, 1991b, 1991a).

However, perhaps most relevant to the development of the Spanish banks is the role played by their leading executives; the chairmen,

Table 3.2   The time-line of the deregulaiton in Spain

1969	Interest rates are set as a function of the Central Bank discount rate. Interbank rates, loan interest rates over three years and industrial banks deposit rates over to years are set freely.
1970	Establishment of a reserve requirement for banks.
1971	Establishment of a reserve requirement for savings banks. Forced investment ratios for commercial and savings banks.
1974	Lifting of restrictions to branch opening for commercial banks. Loan and deposit rates over two years freely determined. Forced investments for savings banks are reduced.
1977	Free determination of one-year loans and deposit interest rates. Forced investment ratios lowered. Savings banks become allowed to discount paper and operate in the foreign exchange market.
1978	Partial lifting of restrictions to foreign bank entry (restrictions on the retail segment remain).
1981	Free determination of interest rates for most assets. Over 6 months time deposit interest rates as well as ESP 1 million deposits become freely determined. Commissions on the liability side liberalized. Forced investments in the form of a compulsory deposit at the Central Bank are established.
1984	Reserve requirements increased. A new forced investment in public debt is set.
1985	New solvency regulation: Capital requirements are set as a function of risk, in 7 buckets. Savings banks free to open branches in their regions of origin. Equalization of the investment coefficient for commercial and savings banks.
1987	All interest rates and commissions free. Reduction of forced investment.
1988	Increase in loan loss provision requirements.
1989	Savings banks allowed to open branches nationwide. A calendar to phase out forced investments is announced.
1990	Strong consolidation among savings banks. Substantial reduction in the reserve requirements.
1991	Mergers among savings banks although quantitatively much less important than the previous ones. Mutual funds start to develop rapidly primarily as a result of changes in taxation.
1992	Changes in capital regulations (adaptation to EU rules).

Source: Salas and Saurina (2003) cited by Gallego et al. (2002).

CEOs, and COOs, whose decision-making made the most of the regulatory environment and indeed influenced the regulatory conditions to enable the radical transformation of the sector. Failure to consider these different leaders, would make it difficult to offer a convincing explanation of the diverging paths taken by different banks facing the same business and regulatory environment – such is the case with Banco Popular and Bankinter on the one hand, and Santander and BBVA on the other.

The relevance given to the CEO's knowledge and skills relates to trends in strategic thinking – the cognitive approach to strategic decisions (Barr, Stimpert, & Huff, 1992; Clapham & Schwenk, 1991; Hart & Banbury, 1994; Kagono, 1988; Mann & Ball, 1992; Mintzberg, 1990a, 1990b, 1990c; Tikkanen, Lamberg, Parvinen, & Kallunki, 2005; Weick, 1979). The cognitive approach is in keeping with the resource-based view of the firm (Barney, 2001; Ulrich & Barney, 1984; Ulrich & Smallwood, 2004).

The following section focuses on the cognitive process of CEOs as strategists so that we may then go on to analyse the success factors of Spanish banks in this context.

Kase, Sáez-Martínez, and Riquelme's (2005) framework, on which this analysis draws, is one of the few that consider the cognitive perspective, analysing top executives. (The detailed description of this framework is set out in the latter part of this Chapter.)

Our theory is that executives of Spanish banks lead their institutions on the basis that the future is an extension of day-to-day operations centred on the generation of a strong cash flow position. As such, their focus is what is called by Kase et al (2005), the Profit-Arithmetic cognitive approach (or PA. See below.)

In their four case studies on some of Japan's highly successful CEOs (Nissan's Ghosn, Yamato's Ogura, Sony's Ohga, and Shin-Etsu's Kanagawa) Kase et al (2005) identified two differing strategic approaches based on two different cognitive processes.[12] They are the value-laden, culture-bound, long-term oriented Proto-Image of the Firm (PIF) and the cash-flow generation, matter-of-fact, and rather short-term surviving Profit-Arithmetic (PA) processes.

While Sony's Mr Ohga has a clear image of what the essence of Sony is, or should be, Shin-Etsu's Mr Kanagawa acts in accordance with his extraordinary business acumen which allows him to discern what levers should be pulled to produce profit. Both succeed despite the huge difference in their business approach. It goes without saying that Mr Ohga does not ignore profit levers entirely, nor does Mr Kanagawa lack a corporate image against which to compare alternative decisions to check their fit with the corporate ethos.

If we call Mr Ohga's way of basing his judgment on a specific image of a firm the *proto-image of the firm (PIF) approach* then, by contrast, Mr Kanagawa operates on the basis of processing data and information through a mental model enabling him to discern which options are profit levers and which are not. This we call *profit arithmetic (PA)* approach.

Kase et al (2005) stress that neither approach is superior. In each and every situation; it depends on the business environment and the skills and experience of the executives concerned. As a rule, the faster the pace of change in the business environment and technology panorama, the better the firm does, if PIF is adopted (provided the firm's financial position is solid). In a more mature business environment or with a predictable pace of change, the better the PA-approach is better, particularly, when the firm is in jeopardy and its survival questionable.

Our theory is that the strategic approach taken by Spanish banks shows clear traits of being PA; their emphasis on daily operations rather than a grand long-term vision, their focus on the continuous improvement of operational cost efficiency, their stress on the creation of value for shareholders as the primary concern, and so on.

The adoption or perhaps emergence of the PA approach may find its origin in the banking crisis and consequent transformation in the 1970s and 1980s in Spain.

Firstly, overcoming the crisis required more focus on profit and cash flow generation. Secondly, the PA approach favoured such focus and helped to foster the improvement of operations management and thirdly, even though in the process the retail banks lost their market shares in favour of savings banks, the approach aided some of the bank CEOs to discover that the fostering of a penchant for growth in size was essential to outmanoeuvre their competitors. The competition for size went through mergers and acquisitions, which ultimately shrank the number of major players in Spain from seven (Banesto, Central, Hispano, Bilbao, Vizcaya, Santander and Popular) to four by the turn of the century and to three (Santander, BBVA and Popular) by 2007. The mergers also highlighted the need to integrate and improve IT systems if the resulting banks wanted to hold sway in the competitive arena.[13] Therefore, the penchant for growth, begun around the time when the PA approach was put in place by the top management at banks, gave rise to excellent IT systems, which combined with other strategic components such as the ferocious pursuit of operational excellence, and contributed to the emergence of a world-class generic business model.

Since, the PIF and PA approaches are a key part of the business model, further explanation can be found in final part of this chapter.

(B) The basic business model

The second component of Spanish retail banks' strategy is founded on the basic business model. It comprises (1) bias towards size resulting in focus on the dual strategy levels – business/competitive, and corporate-level strategies, (2) pursuit of operational efficiency (ratio of efficiency), and (3) strategic use of IT systems, and open and modular product architecture. (See Figure 3.1.2 *IT systems, pursuit of efficiency, and bias towards size and growth.*)

Bias towards size based on dual focus on business and corporate-level strategies

For-profit organisations fight their battles on the basis of business or competitive strategy either by cost leadership or differentiation. Banks are no exception.

In a world characterised by diminishing spread, that is a decrease in the difference between the yield of lending and the interest paid to deposit holders, cost efficiency is essential for prosperity, if not survival.[14]

The Spanish retail banks have been famously successful in lowering costs, as can be seen from their efficiency ratios (operational costs incurred divided by income). Thus, in worldwide and European efficiency ratio rankings they hold the highest positions.[15]

However, in many industries the prevailing key to success has been quietly shifting to corporate-level strategy, defined as 'domain selection'

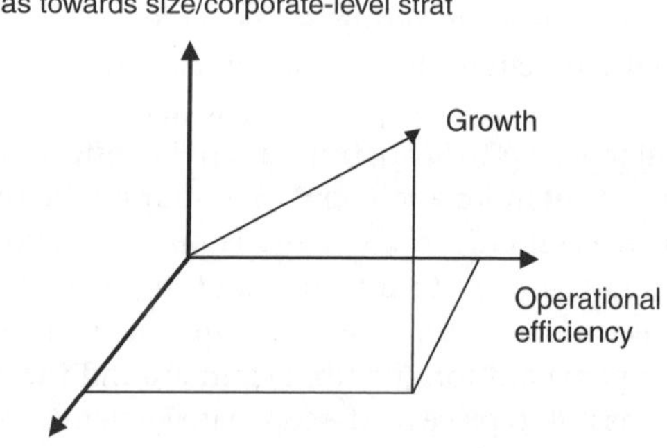

Figure 3.1.2   Graph B

in contrast to 'domain navigation' (Grant, 2004). The purpose of corporate-level strategy is the creation of value at the level of the corporate centre or parent organisation, in pursuit of profit maximisation for the company as a whole (Collis & Montgomery, 1998; Goold, Campbell, & Alexander, 1994). The careful combination of business areas allowing the corporation to generate higher profits is one of the main issues at this level of strategy.

Size of the corporation in terms of market capitalisation has become more important in the banking industry, as it has in other industries such as cement (dominated by Lafarge, Cemex, etc.) and steel (where Mittal is the clear market leader). Globalisation giving rise to an increased need to invest in research and development, above all in Information Technology, plays an important part in bringing this about.

Where the fight for market share takes place over years or decades, effective and continual effort on the business or competitive strategy level may be successful. However, for banking entities that stay focused on their domestic local markets, the time for effective competition is running out. In our interviews with top management of both Santander and BBVA, they emphasised the importance of growth in size, using phrases such as 'growth is in our genes'[16] and 'we are like the Romans'[17] in planning growth and implementing their business plan.

It is probable that, in periods of recession, less efficient retail banks with a wider business scope, particularly in terms of geographical extension and sales volume, find themselves far more exposed than efficient banks with a narrower business scope. If this is so, one of the keys to success will be managing expansion into new areas, including taking different country risks in order to diversify banks' portfolios combining different risks and increase the potential for growth.

In his research on large Japanese banks, Tadesse (2005: 1) points out: 'While diseconomies of scale are shown to be pervasive in the large banks, defying the rationale for consolidation, evidence of an underlying technological progress is presented that operates to significantly increase the industry's efficient minimum size, generating economies at larger banks, thus justifying the ongoing trend in consolidation.'

However, Berger and Allen (1994: 2) do not consider scale and scope economies in banking to be important, except for the smallest banks. On the contrary they maintain that, 'x-efficiency or managerial ability to control costs, is of much greater magnitude – at least 20% of banking costs.'

So the discussion of economies of scale in the academic forum is a moot point. However, considering the behaviour pattern of the large

Spanish banks, there seems to be an underlying belief in the need to create economies of scale that simultaneously guides and binds the banks.[18]

Regardless of whether it is grounded in actual economic benefit or not, the growth in size and the attainment of presence in multiple national markets and geographic regions have become of utmost importance for the major players in the banking industry.[19] Mergers and acquisitions to take over local banks and run local operations are deployed with dexterity and form the core of corporate-level strategy. Thus, in order for banks to compete and become world-players, it is not sufficient for them to have effective competitive or business strategies; they must also design a winning corporate-level strategy.

From observation of the strategy employed by the Spanish banks, it can be concluded that they combine business and corporate-level strategy very well.

Operational efficiency

Why is efficiency one of the cornerstones of the Spanish banks' strategy? What role does IT play in increasing operational efficiency? And how does the replicability of the business model fit in?

Efficiency gain is the quintessential challenge for all retail banking. The commoditisation and securitisation processes in the financial sector are taking heavy tolls on the financial institutions' coffers, as 'improving technology and the continuing decline in transaction costs has added to the intensity of the competition' (Merton, 1995: 26). Crane and Bodie (1996: 109) go further enumerating reasons for the efficiency gains as increased competition from non-traditional institutions, declining processing costs, the erosion of product and geographic boundaries, and less restrictive regulations.

Crane et al. (1995; 1996) maintain that financial institutions perform six functions: (1) making payments, (2) pooling resources to fund large scale enterprises, (3) transfer of economic resources over time and across distances, (4) management of risk, (5) price information to help to co-ordinate decentralised decision-making, and (6) the handling of incentive problems, for example, by imposing loan covenants on borrowers to protect lenders.

Therefore, 'when banks take deposits, they are essentially combining the payment and pooling functions. Lending combines a transfer of resources with risk management' (Crane & Bodie, 1996: 112).

These functions can be discharged by non-bank financial institutions such as money market mutual funds against which the only way to compete is 'by cutting costs and striving to be more efficient' (Crane & Bodie, 1996: 114). From this, it follows that, in order to survive, banks have to pursue the maximum efficiency gain in their operations.

Have the Spanish banks attained efficiency? As shown in Table 3.8 *Evolution Of The Efficiency Ratio In Europe 1997–2004* in Chapter 3, Spain has certainly positioned itself as the top runner in this ratio with 53.87 as compared to the UK with 54.98 and Ireland's 55.12. (See Appendix 'Are they really that efficient?' for a more sceptical interpretation of efficiency gains by UBS researchers.)

Santander's data shows constant improvement – from 62.1 in 1998 to 42. in 2005 (see Chapter 3). Its Portuguese operation, Santander Totta, reached 43.7 as early as 2003, better than the 49.3 which Santander achieved that year.

In search of efficiency, Banco Sabadell's chairman, José Oliu advocates making commercial areas and cost management more dynamic (Oliu, 2006: 8). Working on the first of these comprises (1) productivity increase, (2) focus on customer loyalty, and (3) specialised networks. The second implies a focus on (1) structural adjustments, (2) outsourcing of services, and (3) continual improvement of operational models.

So how do they attain efficiency? To a large extent, the answer can be found in IT systems and product architecture. First, let's have a look at IT systems and their strategic use to see how they contribute to the Spanish banks' operational excellence and cost efficiency. Open and modular architecture facilitates efficiency using IT systems, so we will review and analyse this type of product architecture and the way in which Spanish banks achieve this.

IT systems, and the modular and open product architecture triangle[20]

IT systems.   Three reasons tend to be given for the importance of IT systems in the banking industry. Firstly, due to better access to information across different geographical areas and time zones, the reduction in dissemination time, and a larger capacity to store and process information.

Secondly, in light of the fact that banking fundamentally concerns the handling and management of risk,[21] IT systems can bring about better customer relations and therefore improve the chance of customers buying more products and services. IT systems can also improve operational efficiency and may give rise to better decision-making. Given the huge amount of investment in research and development required, buying more products and services. IT systems can also improve operational efficiency and may give rise to better decision-making. Given the huge amount of investment in research and development required, banking is really one of the pioneering industries.

Thirdly, in the event of a takeover, a strong IT system can allow the acquisition of a target bank with a less developed one. Banco Sabadell's José Oliu (2006: 12) validates the Spanish banks' acquisition of other European ones, since the latter tend to lag behind the former in their use of IT systems. This translates to 6 to 15 points difference in efficiency ratio. Oliu avers that the improvement to the acquired bank's operation efficiency thanks to the use of better IT systems alone can offset the acquisition cost.

Spanish retail banks stand out in their use of IT systems. 60 per cent of banking experts consulted by the Conference of European Banks believe that the Spanish banking industry is equipped with the best technology base.[22] The Spanish banks' core system, namely, the set of basic applications that support standard banking operations, is recognised as functioning perfectly.[23] Spanish banks show the highest efficiency indicators in the use of IT systems.[24] Thanks to the efficient use of IT systems Spanish banks have the lowest number of employees per branch – 6 as against 13 in Italy and 45 in the UK.[25] (For the advantage derived from intensive use of IT, see Table 3.3 *Advantages Of IT – Systems*.)

In line with their PA focus on cash flow generation and operational efficiency the Spanish banks are characterised,[26] in their use of IT systems, by the emphasis on (1) internal advantage (vis-à-vis external advantage) and (2) proven technology (vis-à-vis ground-breaking pioneering technology).

Firstly, Spanish banks make use of IT systems fundamentally to improve in their back-office operations, rather than to differentiate their products and services. Clients benefit from IT systems by way of better quality of service and not so much by external or apparent advantage of differentiated products or services.

Secondly, Santander and BBVA tend to take on proven technology in lieu of adopting a ground-breaking, revolutionary one.[27,28] These banks introduce the technology that clearly yields immediate advantage and apply it across the board to all their operations.

In conclusion, for the Spanish banks technology constitutes an essential element of their business. However these banks tend only to consider technology to the extent to which it is beneficial for their operations – improvement in their efficiency, much in line with their PA mind-set.

Table 3.3   Advantages of IT systems

Factors for success	Leverage	Benefits
The intensive use of IT systems	• High level of core IT systems • Larger horizontal integration between different applications and the incorporation of common modules (score cards, product workshops, and committees) oriented to customers • Larger use of integral packages of software • High level of outsourcing • Automation of back-office processes for their centralisation • Adequate distribution of IT costs between discretionary and non-discretionary costs • Automation of payment services	• Cost reduction • Optimisation of cost structure (discretionary vs. non-discretionary; variable vs. fixed) • Generation of high-level service • Improvement of productivity
The fundamental role of the technology co-operation between financial institutions	• Industry-wide co-operation in compensation and settlement • Intermediation in almost all payment transactions: payment by direct debit and transferences • Interconnection of ATM networks • Utilisation of common standards for payment services	• Cost reduction • Service standardisation • Use of electronic payment methods • Overcoming of geographic fragmentation

Source: Moreno and Avendaño (Moreno & Avendaño : 10)

Product architecture oriented to the open and modular type.   Spanish banks pursue the cost leadership advantage by commercialising similar products and services throughout their geographic spread, homogenising their offer. This gives rise to substantial savings in R&D expenses by applying the skills and knowledge already learnt in one area, and the comfort of offering quality-assured products and services, as described in Nafría (2004). Product design is based in Spain and the bank's effective use of IT systems facilitates the introduction of these products into different markets. (See Figure 3.1.3 *Open and Modular type of Product Architecture.*)

The offering of the same or similar financial products is facilitated by the open and modular nature of the product architecture. The product architecture is the concept relating to the way in which the core components forming a product are combined (Fujimoto, 2003: 59).[29 and 30] There are two types of product architecture: (1) modular and (2) integrated. The modular (and open) type allows the assembly of standard, ready-made components procured from external suppliers without much need to fine tune between them, in contrast, the integrated (and closed) type requires integration and optimisation of an interface between the components (Fujimoto, 2003, 2004a).

The modular-type architecture is based on the combination and assembly of standard parts and components using standard production facilities (without modifying them too much); and the integration-type architecture obtains new product and new product functions by adjusting and adapting pieces and components to each other (Fujimoto, 2004a). Fujimoto (2003: 60) points out that Japan excels in the second type, since it takes advantage of the country's organisational capability; teamwork and the sharing of information.

Product architecture can also be classified by open and closed types (Fujimoto, 2003: 89).[31] An open type is basically modular type but the interface between components is usually standardised across the industry. Product assembly is feasible without the need to interface the differences. A closed type is so-called because of the exclusiveness of the interface

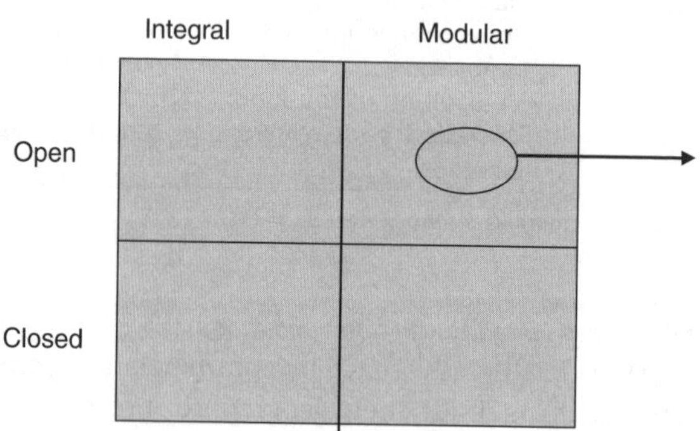

Figure 3.1.3   Graph C

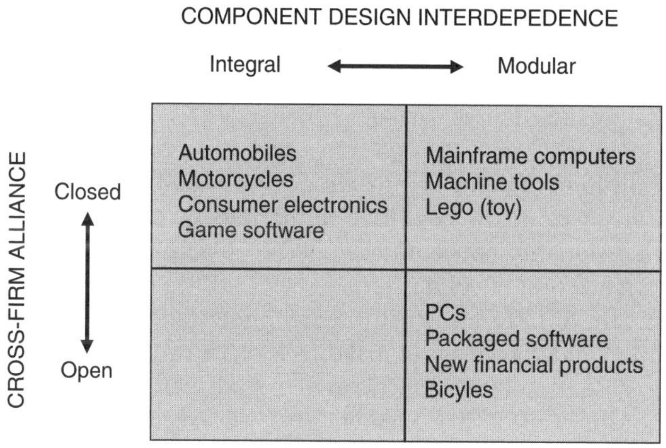

COMPONENT DESIGN INTERDEPEDENCE

Integral ←→ Modular

CROSS-FIRM ALLIANCE

Closed

Automobiles Motorcycles Consumer electronics Game software	Mainframe computers Machine tools Lego (toy)
	PCs Packaged software New financial products Bicyles

Open

Figure 3.2   Graph B Component design interdependence
Source: Fujimoto, (2003: 90).

design. In the case of the automobile industry, the component design is entrusted to external suppliers but basic design including the interface and functions is closed to external suppliers and undertaken by the automobile manufacturers themselves.

Accordingly, a two by two matrix can be constructed by combining modular, integral, open, and closed types as illustrated in Figure 3.2.

The ability of the Spanish retail banks to convert their product architecture into the modular and open type enables them (1) to make the most of the IT systems advantage, i.e. the management control of costs and personnel, and (2) to implant the same or similar products and services in different geographical markets without the need to rely too heavily on the skills and capabilities of local staff.

The open and modular product architecture is very much in line with the trend in the use of IT systems to gain competitive edge. Moreno and Avendaño (2006: 13) list as future trends: (1) industrialisation and standardisation of IT systems (presumably facilitated by open and modular product architecture) and (2) the conversion of branches into 'supermarkets', i.e. places where standardised financial services are sold.

Cognitive process – PIF and PA

The head of the corporation is ultimately responsible for the design of the organisation's strategy, defining the issues and taking strategic decisions in the light of a specific mental framework.

CEOs carry out four functions in transforming their organisations: (1) making the transformation meaningful for their staff; (2) being a role-model leading the staff; (3) bundling and leading a team; and (4) relentless pursuit of targets (Aiken & Keller, 2007).

Strategy in this context is a pattern which gives coherence to the decisions of an individual or organisation (Grant, 2004). The need for the pattern arises from the cognitive limitations of human beings – the bounded rationality concept developed by March and Simon (March, 1978; March & Simon, 1958).

The stream of research which tries to understand how managers use information and knowledge to make decisions is called the cognitive perspective (Kase et al., 2005: 28). It is used to study perceptions and conceptualisation as well as management style of executives (Mintzberg & Waters, 1985).

From the cognitive perspective, based on the four in-depth case studies Kase et al. (2005) identify two different, equally successful, business approaches and name them the Proto-Image of the Firm (PIF) and the Profit-Arithmetic (PA) approaches (Kase et al., 2005: 30).

Proto-Image of the Firm (PIF) approach

When a firm's CEO has a clear image of what his firm stands for, he has the PIF approach. It may be a *personal* theory but can be codified and made explicit to be transmitted to others.

The personal and professional background of the CEO influences his vision of the firm. Organisational culture helps to configure a PIF. The stronger the firm's existing culture, the greater the chances that a new CEO's PIF will be similar to the founder's. When a new employee joins a firm, a socialisation process starts. In the process the employee develops an idea of what the company is. This process also takes place when a new CEO is contracted, although this same individual subsequently influences the culture and develops the PIF.

A PIF as a mental model is an interpretative mode of an organisation. It is determined by the CEO's beliefs on the corporate environment, so the relevance of the corporate environment on the shaping of a PIF is considerable. (See Figure 3.3 Proto-Image of the Firm approach.)

More often than not, PIF is an abstract vision of the firm not based on the actual resources and capabilities.[32] Soichiro Honda offered an example of this when, while his firm was still a small provincial garage, he proclaimed its need to become international (Pascale, 1988, 1996). Obviously, strategic intent (Hamel & Prahalad, 1989) and PIF interweave. A CEO's PIF may be based on core competences, some key capabilities, etc.

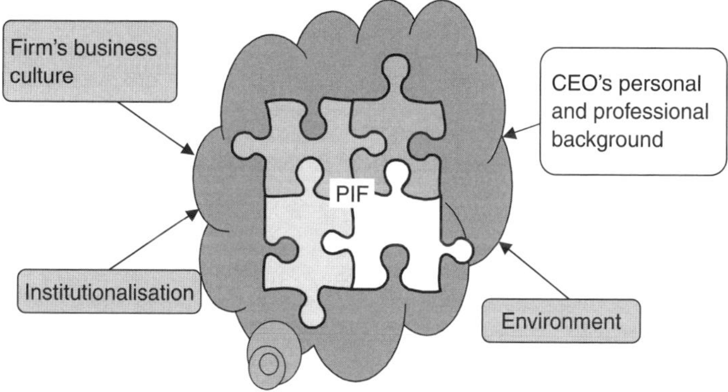

Figure 3.3   Proto-Image of the Firm approach
Source: Kase et al. (2005: 33).

The CEOs with a PIF approach believe they know what their firms are or should be in the future.

If a new investment opportunity arises it will be approved if it meets the principal criterion of whether the investment matches the CEO's PIF. Even if short-term profitability is questioned, the decision will be based on what the CEO believes the firm should be in the future and will overrule the consideration of potential short-term losses.

PIF business leaders understand situations they are faced with by contrasting potential outcomes against their PIF. Associated variables are selected around the PIF and facilitate simplification of the situation.

Profit-arithmetic (PA) approach

CEOs with a PA approach guide their decision-making on the possibility of making profit. Their minds tend to be more analytical and rational than the PIF CEOs'. PA executives' decisions are based on their firm's resources and capabilities, strengths and weaknesses. An important factor in a PA approach is context. A PA CEO knows what profit levers should be pulled.

Analysing a situation involves a simplification process, as in the case of the PIF approach. The simple way of considering the thought process of a PA CEO is that they are classifying the situation into a pattern they have seen or dealt with in the past. Therefore experience is key to this approach, which means that there is no need for a huge amount of

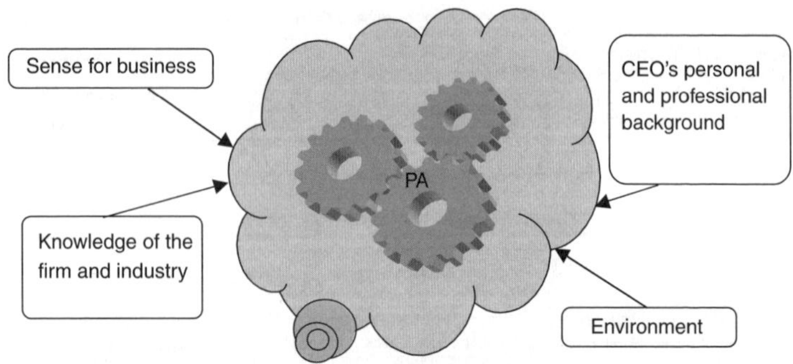

Figure 3.4   Profit-arithmetic
Source: Kase et al. (2005: 37).

information. A PA CEO knows which information is relevant and will only demand that information.

The factors shaping this approach are the CEOs' professional and personal background, their knowledge of the firm and the industry and their business sense. (See Figure 3.4 The Profit-Arithmetic approach.)

As discussed above, pattern recognition of a similar experience is important for the PA CEOs. Essentially, patterns learnt throughout their career allow them to endow meaning to new situations. Experience of previous success or failure guides them since they have formed their own 'theory of the business' (Drucker, 1994).

Business sense forms an essential part of the PA approach. One CEO classified as a PA manager holds that there are things one can do nothing about – will and effort cannot change them (Kase et al., 2005: 38). It is very much in-line with the thinking of the Resource-based View of the Firm (RVF) advanced by Barney (1991) and others.

CEOs with a PA approach prioritise everything that may enhance the firm's profit potential. Cost-cutting and actions biased to daily operations are their concern. A *grand design* for the future does not interest them. Diversification is shied away from if risk is not compensated for by secure profitability.

PIF and PA compared

The difference between PIF and PA regarding applicability, time-frame, and business domain is set out below. (See Table 3.4 *Comparison Of PIF And PA Approaches*.)

Firstly, in essence, a PIF approach is the image of the firm, which leads to the conceptualisation of the business that facilitates the decision-making

Table 3.4   Comparison of PIF and PA

	PIF	PA
Essential element	Image of the firm	Actions oriented to profit levers
Shaping or constituent factors	Professional background, environment, firm's business culture and institutionalization	Professional background, environment, knowledge of firm and industry and sense for business
Familiarity with the firm	Necessary	Not so essential
Time frame	Focus on mid- to long-term	Penchant for short-term
Domain	Wide, new competences and products are fostered	Narrow, existing portfolio
Cash flow position	Affluence required	At the time of crisis, the only option is to survive+++
Explicit or implicit instructions from the top	Implicit, second-guessed	Explicit
Applicable when changing firms?	Difficult	Possible
Succession	Relatively easy to find a person with a similar approach, if they share the belief	Imitability or replicability low
Combination with the other approach	PIF – top management PA – lower management	If PA at the top, PIF not possible at lower levels

Source: Kase et al. (2005: 40).

by the CEOs. A PA approach is, by contrast, more 'pragmatic' in the sense that it favours actions oriented to profit levers.

The constituent factors of each mental model differ: A PIF approach requires the CEOs to possess previous knowledge or familiarity with the firm, its culture, ideology and socialisation process. A PIF is shaped by the firm's culture, but it does not mean that it remains unchanged when CEOs change. The PIF of a new CEO may be different since he may have to deal with a different business environment, which requires a change in the business culture and routines.

Though desirable, familiarity with the firm's culture and ideology is not a necessary condition for a new CEO with a PA approach. His short-term orientation and the palpable good performance flowing from his decisions make him more trusted by his employees. Moreover, the fact that his decisions have such a clear profit-seeking basis make them easier for the staff to understand.

Secondly, regarding the time-frame, the PIF approach has a mid- to long-term propensity, while the PA one is more action- and operations-oriented with the focus on short-term results. Apart from CEOs' personalities the difference may derive from the firm's financial position. If a firm is losing money, it must perforce, prioritise cash flow and a PA approach will suit the situation better.

A PA CEO is short-term profit-oriented. However, this does not mean that he fails to think ahead or to consider long-term results. Pressed for choice between short-term or mid- to long-term during a crisis, he will choose short-term solutions.

Lastly, in terms of business domain, the PIF approach is concerned with new product development, new business exploitation, new core competences, etc. The PA approach, in contrast, is more centred on strengthening existing products and businesses.

PIF and PA approaches and corporate-level strategy

The assumption that underlies strategy is that the primary goal of the enterprise is to be profitable in the long-term (Grant, 2004: 22).

Strategy involves answering two questions: (1) what business should the company be in? and; (2) how should the company compete in a particular business? The answer to the first question concerns corporate-level strategy, while the second relates to competitive or business strategy (Grant, 2004).

Corporate-level strategy decisions include diversification (horizontal, vertical and geographic), acquisitions, new ventures, and resource allocation between different activities.

PIF CEOs undertake diversification investments if they fit their proto-image of the firm. Irrational investments can be made on the expectation that they will lead the firm to the CEO's PIF. PIF CEOs analyse the financial potential of an investment before making it, but this analysis does not become the crux of the decision.

A PA CEO takes corporate-level strategy decisions on the basis of the analysis of profit potential. Where time constraints impede him from conducting in-depth analysis, he relies on his experience and business sense to guide the decision-making.

As shown in Table 3.5 Kase et al. (2005) compare PIF and PA approaches in the light of Porter's (1987) and Goold and Campbell's (1987) corporate-level strategy frameworks.

Table 3.5   Comparison Porter, PIF, and PA

Porter (1987)	PIF	PA
Portfolio strategy (The centre creating value by spotting acquisition candidates)	• Company identification is profit based • Loose financial controls	• Company identification is based on Proto-Image • Strict financial control
Restructuring (The centre creates value by transforming underperforming firms)	Can be accomplish to adjust the new acquired firm to the PIF	Efforts aimed to increase profit levels
Transferring skills (The centre creates value by organizing inter-unit linkages)	It is more accurate on a PIF model	When profit levers are similar among business
Sharing activities (The centre creates value by common physical distribution system and sales force)	• Strong feeling of corporate identity	• Financial incentives that prime coopera-tion among businesses
	• A clear mission that pinpoint the impor-tance of integration among business units	• Multifunctional and multibusiness working groups

Source: Kase et al. (2005: 45).

Porter (1987) classifies the value creation pattern by the corporate centre into four generic corporate-level strategies: portfolio, restructuring, transferring skills, and sharing activities.

For their part, Ashridge Strategic Management Centre's Michael Goold and Andrew Campbell (1987) identify the role of the corporate centre fundamentally as (1) planning and allocating resources and (2) controlling and auditing performance. Based on the way these two influences, namely, planning and controlling, are combined and used by the centre, Goold and Campbell classify the strategic management styles into strategic planning, strategic control, and financial control types. Goold and Campbell (1994) call them parenting styles,[33] since the classification is carried out by the way in which the centre or parent exerts its value-creating influence.

Strategic planning: the centre works closely with business unit managers to develop strategy through extensive planning processes, etc.

Strategic control: the centre leaves the plan development initiative to the business-unit management. It reviews and critiques plans and uses the review to check the quality of thinking in business units.

Table 3.6   Ashridge, PIF and PA comparison

	PIF/PA approach framework	Ashridge framework
Assumptions	Business leaders motivational or mental scheme	• Personal motivation structure (autonomy versus intervention from the center) – balancing of tensions • Consonant remuneration/ compensations
Environment	Organizations and systems contingent on business environment (fast-growing, mature, etc.)	Organizations and systems contingent on business environment (fast-growing, mature, etc.)
Key variables	Business domain Timeframe	Control and planning
Focus	Business leaders	Corporate-wide, systemic co-ordination

Source: Kase et al. (2005: 48).

Financial control: the centre exercises its influence through the budget process, strategy development is limited. The centre focuses on a close review of the annual budget. (Table 3.6 compares Ashridge parenting styles with PIF and PA approaches.)

Value creation by Spanish banks: Empirical validation of the generic business model

Spanish banks have modernised at a rapid pace since the 1980s, due at first to pressure arising from Spain's status as a new EU member state and then the necessity for banking to reach the critical sector size later. Such evolution of the Spanish banking system was mainly pioneered by Santander and BBVA.

Firstly, this section will look at how these two banks outperform the Spanish banking system as well as their European competitors. This phenomenon may partly be explained by a generic environment that has favoured European retail banks over the last decade. However, there have been a number of specific factors that have favoured the creation of value for the shareholders of Santander and BBVA, confirming the excellence of their management and business model.

Secondly, we will delve into the internal mechanism that we believe exists between value creation and the business model, i.e. the pursuit of operational efficiency, the use of IT systems, and the penchant for size and growth.

Empirical validation

Between December 1991 and December 2005 Santander and BBVA experienced a large increase in their market capitalisation, and thus an increase in the shareholders' value and the value created for shareholders, as stated in Table 3.7 *Value Creation By Santander And BBVA*.

These indicators go further to confirm our belief that the Spanish banks have an excellent business model based, as discussed, on a PA approach. As such, we consider that it was the commitment to growth in retail banking, the development of IT and a constant improvement of efficiency, which enabled Spanish banks to outperform their competitors.

Table 3.7   Value created for the shareholders of Grupo Santander and BBVA

	Santander	BBVA
1992	−404	−3,727
1993	3,988	2,532
1994	−2,530	−611
1995	1,082	2,563
1996	3,569	6,729
1997	12,381	19,651
1998	1,227	9,794
1999	8,937	−133
2000	−4,603	1,547
2001	−18,241	−14,515
2002	−22,141	−24,067
2003	14,517	5,140
2004	−3,956	5,551
2005	10,512	5,161

(*) In € millions of 2005.

Source: Fernández and Carabias (2006a; 2006b).

Table 3.8   Efficiency ratio in Europe

		1997			2004
1	Sweden	51,14	1	Spain	53,87
2	Denmark	51,92	2	UK	54,98
3	UK	59,86	3	Ireland	55,12
4	Finland	60,07	4	Portugal	58,23
5	Portugal	60,64	5	Denmark	58,82
6	Ireland	61,59	6	Sweden	60,91
7	Bélgium	64,35	7	Greece	60,93
8	Spain	64,69	8	Finland	61,61
9	Greece	66,84	9	Bélgium	64,02
10	Austria	68,26	10	Italy	65,31
11	Germany	68,72	11	Austria	66,67
12	Holland	68,77	12	France	66,81
13	Italy	72,03	13	Holland	67,89
14	France	72,28	14	Germany	75,47

Source: AEB – Spanish Association of Banks (Annual report, 1997 & 2004).

Table 3.8 compares the efficiency ratio average in different European countries in 1997 and 2004.[34] As we can see, Spain improved its ranking from 8th in 1997, to the lead position in 2004.

Successful Spanish banks emerging from a system with structural difficulties compared to its competitors: Although Spanish banks, savings banks and the Spanish Central Bank have managed to develop a successful banking model, the main players in the financial system have had to cope with adverse conditions in order to compete. With this in mind, we will quickly analyse the Spanish financial system from a macro and micro perspective.

Santander and BBVA: outstanding performance

The performance of Santander and BBVA shows a parallel between two retail banks with a strong emphasis on value creation. The common performance of these entities leads us to consider the existence of a Spanish retail model based on PA management and value creation on the financial markets.

Market capitalisation

The market capitalisation of Santander and BBVA grew by twenty-six times and almost fourteen times, respectively, between 1991 and 2005 as shown in Table 3.9 *Market capitalisation of Santander and BBVA between*

Table 3.9   Market capitalisation
of Grupo Santander and BBVA
1991–2005

	Santander	BBVA
1991	2,665	3,749
1992	2,886	3,249
1993	4,482	4,394
1994	4,838	4,533
1995	5,846	5,902
1996	7,977	9,468
1997	14,658	20,040
1998	19,837	27,316
1999	41,226	29,878
2000	51,477	50,654
2001	44,871	44,422
2002	31,185	29,146
2003	44,775	34,995
2004	57,102	44,251
2005	69,735	51,134

(In millions of euros)
Source: Fernández and Carabias (2006a;
2006b).

1991 and 2005 and Figure 3.5 *Market capitalisation.* Both banks, and indeed most financial institutions across the world, saw their market capitalisation suffer a sharp drop in 2001, which took four or five years to recover to its 2000 level.

Increase in the shareholder value[35]

As shown in Table 3.10 and Figure 3.6, the increase in shareholder value at Santander and BBVA is characterised (1) by the overall positive results, (2) by its almost cyclical tendency; a positive and growing trend followed by a decrease and then a positive and growing trend again, and (3) two consecutive years in which the results were below zero: between 2002–2004.

Shareholder profitability

As demonstrated in Table 3.11, overall the shareholder profitability was positive in the period between 1992 and 2005 with most years showing double digit profitability. However, in 2001 and 2002 the banks suffered double digit loss percentages. While in 1997, profitability reached as high as 88–115 per cent. Figure 3.7 bellow illustrates this.

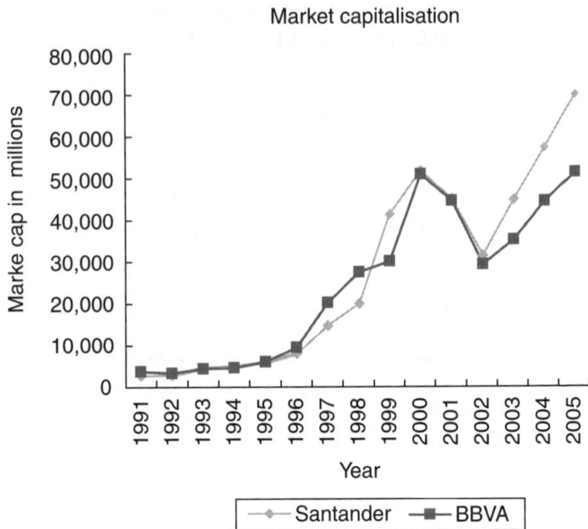

Figure 3.5   Market capitalisation of Grupo Santander and BBVA
Source: Fernández and Carabias (2006a; 2006b).

Table 3.10   Increase in shareholders value at Grupo Santander and BBVA

	Santander	BBVA
1992	1,313	−337
1993	5,730	1,343
1994	−903	327
1995	3,193	1,782
1996	5,429	3,861
1997	14,160	10,850
1998	3,830	7,293
1999	11,559	2,037
2000	2,114	4,161
2001	−11,207	−5,346
2002	−16,065	−14,339
2003	17,698	6,974
2004	127	8,000
2005	14,820	8,455

In millions of euros.

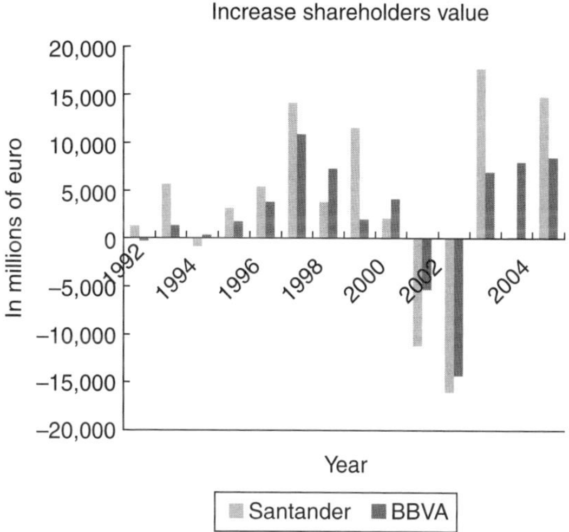

Figure 3.6   Increase in shareholders' value at GS and BBVA
Source: Fernández and Carabias (2006a; 2006b).

Table 3.11   Shareholders profitability

	Santander (%)	BBVA (%)
1992	12.4	−9.0
1993	59.1	41.3
1994	−6.7	7.4
1995	25.8	39.3
1996	41.5	65.4
1997	88.0	115.0
1998	14.2	36.4
1999	34.1	7.5
2000	3.3	13.9
2001	−15.5	−10.6
2002	−28.2	−32.4
2003	48.6	23.9
2004	0.3	22.9
2005	26.0	19.1

Source: Fernández & Carabias (2006a; 2006b).

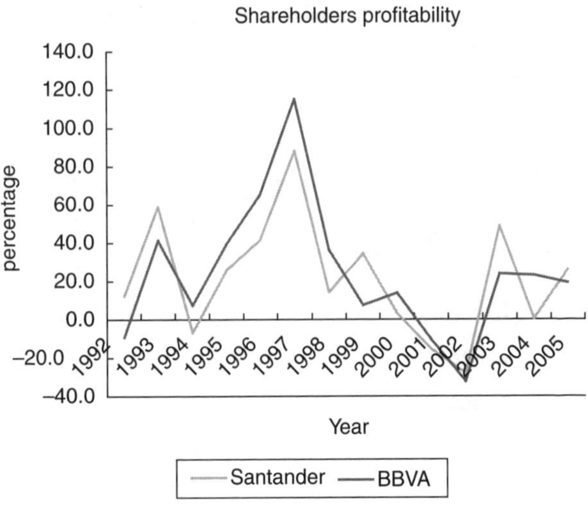

Figure 3.7   Shareholders' profitability
Source: Fernández and Carabias (2006a; 2006b).

Required shareholder profitability compared with actual profitability[36]

Shareholder profitability *per se* is not sufficient for us to get a clear view of the amount of real profitability shareholders are enjoying. The real picture is obtained only by contrasting with expectation: (Ke = long-term treasury bond interest rate plus risk premium).

In the period between 1992 and 2005, Santander's shareholders enjoyed profitability in excess of Ke in all bar four years, while BBVA's shareholder profitability exceeded Ke in all bar five years. (See Table 3.12 *Required Shareholder Profitability Against Actual Profitability*.)

Shareholders' value created[37]

In absolute terms the value created for the shareholders of Santander and BBVA was as shown in Table 3.13. The sum total of the value created by Santander between 1992 and 2005 amounted to 4,158 million euros in contrast to 15,617 million euros by BBVA. Again, 2000–2002 and 2001–2002 for Santander and BBVA, respectively, were years in which their value creation was negative. (See Figure 3.8 value created for the share holders)

Table 3.12 Required shareholders profitability against the actual profitability

	Interest rate (10 yrs) %	Required profitability %	Risk premium %	Santander %	BBVA %
1992	11.3	16.3	5.0	−3.9	−25.3
1993	12.5	18.0	5.5	41.1	23.3
1994	8.1	12.1	4.0	−18.8	−4.7
1995	11.9	17.1	5.2	8.7	22.2
1996	9.7	14.2	4.5	27.3	51.2
1997	6.9	11.1	4.2	76.9	103.9
1998	5.6	9.7	4.1	4.5	26.7
1999	4.0	7.7	3.7	26.4	−0.2
2000	5.6	10.6	5.0	−7.3	3.3
2001	52.0	10.0	−42.0	−25.5	−20.6
2002	5.1	10.7	5.6	−38.9	−43.1
2003	4.3	8.7	4.4	39.9	15.2
2004	4.3	8.5	4.2	−8.2	14.4
2005	3.6	7.5	3.9	18.5	11.6

Source: Fernández and Carabias (2006a; 2006b).

Table 3.13 Value creation by Grupo Santander and BBVA

	Market cap increase (*)	Shareholders' value increase (*)	Value created for shareholders (*)
Santander	67,070	32,114	4,158
BBVA	47,386	35,001	15,617

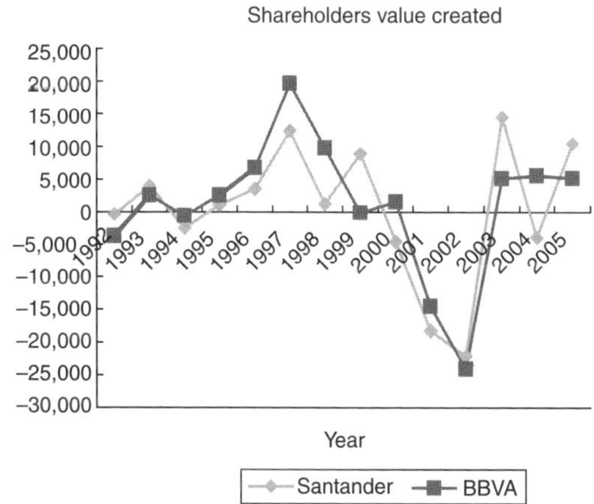

Figure 3.8 Value created for the shareholders of Grupo Santander and BBVA
Source: Fernández and Carabias (2007: 39).

Santander and BBVA compared with other Spanish banks in terms of value creation

Before concluding this section it is worth comparing the value creation by Santander and BBVA with that of other banks in Spain in order to put these two banks' excellence into perspective.

The following Table 3.14 clearly shows that Santander and BBVA are set apart from Banco Popular and Bankinter in value creation in terms of absolute amounts in billions of euros, over the period 1991–2006. The first two have shown consistently higher rates of value creation, with the exception of the period 1999–2001.

Linking the empirical validation to the components of the business model

How does the Spanish banks' value creation business model work? Can the penchant for size, growth and operational efficiency be justified in the light of value creation?

Value formula

To answer this, we need to have a look at the value creation formula (McKinsey & Company, Koller, Goedhart, & Wessei, 2005: 62), expressed as a perpetuity rent, where the growth rate of free cash flow is constant. Value here means the sum of "present value of the cash flow during explicit forecast period + present value of cash flow after explicit forecast period." (McKinsey & Company, Copeland, Koller, & Murrin, 2000: 267).

$$\text{Value} = FCF_{t=1}/(WACC - g)$$

Where FCF equals free cash flow, WACC equals weighted average cost of capital, and g equals annual growth rate of FCF considered to be constant.

$$g = ROIC * IR$$

with ROIC being the return on investment and IR, the investment rate (i.e., Net investment/NOPLAT or Gross investment/Gross Cash flow). Therefore, $IR = g/ROIC$

The free cash flow is defined as:

$$FCF = NOPLAT * (1 - g/ROIC)$$

Where NOPLAT is net operating profit less adjusted taxes.

Table 3.14 Value creation by Grupo Santander and BBVA(*) (**)(in billions of euros)

		A														
		1992	1993	1994	1995	1996	1997	1998	1999	2000	2001	2002	2003	2004	2005	2006
SAN	1991	−0.4	3,9	1,1	2,3	6,1	19,4	20,8	30,4	25,4	5,6	−18,2	−2,6	−6,8	4,5	20,7
	1992		4,3	1,6	2,7	6,6	19,9	21,2	30,8	25,9	6,1	−17,7	−2,1	−6,4	4,9	21,1
	1993			−2,7	−1,6	2,3	15,6	16,9	26,5	21,6	1,8	−22,0	−6,4	−10,7	0,6	16,9
	1994				1,2	5,0	18,3	19,6	29,2	24,3	4,5	−19,3	−3,7	−8,0	3,3	19,6
	1995					3,8	17,1	18,5	28,1	23,1	3,3	−20,5	−4,9	−9,1	2,2	18,4
	1996						13,3	14,6	24,2	19,3	−0,5	−24,3	−8,7	−13,0	−1,7	14,6
From	1997							1,3	10,9	6,0	−13,8	−37,6	−22,0	−26,3	−15,0	1,3
	1998								9,6	4,7	−15,1	−38,9	−23,3	−27,6	−16,3	−0,1
	1999									−4,9	−24,7	−48,6	−32,9	−37,2	−25,9	−9,7
	2000										−19,8	−43,6	−28,0	−32,2	−20,9	−4,7
	2001			52 Periodos < 0								−23,8	−8,2	−12,4	−1,1	15,1
	2002												15,6	11,4	22,7	38,9
	2003													−4,3	7,0	23,3
	2004														11,3	27,5
	2005															16,2

Continued

Table 3.14 Continued

		1992	1993	1994	1995	1996	1997	1998	1999	2000	2001	2002	2003	2004	2005	2006
BBVA	1991	−4,0	−1,3	−1,9	0,8	8,0	29,2	39,7	39,6	41,2	25,6	−0,3	5,3	11,2	16,8	25,4
	1992		2,7	2,1	4,8	12,1	33,2	43,7	43,6	45,2	29,6	3,8	9,3	15,2	20,8	29,4
	1993			−0,7	2,1	9,3	30,5	41,0	40,8	42,5	26,9	1,0	6,6	12,5	18,1	26,7
	1994				2,8	10,0	31,1	41,6	41,5	43,2	27,6	1,7	7,2	13,2	18,7	27,4
	1995					7,2	28,4	38,9	38,7	40,4	24,8	−1,1	4,5	10,4	16,0	24,6
	1996						21,1	31,7	31,5	33,2	17,6	−8,3	−2,8	3,2	8,7	17,4
	1997							10,5	10,4	12,0	−3,6	−29,4	−23,9	−17,9	−12,4	−3,7
From	1998								−0,1	1,5	−14,1	−40,0	−34,4	−28,5	−22,9	−14,3
	1999									1,7	−13,9	−39,8	−34,3	−28,3	−22,8	−14,1
	2000										−15,6	−41,5	−35,9	−30,0	−24,4	−15,8
	2001											−25,9	−20,3	−14,4	−8,8	−0,2
	2002												5,5	11,5	17,0	25,7
	2003					38 Periodos < 0								6,0	11,5	20,2
	2004														5,5	14,2
	2005															8,7

POP	1991	−0,47	1,80	1,00	3,14	3,47	8,80	7,98	7,55	8,50	7,71	7,72	9,53	9,30	9,61	13,43
	1992		2,27	1,47	3,61	3,94	9,27	8,45	8,01	8,97	8,18	8,19	9,99	9,77	10,08	13,89
	1993			−0,80	1,34	1,67	7,00	6,18	5,75	6,70	5,91	5,92	7,73	7,50	7,81	11,63
	1994				2,14	2,47	7,80	6,98	6,55	7,50	6,71	6,72	8,53	8,30	8,61	12,43
	1995					0,33	5,66	4,84	4,40	5,36	4,57	4,58	6,38	6,16	6,47	10,28
	1996						5,33	4,51	4,08	5,03	4,24	4,25	6,06	5,83	6,14	9,96
From	1997							−0,82	−1,25	−0,30	−1,09	−1,08	0,73	0,50	0,81	4,62
	1998								−0,43	0,52	−0,27	−0,26	1,55	1,32	1,63	5,45
	1999									0,95	0,17	0,17	1,98	1,75	2,07	5,88
	2000										−0,79	−0,78	1,03	0,80	1,11	4,92
	2001											0,01	1,81	1,59	1,90	5,71
	2002												1,81	1,58	1,89	5,71
	2003			13 Periodos < 0										−0,23	0,09	3,90
	2004														0,31	4,12
	2005															3,81

Continued

Table 3.14 Continued

		1992	1993	1994	1995	1996	1997	1998	1999	2000	2001	2002	2003	2004	2005	2006
BKT	1991	*−1,01*	0,94	0,39	0,28	1,73	2,46	3,02	5,35	3,19	2,51	1,35	2,10	2,55	3,05	3,88
	1992			1,94	1,40	1,28	2,74	3,47	4,03	6,35	4,19	3,52	2,36	3,11	3,55	4,06	4,88
	1993				−0,55	−0,66	0,80	1,52	2,08	4,41	2,25	1,58	0,42	1,16	1,61	2,11	2,94
	1994					−0,11	1,34	2,07	2,63	4,96	2,80	2,12	0,96	1,71	2,16	2,66	3,49
	1995						1,46	2,18	2,74	5,07	2,91	2,24	1,08	1,82	2,27	2,77	3,60
	1996							0,73	1,29	3,62	1,45	0,78	−0,38	0,37	0,81	1,32	2,14
	1997								0,56	2,89	0,73	0,05	−1,11	−0,36	*0,09*	0,59	1,42
From	1998									2,33	0,17	−0,51	−1,67	−0,92	−0,47	0,03	0,86
	1999										−2,16	−2,83	−3,99	−3,25	−2,80	−2,30	−1,47
	2000											−0,67	−1,83	−1,09	−0,64	−0,14	0,69
	2001												−1,16	−0,41	0,03	0,54	1,36
	2002													0,75	1,19	1,70	2,52
	2003														0,45	0,95	1,78
	2004															0,50	1,33
	2005																0,83

(*)
SAN: Santander
POP: Banco Popular
BKT: Bankinter
(**)
In Y-axis, 'desde' means since.

Substituting for free cash flow, the value is defined as:

$$\text{Value} = \text{NOPLAT}_{t=1}(1-g/\text{ROIC})/(\text{WACC}-g)$$

On the basis of this last mathematical expression, the internal working of the value creation is analysed below in its relationship with the Spanish banks' business model.

The relationship between Value and the terms is summarised as follows:

Value ↑	When
	NOPLAT ↑
	ROIC ↑
	g ↑
	WACC ↑

Perhaps the difficulty may lie in understanding why Value increases when g increases. It can be clearly seen by the fact that (1) g is placed both as numerator and denominator, and (2) the effect of the increase in g as numerator is direct, while that of g as denominator is the inverse of 1, which means the multiplying effect (i.e., $1/(\text{WACC} - g)$) increases exponentially. Where the WACC and g carry the same value, the effect is infinite. In the following Table 3.15 and Figure 3.9, WACC and g show this effect assuming WACC equals ten per cent.

Spanish banks' business model in the light of the value formula

NOPLAT, and (a) the penchant for size and growth and (b) operational efficiency

NOPLAT increases when income grows and the cost is reduced. Therefore value is created, which means that the size concern and relentless efforts to improve operational efficiency are justifiable.

ROIC, and (a) the penchant for size and growth (b) operational efficiency

The return on investment increases (1) when the return in absolute figures or NOPLAT increases and/or (2) the amount of investment decreases.

Therefore, supposing that the amount of investment is maintained, the increase in the return or NOPLAT increases, and accordingly, ROIC increases. By virtue of what we have just analysed in 2.1, NOPLAT increases when the income by growth in size increases and operational efficiency is pursued.

Table 3.15   WACC and *g*

WACC	*g*	WACC–*g*	1/(WACC–*g*)
0.1	0.09	0.01	100.00
0.1	0.08	0.02	50.00
0.1	0.07	0.03	33.33
0.1	0.06	0.04	25.00
0.1	0.05	0.05	20.00
0.1	0.04	0.06	16.67
0.1	0.03	0.07	14.29
0.1	0.02	0.08	12.50
0.1	0.01	0.09	11.11

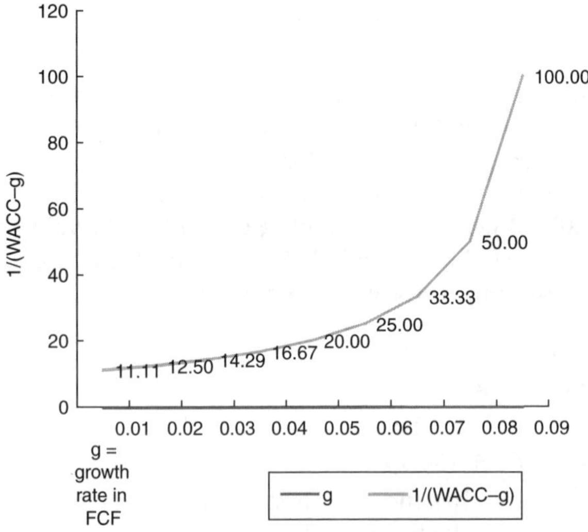

Figure 3.9   WACC and *g*

However, an increase in size may mean an increase in investment. Thus, it may annul the positive effect of cost reduction by operational efficiency.

WACC, and (a) the penchant for size and growth and (b) operational efficiency

WACC may increase if the growth in size forces the banks to seek financial resources at over optimum cost and may also increase if the leverage ratio of a firm becomes higher, since "it pushes up the risk of the common stock and leads the stockholders to demand a correspond-ingly higher return." (Brealey & Myers, 2000: 213).

Empirical proof to confirm or negate whether this is actually happen-ing would constitute another interesting research project.

g and (a) the penchant for size and growth and (b) operational efficiency

We have seen above that g ought to be studied in conjunction with WACC, since the negative effect of the increase in g through the numer-ator (i.e., $(1 - g/ROIC)$) is compensated by the exponential increase in the denominator (i.e., $(1/(WACC - g))$).

g will increase if NOPLAT increases. As seen in 2.1) NOPLAT increase is achieved by the growth in size and/or operational efficiency, so the business model favours growth in g.

Once again, however, growth in size may lead to growth in WACC, although we do not have any empirical evidence to support this hypothesis.

In conclusion

The above can be summed up as follows:

Value ↑	When		
NOPLAT ↑	Size ↑	Operational efficiency ↑	
ROIC ↑	Size (?)	Operational efficiency ↑	
g ↑	Size ↑	Operational efficiency ↑	
WACC ↑	Size (?)	Operational efficiency ↑	

Conclusions

In this chapter we put forward the theory that there is a common strate-gic configuration in the Spanish banks. The configuration includes (A) the general framework consisting of the CEO, his team (COO/staff), and the regulatory environment, and (B) the basic business model comprising (1) a bias towards size which leads to the focus on dual strategy levels – business or competitive, and corporate-level strategies, (2) the strategic use of IT systems, the efficiency of which is aided by the modular and open product architecture, and (3) the pursuit of operational efficiency.

We sought to validate the success brought about by this strategic business model from the empirical results on the basis of exhaustive studies conducted by Pablo Fernández and José María Carabias, two Spanish researchers on the creation of shareholder value. Their find-ings amply demonstrated value creation by Santander and BBVA. These banks constantly increased the shareholder value created, between 1992 and 2005 (with the exception of 2001–2003) to the tune of €16 billion, in the case of BBVA and €4 billion in the case of Santander.

In the following chapters we will discuss the application of this model to each particular situation of Santander and BBVA, including supplementary information on Banco Sabadell.

Appendix

"Are they really that efficient?"

As a contrast to our theory we summarise below Van Rooyen and Chiavarini's (2006) interpretation on the efficiency gains by Spanish banks.

Van Rooyen's work consists of researching following issues:

A. The apparently low reported cost/income ratios
B. The drivers of efficiency

The apparently widely-reported cost/income ratios

The Bank of Spain puts the low cost/income ratio down to low in-branch staffing and increased use of technology/limiting manual transactions. Branches are staffed with an average of five employees compared to 12 on average in the EU. Only one in five transactions is carried out manually, versus three out of five in 2001. This has meant the number of administrative staff has declined by 40 per cent, while sales and marketing personnel has increased by 50 per cent since 2001.

But, Spain has (1) more high street banks than any other European country, (2) more ATMs than any other European country, (3) the highest branch/customer ratio in the world, and (4) higher wage inflation than elsewhere in Europe.

Despite these factors, however, Spanish banks enjoyed far better efficiency by 2005 than French ones that used to boast a similar level of efficiency until 1999 (Van Rooyen & Chiavarini, 2006: 6).

The drivers of efficiency

The Bank of Spain's explanation for the efficiency of Spanish banks (smaller branches and the use of technology replacing manual transactions, pushing down costs, etc.) stresses Spanish banks' focus on costs.

The cost focus resulted in operational leverage, thanks to which Spanish banks had a compound annual growth of 12 per cent in gross operational profit between 1998 and 2004 (against 7 per cent by French banks in the same period).

Van Rooyen and Chiavarini (2006: 7) points out that this difference in growth at a gross operation profit level cannot solely be explained as a result of cost containment (5 per cent in Spain and 4 per cent in France) but that stronger revenue growth also plays its part (7 per cent in Spain and 5 per cent in France).

Therefore, Van Rooyen and Chiavarini suspect that the low cost/income ratio in Spain is attributable to reasons other than those given by the Bank of Spain, and argues that the cost efficiency ratio was a function of (1) the significant volume growth creating operational leverage, (2) the high portfolio share of the banking system with respect to financial products, and (3) the accounting treatment of early retirement costs in Spain.

Volume growth resulting in operational leverage

The private sector debt/GDP in Spain grew from 71 per cent to 136 per cent between 1994 and 2005. France's corresponding data in the same period was from 87 per cent to 100 per cent. The difference implies that while Spain's year on year compound growth in lending was 14 per cent, France's was 5 per cent.

In contrast to the difference between Spain and France in the compound annual growth in lending, the compound growth in operational expenses was similar in the two countries: Spain 5 per cent and France 4 per cent in 1998 to 2005 period. This suggests little difference in absolute cost containment.

However, as a result of the greater volume in lending, firstly, unit cost in Spain declined faster. Van Rooyen (2006: 8) estimates the reduction of the cost of delivery per euro of debt from €0.06 to €0.03 between 1998 and 2005. Secondly, increased volumes led to a decline in the cost per unit of debt and therefore the overall profitability of the banking system in Spain. Thirdly, increased volume also helped the sums spent on IT systems to become diluted in the larger volume of transactions, bringing unit costs down. This is an indication of the effect of economies of scale.

Despite the volume effects on operational costs, Van Rooyen (2006: 4) argues that (1) the expense/debt ratio is similar in Spain and France (3.12 per cent in Spain and 3.08 per cent in France), suggesting little difference in efficiency between these two countries, and (2) the reason for the lower cost/income ratio in Spain is therefore higher revenue yield – revenue/debt – (Spain's 5.47 per cent against France's 4.82 per cent) as a result of less price competition in Spain due to the strong volume growth.

Basically:

Efficiency ratio = expense/revenue = (expense/debt) * (debt/revenue).[38]

Therefore if expense/revenue is to go down, with expense/debt higher or similar in the two countries, debt/revenue has to go down. As the revenue yield is the inverse of debt/revenue, the revenue yield has to go up.

Higher share of portfolio with respect to financial products

Judging from the foregoing discussion on the revenue yield improvement Van Rooyen (2006: 10) appears to wish to emphasise that the low cost/income ratio of Spanish banks is less due to a more efficient cost structure that it would appear.

He further stresses that the higher yield could be thanks to the fact that Spanish banks have a higher share of portfolio in comparison with other European banks.

As a proof of Spanish banks' higher share of portfolio, Van Rooyen cites the examples of the percentage of mutual and pension funds being sold through bank networks. For both funds Spanish banks have higher percentage in business. Specifically, 91 per cent and 74 per cent, against France's 64 per cent and 60 per cent.

The bone of contention is, as recognised by Van Rooyen, the size of the mutual and pension fund market in Spain being as low as 26 per cent of that in France. So this evidence is not too convincing.

Early retirement benefit

Volume impact and share of portfolio do not address the issue of higher wage inflation in Spain and how it might affect the low cost/income ratio.

Perhaps in order to contain higher wages of existing employees, Spanish banks offered the option to take early retirement. The accounting treatment of the cost implied for the banks in implementing this option is different before and after 2003.

Until 2003 the Bank of Spain allowed the Spanish banks:

> the removal of all costs in the payroll associated with such employees (e.g., salary and other commitments to these employees) *from the time they accept early retirement to the date of effective retirement.* Rather than an expense in payroll, costs associated with these employees are therefore allocated against this provision for the duration of future employment. As such, group earning and ROE are boosted,

but there is a negative impact on NAV (net asset value) growth for these banks. (Van Rooyen, 2006: 10)

From 2004 onwards, this treatment has not been allowed. Van Rooyen stresses that Santander still has €4.2 billion as early retirement cost provision on its balance sheet, and BBVA €2.5 billion.

Van Rooyen and Chiavarini (2006: 11) argues that the amortisation of the total provisions may be the reason for the increase in the cost base of BBVA by €619 million in 2005 or 10 per cent, €892 million or 8 per cent at Santander, and €18 million or 2 per cent at Banco Sabadell.

Van Rooyen and Chiavarini conclude by stating that:

If we therefore adjust the cost base of these operations, then we find that BBVA has a cost/income ratio of 62 per cent rather than 48 per cent ... Santander ... 58 per cent rather than 42 per cent ... The reason for the apparently relatively "high" cost/income ratio of Sabadell also becomes clear with this calculation: the adjustment is only 1 per cent, from 50 per cent to 51 per cent. (Van Rooyen and Chiavarini, 2006: 12)

4
Santander's Business Model

In *Chapter 3, Business Model,* we described and analysed the generic model (or 'ideal type') of the most successful Spanish retail banks. In this chapter, we now explore our theory that Santander uses a Profit-Arithmetic (PA) model that follows the strategic course set by the top executives, namely, Emilio Botín and Alfredo Sáenz.[1 and 2] This claim helps to explain the success of the bank, and assumes that the ability of Santander to remain focused on retail banking is based on three factors – a penchant for size and growth, operational efficiency, and IT systems.[3]

The strategic vision of the business model will be reviewed first, to provide an insight into how components of Santander's business model coincide with the characteristics of the PA approach. In the second place, the business model of Santander will be explained using its three main axes as described in Chapter 3 Business Model, and in the third place, the 'replicability' of this model will be studied.

Introduction[4]

When Emilio Botín was appointed Chairman of Banco de Santander in 1986, Santander was ranked 6th in the Spanish banking sector and 152nd in the world. Back then, the focus was different from the current one – the bank aimed at profitability rather than size. Thus, prior to the concentration of Spanish banks at the end of the 1980s, Santander and Banco Popular had been similar in this sense, although unlike Banco Popular, Santander already had international presence and the vocation to be international.

20 years on, Santander has taken a qualitative and quantitative leap that has enabled the bank to become the leader in Spain and the Eurozone, and tenth (and eigth if ABN-AMRO acquisition is successfully concluded with other partners) in the world in terms of market capitalisation. The qualitative and quantitative leap refers to the adoption of a new business

model and the growth resulting from it. Following the dictates of the new business model, Santander acquired other Spanish banks, such as Banesto, merged with Banco Central-Hispano, and acquired international banks including, among others, Banespa, Serfin, Totta and Abbey National (See Table 4.1 Santander's historical landmarks).

Table 4.1   Grupo Santander's historical landmarks

Grupo Santander's history began on 15 May 1857, when Queen Isabel II signed a royal decree authorising the incorporation of the founding of Santander. Right from the start it was a bank open to the outside world, being initially linked to trade between the port of Santander in the north of Spain and Latin America.

- In 1947, it opened its first regional office in the Americas, in Havana (Cuba), which was followed by others in Argentina, Mexico and Venezuela, and also an office in London. In 1956 the bank's Latin American Department was set up.

- By 1957, on its hundredth anniversary, the Banco de Santander had become the seventh-ranked finance house in Spain.

- In 1960, Emilio Botín Sanz de Sautuola y García de los Ríos joined the bank's board. This period saw the purchase of the Banco del Hogar Argentino, Santander's first subsidiary in Latin America. In 1965, Banco Intercontinental Español (Bankinter) was founded.

- In 1967, Emilio Botín Sanz de Sautuola y García de los Ríos was appointed managing director of the bank and later on, in 1977, CEO.

- With the 1976 acquisition of First Nacional Bank of Puerto Rico, and that of Banco Español-Chile in 1982, Grupo Santander became a commercial banking pioneer in Latin America.

- In 1985, Banco Santander de Negocios was set up in Spain to build on the investment banking and wholesale markets activities as a result of the alliance with Bank of America, the then world's largest bank.

- In 1986, current chairman Emilio Botín Sanz de Sautuola y García de los Ríos, then Vice-chairman and CEO, was chosen to cover the vacancy opened up by his father's retirement after 36 years at the helm of the bank. His first two years as chairman were spent laying the foundations for the challenge of the bank's modernisation and expansion.

- In the late 80s, Grupo Santander bolstered its presence in Europe by acquiring CC-Bank in Germany, a bank with over three decades of experience in the vehicle finance market, from Bank of America. A stake was also acquired in Banco de Comercio e Industria in Portugal, and, what was the most important strategic landmark, an alliance formed with The Royal Bank of Scotland in 1988.

Continued

Table 4.1   Continued

- In 1989, the "Supercuenta Santander" was launched, one of the most innovative products in the history of Spanish banking, which did away with the "status quo" and opened up the Spanish financial system to competition.

- In 1994, the acquisition of Banco Español de Crédito (Banesto), traditionally one ot the most important banks in Spain, became a major historic event in the history of Grupo Santander, making it the leading player in the Spanish market.

- In 1995, a second flurry of expansion in Latin America began, which allowed it to develop its business in Argentina, Brazil, Colombia, Mexico, Peru and Venezuela. At the same time, there was a renewed boost to the businesses already acquired in Chile, Puerto Rico and Uruguay.

- In January 1999, Banco Santander and BCH were the protagonists in the first major banking merger in Europe under the euro. Subsequently the bank bought financial group Totta y Açores and Crédito Predial Portugués in Portugal.

- From the year 2000, the Group acquired Banespa in Brazil, Grupo Serfín in Mexico and Banco Santiago in Chile. This consolidated the Group's position as the leading financial franchise in Latin America.

- In 2003, the Group set up Santander Consumer when it merged German company CC-Bank, the Italian Finconsumo, Hispamer in Spain and other Group companies. This new consumer banking franchise today has a presence in 12 European countries (Spain, the UK, Portugal, Italy, Germany, the Netherlands, Poland, the Czech Republic, Austria, Hungary, Norway and Sweden), in the USA, through Drive Finance, and it has recently struck an agreement to start up its first operation in Latin America, in Chile.

- In April 2004, it moved its Central Services in Madrid to the new headquarters, Grupo Santander City, where 6,800 people work today.

- That same year, in November, another major landmark was reached with the Group's takeover of Abbey, the sixth largest bank in the United Kingdom.

- In 2005, Santander reached agreement to take a 19.8 percent stake in Sovereign Bancorp, the 18th biggest bank in the USA.

- In 2006, Santander made record profits of € 7.596 billion, the biggest of any Spanish company, spurring heavy investment in retail banking and quality of service. "We want to be your bank" (Queremos ser tu banco) in Spain and other enterprising action in Portugal, at Abbey and in America are examples of this drive.

- In 2007, Santander held its 150th anniversary as the world's 12th largest bank by market cap, the 7th in terms of profit and the bank with the largest retail network in the western world, with 10,852 branches.

Source: Adapted from Santander's web site (http: www.santander.com).

The organisation led by Emilio Botín, Chairman, and Alfredo Sáenz, CEO, can be defined as an international financial group with strong local retail activities combined with global capabilities such as wholesale banking. (See Table 4.2 Santander's business domain.)

Table 4.2   Santander's business domain

Principal level

The principal or geographic level is divided into three large areas:

Continental Europe. This covers all retail banking businesses, asset management and insurance and wholesale banking in Europe except for Abbey. The main units are:

  - Santander Network in Spain
  - Banesto
  - Santander Consumer Finance
  - Santander Totta
  - Banif

United Kingdom: Including Abbey and largely retail banking.

Latin America. All the Group's activities conducted via its affiliated banks and subsidiaries, mainly:

  - Brazil
  - Mexico
  - Chile
  - Argentina
  - Puerto Rico
  - Venezuela
  - Colombia

Secondary level

The secondary level, or by type of business, covers three areas and their total activity is equal to that of the three geographic areas:

Retail Banking
Asset Management and Insurance
Global Wholesale Banking

The Group continues to maintain the area of Financial Management and Equity Stakes.

Source: Santander's web site.[5]

Organisational structure

From the information on the group's organisational structure regarding the Board of Directors obtained from its web site, we analysed the significance given to different management aspects on the assumption that relevant issues or areas for the Bank will be taken care of directly by its top two executives.

The board, to better concentrate on different major issues or areas, is organised into six committees – Executive Committee, Risk Committee, Audit & Compliance Committee, Appointment and Remuneration Committee, International Committee, and Technology, Production & Quality Committee.

It should be noted that the top two executives, Emilio Botín, Chairman, and Alfredo Sáenz, CEO, only participate in three committees, but coincide in each of them: (1) Technology, Productivity, and Quality Committee, (2) Executive Committee, and (3) International Committee.

The Executive Committee is the most important of all, since, according to the group's website, 'all the powers of the Board of Directors have been permanently delegated to the Executive Committee' except for some issues such as the approval of the general strategies of the Company.

The fact that Botín and Sáenz personally participate in the remaining two committees indicates that technology strategy and its management and growth in overseas markets are considered high priorities for the bank.

Strategic approach of Santander's business model

Before Emilio Botín took over the management of the Spanish bank from his father in 1986, Banco de Santander had traditionally grown both organically and through mergers and absorption of other banks. But uncertainties surrounding the banking business, the relative weakness of Spanish banks in terms of expertise and financial health compared to their competitors in Europe and elsewhere, and the imminent entry of Spain into the EEC (European Economic Community), all clearly signalled the appropriateness of a PA approach, insofar as this approach tends to focus on short- to medium-term financial health and helps to channel staff energy in this direction.[6]

The arrival of Alfredo Sáenz at Santander, upon its acquisition of Banesto, turned out to strengthen the success garnered previously by Emilio Botín, because, in addition to his success as CEO in turning

Table 4.3 Committee structure shows who takes part in which committees

		Technology, productivity and quality committee	Executive committee	Risk committee	Audit & compliance committee	Appointment & remuneration committee	International committee	Frequence of participation in committees (%)
Basagoiti	Antonio	1	1	1				50
Benjumea	Ignacio	1	1	1	1			67
Botín	Ana Patricia		1				1	33
Botín	Emilio	1	1				1	50
de Azúa	Fernando		1	1	1	1		67
de la Dehesa	Guillermo		1			1	1	50
Echenique	Rodrigo		1	1		1	1	67
Escnámez	Antonio	1	1	1			1	67
Francisco	Luzón		1					17
Luzón	Francisco						1	17
Matutes	Abel				1		1	33
Rodríguez-Inciarte	Matías		1	1				33
Rojo	Luis Angel				1	1		33
Sáenz	Alfredo	1	1				1	50
Salazar-Simpson	Luis Alberto	1			1			33
Soto	Manauel	1			1	1		50

1= yes, 0= no

Source: Santander's web site (http://www.santander.com) as of May 22nd 2007.

around the failing Banca Catalana and Banesto, he also had experience in the merger of Banco de Bilbao and Vizcaya. Thus, the joining of Alfredo Sáenz and his team from Banca Catalana in Santander marked a milestone in the historical evolution of the Spanish bank.

The strategic approach that guided the evolution of Santander was based on achieving profit in the short term, which helped to reach sufficient size to be able to face competition firstly from the other Spanish banks and secondly, and more importantly, the European banks. Santander (2004a) lists as the main elements of their business model (a) the pursuit of high market share plus diversification, (b) a 'vibrant' sales culture leading to revenue growth, (c) efficiency-targeting cost discipline,[7] (d) risk management for high credit quality, and (e) capital strength and discipline allowing growth potential.

The business model that came into being is built on a 'virtuous circle' revolving around cost efficiency and revenue growth. High market share/diversification will ultimately lead to economies of scale resulting in the reduction of cost. A sales culture centred on income growth will certainly help to gain the economies of scale and cost efficiency through lower overheads allocated to each unit of product sold. It is also true that to achieve growth the bank needs to be prepared with a strong capital base, and greater size provides greater bargaining power in the financial market. Thus, the chain of cause and effect bring about cost efficiency aided by a sales culture centred on income growth for profit maximisation.

Santander (2004a: 19) stresses the growth opportunities in Spain, the European consumer sector (potential opportunities), and Latin America (tangible opportunities), but also puts emphasis on Santander's core competence being centred on (1) managing retail banking networks, (2) improving them by means of restructuring for which IT exper tise plays a pivotal role, and (3) entering new markets for which its business model is adapted. (See Appendix 2 for a detailed explanation on the working of this model.)

Firstly, the focus on retail banking can be confirmed by viewing the 49 banks that Santander has acquired over the past 15 years (Euromoney, July 2005). All of them, from Banesto to Banespa or Serfín to Abbey National, had an important customer base and were focused on the management of the same kinds of risk. This fact helped Santander to benefit from the learning curve, with the acquisitions serving as benchmarks leading to best practices, on which we will elaborate later in this chapter.

Secondly, Santander, as with the majority of Spanish banks, did not have any IT legacy problems, unlike some of their main European competitors. This made it possible for Spanish banks to develop and make use of very advanced systems. Acquisitions also permitted access to best-of-class technology.[8] Such was the case with Santander when it acquired Banesto.

Last but not least, the Bank emphasises the importance of replicating the Santander business model in the acquired entities. The advantages of this replication translate into (1) less risk because of the model having been tested and improved in the bank's home market and (2) the establishment of a wider bank network with one business model, allowing the standardisation of products, the centralised use of IT systems for the benefit of cost advantage, and so on.

This endeavour to set up a global bank network across borders,[9] sharing the same modular and open architecture product design, is the activity in which Spanish banks excel and it was a main driver of their success. Actually, they are good at sharing the process and put together product concepts, adjusting them to different national regulations in Europe and Latin America. (See Figure 4.1 Global synergies.) For instance, in Abbey National, which operated as a building society with strong origins in real estate business-related mortgages,[10] Santander identified the opportunity to create value and benefit from two main aspects. Firstly, by improving its efficiency ratio difference – Abbey's 63 per cent compared to Santander's 52 per cent – and, in this, the use of IT systems was essential. Secondly, by creating new product silos in which Santander is already a main player and where the experience can be transferred easily to Abbey thanks to its current business sphere.

By contrast, the businesses of wholesale, consumer finance, cards, asset management and insurance obey an opposite logic because they have to be centralised as a foothold for Santander's gradual expansion into the rest of the world. As these businesses do not constitute Santander's core, the priority is, above all, on retail banking.

Alfredo Sáenz (2005), Santander's CEO, completes the aforementioned point of view by adding that those with 'winning' business models will continue to grow thanks to three fundamental elements: (1) a wish (or strategic intent) to become a global player, (2) customer orientation, and (3) continuous renewal.

In the first place the globalisation of competition and growth on a global scale will strongly affect both the cost and income of the bank's Profit & Loss account. For example, a data processing centre covering various national markets will be more efficient in terms of cost than one owned by a single national or local bank. Similarly, a global business unit handling bank cards for the whole world will accumulate

6. The case for <u>global synergies</u>: Global organisations such as Santander are in a unique position to create value by developing <u>global bussiness units</u> in areas such as creditcards, asset management or insurance

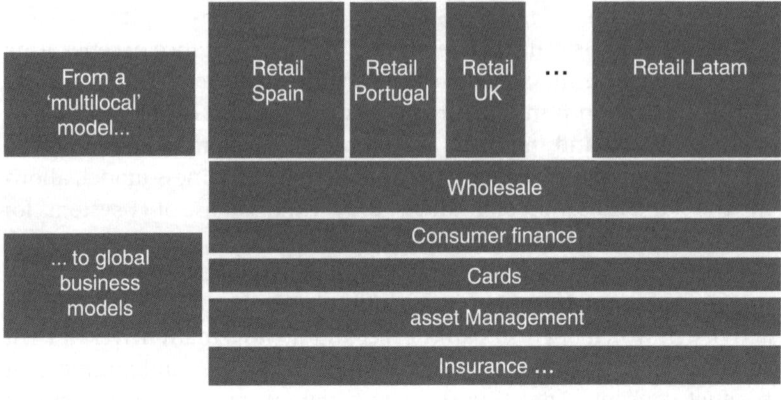

Figure 4.1   Global synergies

strong know-how on the card business and the use of IT systems thanks to a steeper learning curve effect. In other words, the success factor in global businesses does not so much lie in the physical location as in the business model that allows the integration of these businesses by the exchange of best practices amongst different territories.

In the second place, focus on customers comprises five 'principles' (Sáenz, 2005: 34).[11] Service quality recognises the importance of long-term relations with the customer, since they are prioritised to 'maximise the present and future profit of the bank'. As many financial services, especially those of retail banking, are open to easy replication by other competitors, and innovations are strictly controlled and channelled by regulatory institutions, only the service quality and, above all, the increased pace of product innovations can stabilise the long-term relations with customers and help to differentiate them from their competitors.

Other principles are a strong sales culture, empowerment of the commercial network, and larger-scale segmentation of the market to adapt the products and services to the heterogeneous needs of customers.

Santander excels at developing and launching new products. An illustration of this can be found in the launch of products such as the *'supercuenta'* (1989),[12] the *'superdepósito and superfondos'*[13] (1991), the *'supercrédito vivienda'* (1992), the *'superhipóteca'*[14] and *'superlibretas'* (1993)...the '*superseguridad* pension funds '(2001), the '*depósito supersatisfacción*'[15], the '*hipóteca Superoportunidad*' and '*fondo superelección*' (2003), the '*supergestion* fund' and '*superoportunidad* mortgage plan'[16] (2004) as well as the campaign '*Queremos ser tu banco*' in 2006 publicising commission-free services (Sáenz, Seven Growth Driver Presentation at Merril Lynch, 2007).

In the third place, regarding continuous organisational renewal for the enhancement of operational productivity and efficiency, Sáenz (2005: 35) considers technology as a necessary condition but not sufficient in itself, and advocates the continuous 're-engineering' of the bank. This willingness to maintain pressure on the organisation comes from the fact that Santander is a PA organisation that has emerged as a leader in Spanish banking thanks to its capacity to cope better than its competitors with the uncertainties resulting from the restructuring of the Spanish banking industry in the 1980s. The *modus operandi* of the PA approach keeps the organisation alert and quick to react to any changes and to keep pace with innovations, on account of its preference for short-term, day-to-day operations over long-term, vision-based activities. (See Figure 4.2 *Drivers For Growth*.)

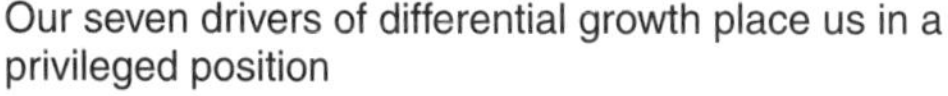
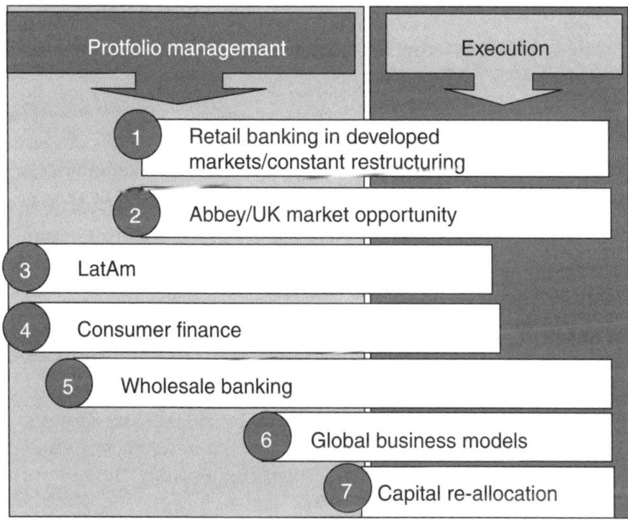

Figure 4.2   Drivers for growth

Sáenz (2005: 39) emphasises that the maximum mandate for management is the maximisation of shareholder value, for which EVA (Economic Value Added)[17] was adopted from 2005 as one of the KPIs (Key Performance Indicators). In line with its philosophy, Santander's budget system aims (1) to optimally manage the capital assignment to maximise the return, (2) to keep control of the demand on capital derived from the bank's growth, both organic and by mergers and acquisitions, (3) to assign the capital adequately to the businesses by setting priority criteria, and (4) to set business unit objectives, based on the shareholders' value creation, that are linked to the incentives of business unit managers. (See Table 4.4 *Santander's Mission Statement.*)

Santander business model

In line with the generic business model explained in Chapter 3, Santander's business model revolves around the pursuit of operational efficiency measured by efficiency ratio:[18,19] (1) penchant for size and growth in search of size, (2) efficiency enhancement and (3) the strategic

Table 4.4   Santander's Mission Statement

Vision Towards a global bank	Santander wants to consolidate itself as a large international financial group, which provides an increasingly high return to its shareholders and meets all the financial needs of its customers. In order to achieve this, it combines a strong presence in local markets with corporate policies and global capacities.
Corporate values Dynamism	The initiative and agility to discover and exploit business opportunities before our competitors and the flexibility to adapt to market changes.
Strength	Our strong balance sheet and prudent credit management are the best guarantees of our capacity to grow and generate shareholder value over the long term.
Leadership	Leadership vocation in all the markets where we operate, with the best teams and always focused on the customer and on results.
Innovation	Constant search for products and services that meet customers' new needs and enable us to obtain returns higher than those of our competitors.

Source: Santander's web site (www.santander.com).

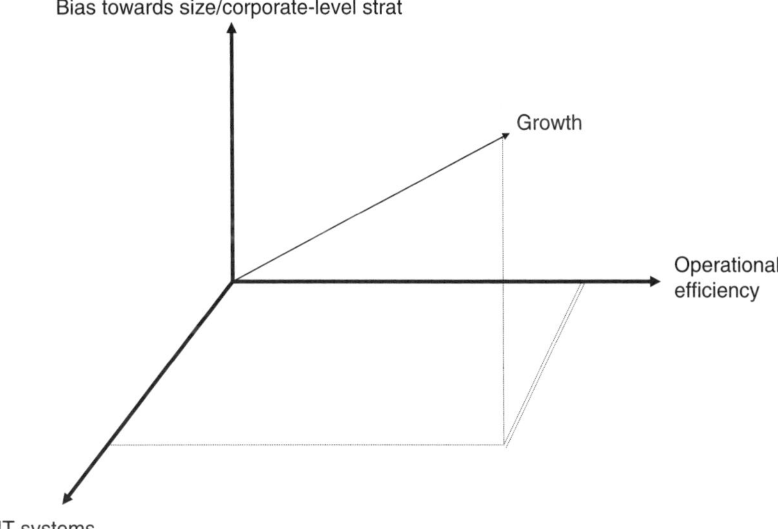

Figure 4.3   Santander's Business Model

use of IT systems predicated on the open and modular product architecture. (See Figure 4.3 *Santander's Business Model*). In the following sections each component will be analysed.

Penchant or bias for size and growth after size

Santander's bias to growth can be brought into relief from a different perspective. Firstly, geographical expansion through mergers and acquisitions is the unequivocal signal of this trend. Secondly, the willingness to constantly launch new products on the basis of relentless innovation for expansion and growth provides further evidence. Thirdly, and to a lesser degree, the search for economies of scale – despite their arguably reduced impact on the banking industry – confirms the intent (that lies behind this penchant) to become the leading bank.[20]

Geographical expansion, product expansion and retail banks

According to Santander (2004a), Santander's strategy regarding its business portfolio rests on high-growth businesses including (1) Iberian retail, (2) European consumer finance, (3) Latin American retail, and (4) the diversified international expansion.

From penchant for profitability to growth-centred bias

Although Santander has maintained several alliances with different banks; among others, Société Générale, Commerzbank, Fidelity and San Laulo IMI, the time-line of Santander's expansion started with its strategic alliance in 1988 with Royal Bank of Scotland and 'all (Santander's discussions with RBS Board) were on how to grow income' (Inciarte, Euromoney, July 2005). The connection with the Edinburgh bank – still existing today as exemplified by the takeover bid of ABN-Amro in 2007 by these two banks along with Fortis – marked a turning point from the pursuit of profitability to the pursuit of growth.[21] This strategic alliance would change Santander's strategic approach at the outset of the merger process taking place among Spanish banks. Botín emphasised that 'the importance of the relationship cannot be underestimated. Each time we met, we challenged each other, shared ideas and offer our support (...). Analysts cannot understand the importance of such relationships.' (Euromoney, July 2005).

This situation logically led to acquisitions, first in Spain. In 1994, Banesto was acquired, and the merger with BCH followed suit five years later, in 1999. Comparing the different acquisitions made,[22] Santander commented that they 'are really proud of Abbey, which today represents one third of Santander. The takeover of Central Hispano was also crucial. Nevertheless, without a doubt, the most important development in (the bank's) history was buying Banesto. It changed the fabric of the bank. (Santander) knew if (it) wanted to be an international bank, (it) needed to be the number one bank in (its) home market. Banesto made that possible. It was a quantum leap for Santander.' (Botin interviewed by Euromoney, July 2005.) The interest in external growth and the ability to close deals in a short amount of time were the main lessons learnt from this experience, having provided the bank with a temporary advantage over their competitors. This was the first move before positioning the bank in Latin America.

Expansion in Latin America

The Latin American market's growth potential was evidenced not only by their 450 million inhabitants, but also by the fact that, according to the IMF, the ratio of loans to GDP ratio in Spain is 129 per cent (and 142 per cent in Europe) in contrast to Mexico (16 per cent), Brazil (29 per cent), and Chile (62 per cent); clearly, the market penetration is still far from complete (Santander, 2004).

The penetration of Santander in Latin America was realised in two 'waves'. The first one, between 1996 and 1998, started with the acquisition of Banco de Venezuela and of Banco Río in Argentina in 1997, a year in which Santander also bought a stake in a Mexican bank. The first wave concluded with the purchase of Bancos Geral de Comercio y Noroeste in Brazil. These acquisitions were carried out in the wake of privatisations of state-controlled entities and Spanish multinationals subsequently penetrating this geographical area.

The second 'wave' coincided with privatisations in the remaining Latin American countries that applied the recommendations of the Washington Consensus later:[23] that is, the liberalisation of the economy and free market. The acquisitions included Serfin in Mexico and Banespa in Brazil.

The learning curve effects that took place during the two waves were considered a success by Santander's management, and the strategy to take advantage of the efficiency ratio difference and to enhance the value of the acquired banks in Latin America proved to be valid. As a consequence, between 2000 and 2002 Santander carried out even larger operations, such as the acquisition of Banespa in Brazil for €8,228 million, Grupo Financiero Serfín in Mexico for €2,323 million, and Banco Santiago in Chile for €2,179 million.

Santander's investments in Latin America were not made on the spur of the moment nor to take advantage of speculative movements, but rather in the expectation that the region would offer great opportunities in future, on account of its high economic growth potential coupled with a large population and productivity growth (Francisco Luzón Presentation on Latin America Day on November 15, 2005 and Alfredo Saénz Presentation at Merrill Lynch, March 2007). This would lead to a higher demand for banking services, as well as a higher level of bank usage by people who had previously remained in the informal or 'black' economy.

As shown in the following Tables 4.5 *Santander In Latin America*, and 4.6 *Profit Attributed By Operation Unit* Santander is currently operating in eight countries (Brazil, Mexico, Chile, Venezuela, Argentina, Puerto Rico, Colombia and Uruguay) where Santander's market-share is 10 per cent in terms of loans, deposits, mutual funds plus pension funds (Santander, 2004a). Nevertheless, Santander withdrew in recent years from Bolivia and Peru, due more to the markets not being big enough to develop a retail banking business than to potential political complications and the ensuing potential increase in the country risk premium (bearing in mind that a problem in any country affects the global rating of the bank). By way of example, when on 1st May 2006 the newly elected President Evo Morales in Bolivia decided to national-ise the oil reserves held by Spanish energy giant Repsol, the market capitalisation of the Spanish company decreased by 2 per cent in one day and affected the position of the whole company.[24]

Expansion in Europe

The expansion of Santander in Europe was undertaken at two levels. Firstly, Santander Consumer, a group company specialising in consumer

Table 4.5 Grupo Santander in Latin America

Countries	10
Number of offices	4,100
Employees	62,746
Clients of commercial banking	20.3
Participants in pension funds	8.0
Outstanding loans (in millions of US dollars)	59,884
Resources of clients managed (ditto)	145,446
Operational margin (ditto)	3,886
Profit attributed (ditto)	2,208

Source: Santander's Annual report (2006a).

Table 4.6 Profit attributed by operation unit (*)

Brazil	734
Mexico	468
Chile	420
Venezuela	165
Argentina	97
Puerto Rico	60
Other countries	120
Santander Private Banking	144
Total	2,208

(*) In millions of US Dollars

Source: Santander's Annual report (2006a).

finance especially for car purchases (and thus its customers are car deal-ers), enabled Santander to enter a new market niche in Europe that was complementary to retail banking, and to reach critical size early on. Secondly, Santander developed its retail bank network in Europe thanks to its 'acquisition of Totta and Abbey National, in Portugal and the UK respectively' (Sáenz, 2006).

The expansion in Portugal, Germany, Poland and Norway was achieved through the acquisitions of Grupo Totta (for the retail busi-ness) in 2000, AKB in 2002, PTF in 2004 and Elcon, respectively. (See Table 4.7 *Santander's Presence In The World*.)

In 2006, Santander Consumer continued its European penetration, with operations in the UK, Italy, the Netherlands, Hungary, Austria, the Czech Republic, Sweden and Russia.[25] This new business unit headquar-tered in Madrid comprises 5,234 employees and 256 branches (Rodríguez Inciarte, 2006).

Santander Consumer is dedicated to providing consumer loans, with its main product being car loans (over one million taken out each year) (Sáenz, 2006), although other short-term consumer credit operations exist.

Santander Consumer Finance's business model is unique in that it copes with one of the weaknesses in current retail banking, namely high fixed costs.

Indeed, Santander Consumer acquires many new customers thanks to indirect products (without the Santander brand) which, crucially, do not incur the costs linked with the opening of branches and recruiting staff. Despite the resulting brand recognition being far lower at the beginning, this strategy nevertheless enables Santander to contemplate the parameterisation of credit risks in a wide variety of countries at the same time, leaving open the possibility of further acquisitions by Santander in those countries as soon as any opportunity arises.

Also, in contrast to retail banks that may suffer in the event of a crisis in the real estate sector in Spain,[26] the consumer finance division does not incur the same cost, even if the credit risk is higher for these products.

Last but not least, the aim of Santander Consumer Finance is to ensure that customers who obtained consumer credit for their car subsequently move to higher-margin credit operations such as credit cards or real estate. The key success factor in managing an upgrade of the purchased product depends on the ability to build the database first and to exploit it afterwards.

Table 4.7 Santander in the world

	Clients (millions)	Offices	Outsanding loans (1)	Clients' resources managed	Operational margin	Profit assigned	Efficiency (2) in per cent
Santander Spain	7.6	2,699	92,145	97,627	2,101	1,285	44.0
Banesto	2.3	1,703	49,973	71,231	1,140	498	42.6
Santander Consumer Finance	7.7	267	30,008	18,868	1,073	487	33.9
Santander Totta	1.8	693	25,861	26,613	498	345	49.4
Banif	0.1	42	2,130	24,400(3)	61	24	54.6
Santander Banespa	7.1 (4)	1,897	12,584	29,494	1,524	734	52.5
Santander Serfín	9.4	1,005	15,616	42,690	816	468	54.1
Santander Santiago	2.9	401	17,657	30,221	742	420	45.4

(1) Securitisations effects deducted
(2) Depreciations included
(3) Comprises the asset in total including deposited securities
(4) Clients of commercial banking and participants in pension plans

Source: Santander's annual report 2004 and 2005.

In that sense, Santander has achieved a good balance between emerging and mature markets. Mature markets are characterised by low growth and strong competition, i.e. they require customer focus, R&D, innovation and technology efficiency, while emerging markets offer high growth potential due to current low market penetration but are highly demanding in terms of investment in customers, distribution networks and channel products. Nevertheless, in the future they are likely to increase efficiency for the bank.

For this reason acquiring other retail banks in Europe enables the bank to improve its efficiency ratio. Indeed, increasing the number of customers is a key success factor in order to obtain better ratings and in order to expand the IT system to other entities, particularly considering that the acquired banks are unlikely to have optimised their IT systems. The future of banking in Europe passes through the integration of IT systems because the back-drop for the above 'theory of the business' is the conviction that 'the less efficient banks will end up being acquired by the most efficient in the process of European consolidation.' (Santander, 2006b). Convinced by this 'new Darwinian theory of evolution', Santander has adopted a pro-active attitude in order to grow as fast and as much as possible though, of course, not oblivious to profitability and value creation.

Economies of scale

The last factor concerning Santander's willingness to grow relates to economies of scale. Mainly due to regulations in each territory, preventing banks from standardising and homogenising their financial products and management systems, economics of scale may be hard to gain in this industry.

In their study of American banks, Berger and Humphrey (1994) argue that mergers and acquisitions can lead to a 1–5 per cent reduction in costs. Santander's Alfredo Sáenz recognised that,[27] with the acquisition of Abbey National, his bank did not seek to achieve immediate economies of scale or other 'visible' benefits in the immediate term. On the contrary, he considers the acquisition as rather 'diluting' the shareholder value in the short term, even if that value might be boosted in future (by 2007). What Santander foresees is, firstly the generation of cost-saving synergies followed by revenue-generating synergies later on.

Be that as it may, we assume that in the current time framework, in which cross-border merger and acquisition transactions throughout Europe are starting to materialise (Expansión, 2007a: 30), the ability to outperform competitors in operational efficiency, perhaps resulting from economies of scale, will give a competitive edge over rival banks.

Efficiency

This is the core part of Santander's business model. As shown in Table 4.1 the history of the group was that of continuous improvement in its efficiency ratio, defined by Santander (2004a) as personnel and general expenses/net operating revenue.

Spanish banks have a good track record regarding fixed-cost management despite the fact that they have higher fixed costs than retail banks. The lower efficiency ratio is obtained thanks to one of the special features of the Spanish banking system: a capillary system of branches capturing the customer, at low cost, supported by IT systems, and with a strong focus on sales.

Some observations can be made about the data in Table 4.8. Firstly, in all three banks the efficiency ratio experienced a steady improvement. Secondly, the subsidiary banks, Banesto and Santander Totta had better ratios than Santander as a whole. Thirdly, Santander Totta had better ratios than Banesto.

It may be hypothesised that (1) smaller banks, because of their relatively small size, have a better chance of seeing quicker results after an improvement measure has been adopted, (2) best practices are first tried at smaller units, or (3) smaller and newly acquired banks have fewer legacy problems (perhaps due to the restructuring and modernisation process they may have been through) by which a measure implemented has a backlash effect.

Table 4.8   Efficiency ratio (*) (in per cent)

	1998	1999	2000	2001	2002	2003	2004	2005
Santander	62.1	57.7	56.1	54.0	52.3	49.3	46.79	42.91
Banesto	62.6	58.8	55.4	52.1	50.3	47.2	46.4	42.6
Santander Totta			53.1	50.4	45.6	43.7		
Abbey								63

(*) with depreciations
(**) However, according to the 2006 Annual Report of Santander, the efficiency ratios are 48.53% for Santander, 40.95% for Santander network in Spain, 45.27% for Banesto, 47.33 for Santander Totta and 55,10 for Abbey. The differences may arise from different calculations methods.

Source: Santander (2004) and annual report (2005).

The ratio is a useful tool to determine how efficient a bank is in generating revenue (McCune, 2005). Citing John Walker, director of BNK, Cocheo (2005: 12–13) lists net interest income, net overheads, and capital efficiency as the three most important factors in banking and argues that, with the exception of capital efficiency, the efficiency ratio reflects them.

However, the shortcomings of any banks specialising, for example, in retail are (1) that the comparison of banks across the entire spectrum, that is, banks in different sectors, cannot be made 'intelligently', (2) that the comparison of banks within different size categories is doubtful because of the economies of scale, (3) that the ratio can be ambiguous because of banks putting emphasis on different components of the profit and loss account, in particular revenue increase or cost control, (4) that the ratio can be 'a weapon for self-inflicted wounds' because of its 'quasi-religious status' giving rise to overemphasis, and (5) that by itself the ratio may be deceiving, with some doing well in shareholder return but with poor efficiency ratios (Cocheo, 2005: 12). Bankecon (2002: 5) also warns of scant correlation between bank profitability as measured by return on equity and apparent efficiency as measured by the cost/income ratio.

For instance, the financial benefits of the acquisition of Abbey National are the 'improvements in Abbey's customer offering and implementation of technology-based efficiency' (Ghemawat et al., 2005: 7). Cost savings amounting to €450 million within three years of the acquisition are to be derived from improvements in information technology (€128 million), customer operations (€83 million), sales (€45 million), and others (€45 million) according to Ghcmawat et al (2005) citing the data published by Santander. The *Parthenon* banking platform is expected to obtain €220 million by 2007 according to the USB researchers. USB (Van Rooyen & Chiavarini, 2006a, 2006b) estimates Santander's capital gains at €2.2 billion in 2005 which will be used to create a provision for restructuring costs at Abbey for the amount of £450 million.

Improvements in productivity open new possibilities for future acquisitions because the increase in Santander's productivity gives rise to a virtuous circle that in turn leads to further acquisitions and further reduction of the efficiency ratio. The reinforcement comes from information technology, as will be described in the following section.

Information Technology (IT)

The Spanish banks have managed to use IT as a source of competitive advantage over their competitors, mainly due to the absence of legacy problems and the relatively-early modernisation of their IT systems at the end of the 1980s and at the beginning of the 1990s. The emphasis on IT systems began to be placed around 1990 and 1993. In July 2005, José María Fuster, Global Chief Information Officer of Santander explained Santander's interest in the Parthenon IT platform, 'Banesto had started something which had real potential. The senior management of Santander recognised Parthenon's potential and invested heavily in it'. Thus, despite massive investment of more than 500 million euros, the reduced costs achieved by this move are estimated at around 265 million euros a year (Euromoney, July 2005). In retail banking, the synergies created by an IT system stem from the integration of the customer and channel management. In Santander's case, the issue has been to develop cross-selling applications that include all the banking operations carried out by each of the banks in the group, enabling any Santander entity to develop new products at a lower cost through the replication of an existing product.

Former Banesto chairman, Alfredo Saénz (2005) oversaw Banesto becoming a highly technologically-advanced Spanish bank, with well-qualified staff inherited from the acquired bank. Santander took

Table 4.9   Evolution of IT systems at Grupo Santander

Year	Concept
2002	• Partenón project initiated to modernise the group's IT systems in Spain and Europe and to reduce technology costs • Altair project (a platform for Latin American operations) continued
2003	• Approval of Technology and Systems project to "increase the efficiency and improve service, making of the IT system the core of it."
2004	• Appointment of CIO (chief information technology officer) and Technology Strategy Committee chaired by the CEO • Launch of Alhambra project to develop the future technology strategy of the group, based on Partenón and Altair platforms
2005	• Partenón project completed in Spain. • Implemetation of Alhambra project at Banesto • Development of technology service shared across the board

Source: (Santander, 2003, 2004b, 2005a, 2006a).

advantage of at least some major elements of its IT strategy using Banesto as an IT laboratory for the group. (See Table 4.9 *Evolution Of IT Systems At Santander*). He distinguishes three phases in the continuous improvement of productivity. Firstly, he foresees expenses control by the application of partial technology solutions.

Secondly, as cost savings were hampered by limits imposed by the official regulations and by differences in the national credit management system among Spanish banks, the implementation of common IT systems was needed to simplify the technological architecture of the business. Santander implemented IT systems in its branches in Latin America (the system was called 'Altair') and in Europe ('Parthenon')[28] (Santander, 2007: 53).

By the automatic handling of transactions, Parthenon (1) allows access to resources for administrative purposes, (2) flattens the back office structure and (3) reduces the maintenance costs of obsolete information 'silo systems'.[29]

Table 4.10   IT situation in Latin America

Bank	Not tallying	Environments	Organisations	Year 2000
Banco Mexicano	A	B	A	A
Banco Venezuela	A	A	A	A
Bancoquia	A	A	C	A
Banco Río de la Plata	A	A	C	A
Banco Santiago	B	A	A	A
Banco Sur	B	A	A	A
Banco Tornquist	B	A	A	A
Banco Santa Cruz	A	A	A	A
Banco Asunción	B	A	A	A
Banca Serfin	B	B	C	n.a.
Banco Caracas	A	A	B	n.a.
Banco Geral	B	B	C	A
Banco Noroeste	A	A	A	
Banco Meridional	A	A	A	A
Banco Bozano	A	A	A	A
Banespa	A	A	A	n.a.

A: > 75 per cent with problems, B: = 50 per cent with problems, C 25 per cent with problems
Source: Adapted from Santander (2005b: 5).

By way of contrast, the situation facing Santander in Latin America regarding its Altair IT system is summarised in Table 4.10, explaining the difficulties Santander faced before implementing its own systems in those markets.

The Altair system was implemented in Banco Santander Chile, Banco Río de la Plata, Banco Venezuela, Banco Santander Colombia, Banco Santiago, and in Banco Santander Puerto Rico and Mexico. The service centres were concentrated in Chile and Mexico. By 2005 the system was up and running smoothly. Its contribution to Santander is summarised in Table 4.11 *Altair: Operational Figures*. The diminishing investment in IT in Latin America seems to point to economies of scale as the IT systems were implemented throughout the group's bank network. In 2001 the amount was US$925 million which dwindled to US$610 million and US$500 million in 2005 and 2006, respectively (Santander, 2005b: 15).

The third phase introduces a new operational process architecture for cost-saving and the enhancement of commercial activities. IT management is led in concrete terms by Santader's three affiliated companies, ISBAN, PRODUBAN and GEOBAN, which are responsible for information systems, production and support systems, and business processes outsourcing respectively. (See Figure 4.4.)

Accenture's Moreno (2006: 9) holds that 60 per cent of the top executives of European banks consider the Spanish banks to be the best equipped in terms of IT systems. Santander illustrates this being a front-runner in the IT area, enabling the bank to boost its efficiency and its growth through the exploitation of silos and through the synergies existing from external growth.

Table 4.11   Altair: operational figures

	Latin America	Spain
Nº branches in total	3,653	4,655
Nº clients in total	14,215,538	8,740,000
Nº monthly transactions at branches	263,097,463	18,500,000
Nº monthly transactiona at automatic banking	47,498,241	7,000,000
Nº monthly operations telebanking	11,729,573	7,000,000
Nº monthly transactions by virtual banking	28,235,475	4,000,000
Nº own cheques monthly processed	22,584,050	1,200,000
Nº cheques of other banks monthly processed	12,772,938	1,000,000
Nº payment by direct debit by bank	6,319,191	19,070,000

Source: Santander (2005b: 14).

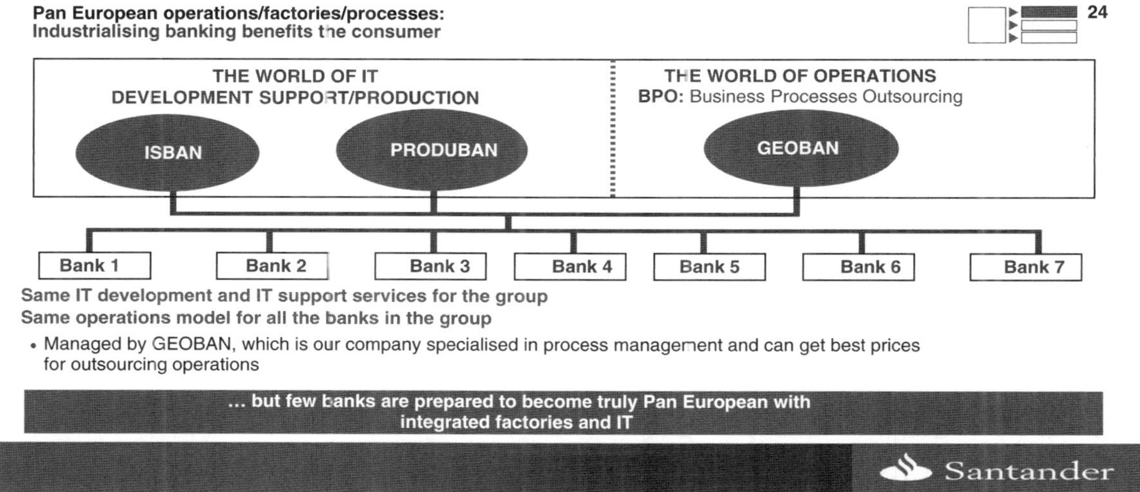

Figure 4.4   Pan European operations factories processes

Conclusion

In less than 20 years, Santander has managed to become one of the ten most highly-capitalised banks. The alliance of two exceptional people, Emilio Botin in particular but also Alfredo Sáenz, explains this success. Both of them have been surrounded by a permanent climate of crisis in Europe in general and especially in Spain. Such a situation has led to them remaining focused on operational efficiency and day-to-day operations prioritising immediate cash flow generation – a clear PA model. Its previous successes, its own structure and business model maintain focus on external growth through mergers and acquisitions, efficiency through internal productivity, and also a strong focus on IT in order to develop best practices and establish benchmarks.

In the future, the ability to have a superior execution of banking best practices and a good portfolio management that helps Santander to identify possible institutions where they can replicate their own model – as they are currently doing – should be decisive factors in increasing the bank's leadership in the sector.

Appendix 4.1

	Santander network	Banesto	Santander consumer finance	Santander Totta	Banif	Santander Banespa	Santander Serfin	Santander Santiago	Abbey
Customers (millions)	7,5	2,3	7,7	1,8	0,1	7,1	9,4	2,9	18,3
Branches	2669	1703	267	693	42	1897	1005	401	712
Credit investment*	92145	49973	30008	25851	2130	12584	15615	17757	117732
Customer assets managed	97727	71231	18858	26613	24400**	29494	42690	30221	155609
Exploitation margin	2101	1140	1073	496	61	1524	816	742	963
Benefits	1285	498	487	345	24	734	468	420	555

- The securitization effect deducted
- All assets managed. Abbey figures are in Sterling Pounds

	Banca Comercial	Europa Continental	11.732.831
		Reino Unido	18.267.197
		Iberoamérica	20.247.401
Clientes	Consumo	Santander Consumer Finance	7.702.324
	Otroa	Gestoras de Pensiones	8.040.000
		Banca Privada	81.948
		Banca Mayorista Global	11.498
		Total clientes	66.083.199

Iberoamérica. 10 paises, 62.746 emplendos, 4.100 oficinas. 20,3 milliones clientes de banca comercial

Milliones de euroe	Margen ordinario		Margen de explotacion		Beneficioa atribuido al Grupo	
	2005	Var. (%)	2005	Var. (%)	2005	Var. (%)
Brasil	2.697	32,91	1.226	42,62	591	3,89
México	1,572	22,34	656	24,12	376	15,02
Chile	1.101	22,14	596	29,92	338	45,19
Venezuela	409	8,44	186	3,11	133	38,39
Argentina	384	31,8	157	63,21	78	188,04
Puerto Rico	255	2,86	92	10,6	49	2,5
Colombia	115	24,15	44	33,99	40	81,83
Resto	316	16,3	168	23.98	171	12,57
Total	6.860	24,57	3.125	31,58	1.776	20,77

Banca comercial Millones de euros	Margen ordinario		Margen de explotación		Resultado antes impuestos	
	2005	Var. (%)	2005	Var. (%)	2005	Var. (%)
Europa Continental	8.172	11,29	4.747	21,25	3.789	39,14
de la que: Espana	6.124	9,61	3.551	19,45	2.939	37,7
Portugal	884	7,1	425	19,31	354	40,93
Reino Unido (Abbey)	3.232	–	1.228	–	986	–
Iberoamérica	5.516	26,42	2.179	38,22	1.514	36,23
de la que: Brasil	2.153	35,92	774	60,7	403	36,31
México	1.253	21,45	458	22,35	369	2,18
Chile	903	27,33	458	42,3	338	70,69
Total Banca Commercial	16.920	44,54	8.154	48,49	6.289	64,01

Gestión de Activos y Seguros. Resultados Millones de euroe	Margen ordinario		Margen de explotación		Resultado antea impueatos	
	2005	Var. (%)	2005	Var. (%)	2005	Var. (%)
Fondos de inversión	295	25,63	189	22,27	189	22,19
Planes de pensiones	296	18,53	160	33,35	160	38,19
Sequors	776	397,51	336	232,84	340	237,33
de los que: Abbey	555	–	179	–	179	–
Total Gestión de Activoa y Saguroa	1.367	113,39	685	82,51	688	85,61

Distributción Capital Económico

Por tipoas de rieago

Crédíto	55,4%
Mercado (Participaciones de Renta variable)	11,4%
Resto Mercado	7,6%
Interés Estructural	8,4%
Negocio	8,4%
Operativo	6,8%
Seguros (Abbey)	2,0%

Por Unidades de negocio

Iberoamérica	32,5%
Gestion Financiera y participaciones	17,8%
Abbey	14,2%
Red Santander en España	11,1%
Banesto	8,9%
Banca Mayorista en España*	7,0%
Portugal	4,2%
Santander consumer	3,8%
Gestion Activos y Sequros España	0,4%
Grupo Banif	0,1%

* Banca Mayorista Global representa un 13,5%

Appendix 4.2   Detailed interpretation of the working of Santander's business model

With the benefit of hindsight we can discern a certain direction in the behaviour and performance of Santander, and we may call it the group's 'strategic intent', a concept advanced by Hamel and Prahalad (1989) who maintain that companies with a long-term vision may end up reaching their goals even if their short-term manoeuvrability is restricted due to limited resources. We will elaborate on this point later in this chapter.

Santander (2004a) list, as main components of their business model, (a) high market share plus diversification, (b) 'vibrant' sales culture leading to revenue growth, (c) efficiency targeting cost discipline, (d) risk management for high credit quality, and (e) capital strength and discipline allowing growth capacity.

How do all these components coalesce into an integral business model or system? To answer the question, the following profit equation is useful:

$$\pi = pq - k$$

where π = profit, p = price, q = quantity, and k = cost.

Now we must remember that the purpose of a company is to maximise the profit (Grant, 2004). So a company must either increase 'pq' or reduce 'k' or do both. How does this relate to the handling of Santander's business model components?

High market-share plus diversification and revenue growth resulting from a sales culture point to the increase in sales volume and/or price, namely 'pq'; the efficiency gain and risk management concern 'k'. The capital strength will strengthen the firm's capacity to grow, namely, the increase in 'pq'.

Overall, the model aims at creating a 'virtuous circle' around cost efficiency. (See Figure 4.5 *Model Around Cost Efficiency.*) Therefore, the following scheme seems to cover the working of all these components.

High market share and diversification will ultimately lead to economies of scale resulting in reduced costs. A sales culture boosting revenue growth will also certainly help to achieve economies of scale and cost efficiency through the spread of overheads. It is also true that for growth the bank needs to be prepared with a strong capital base. Thus, the concatenation of cause and effect bring about cost efficiency for the benefit of profit maximisation.

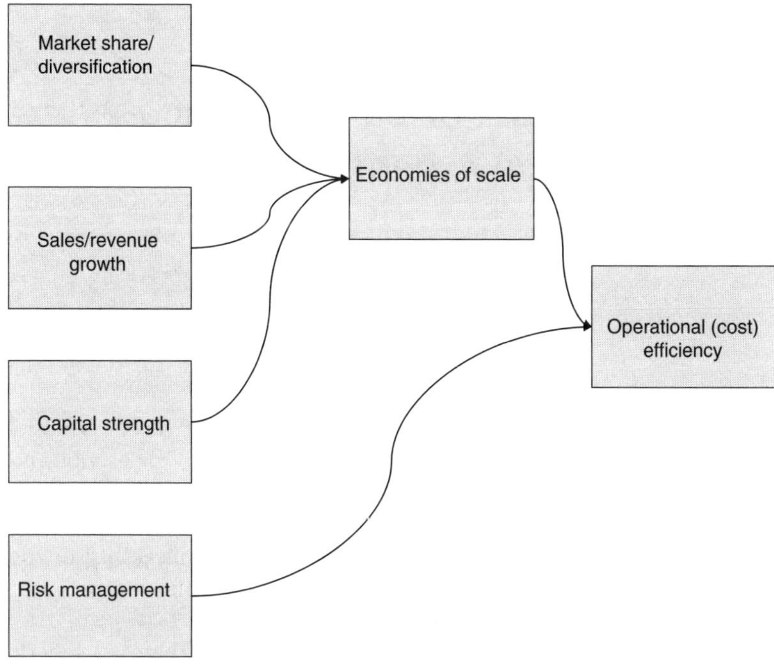

Figure 4.5   Santander's model around the operational/cost efficiency
Source: Authors

Obviously the penchant for growth is a fundamental part of the bank's culture. In an interview with the authors, Alfredo Sáenz, the bank's CEO, emphasised that 'the Group's DNA is to grow; we don't know why it should be, but we feel strong if we grow'.[30] Santander (2004a: 19) stresses the growth opportunities in Spain, the European consumer sector (as potential opportunities), and Latin America (as tangible opportunities), but also puts emphasis on Santander's core competence remaining focused on (1) managing retail banking networks, (2) improving them by means of permanent restructuring for which IT expertise plays a key role, and (3) expanding to new markets to which its business model is well-suited.

5
Business Model of BBVA – Banco Bilbao Vizcaya Argentaria

In Chapter 3 we looked at Spanish retail banks' generic business model as an *ideal type* or *construct*, before going on in Chapter 4 to describe and review Santander's model based on the way it works, its strategic approach, and other components.

In this chapter, as further confirmation of the applicability of the generic business model to other major banks in Spain, we turn our attention to BBVA.

For the purpose of the *triangulation* of the proof that there is a generic business model in Spanish retail banks, we will review the business model of Banco Sabadell in Annex 3.

Introduction[1]

The final throes of the dominance of Spain's banking industry by the 'Big Seven' large banks began when in 1987, Sánchez Asiaín, then CEO of Banco de Bilbao, initiated the race for growth by mergers and acquisitions. Even though his first attempt at a merger with Banesto was not successful, his second attempt this time with Banco de Vizcaya, led to the creation of Banco de Bilbao Vizcaya in 1989 (See Table 5.1 the merger history and birth of BBVA.) It was agreed between the heads of the emerging banks that the new entity would be led by Sánchez Asiaín for the first year and thereafter by Pedro de Toledo, the chairman of Banco de Vizcaya (even though Bilbao had six times as many customers as Vizcaya) (Cacho, 1990). It was supposed to be a merger between equals, because at the time, it was widely believed that a hostile takeover in the banking industry was destined to fail. As Vizcaya was a more dynamic bank in terms of process, the balance of size versus process could have justified the transaction (Gómez Escorial, 2004).

Table 5.1   The mergers and acquisitions, and the birth of BBVA

During the 1980s Banco de Bilbao's strategy was to attain sufficient size in order to participate in financial operations generated by advances in technology, deregulation, securitisation and the interrelationship between domestic and international markets.

Banco de Vizcaya contributed to the refloating of banks affected by the economic crisis and pursued a policy of strong growth through acquisitions. This turned it into a large banking group. The most important operation was the acquisition of Banca Catalana in 1984.

In the meantime the official credit entities expanded their business through market operations. In 1982 BEX lost the exclusive right to provide export finance. It refocused its goals on becoming a universal bank and on building a financial group. During this process it acquired Banco de Alicante in 1983.

In 1988 Banco de Bilbao and Banco de Vizcaya merged to form BBV.

Corporación Bancaria de España (CBE) was set up in 1991 as a government corporation and credit entity with bank status. Argentaria started out with a federated banking model. However in 1998 Corporación Bancaria de España (already privatised via IPOs), BEX (which had merged with BCI), BHE and Caja Postal were merged into a single bank: Argentaria.

BBV and Argentaria announced their planned merger on 19th October 1999. The goal was to continue creating value. The new group had the advantages of significant size, a strong capital base, a considerable financial structure and appropriate geographic diversification of its business and risks. As a result there was a greater profit potential.

Customers now had access to a bigger network and a wider range of products. They also enjoyed easier access to new channels and a considerable international presence. Employees also had more opportunity for career advancement.

The integration of BBVA went very smoothly. This was attributed to the following:

- the speed of strategic decisions
- the immediate definition of the new organisation and a framework agreement with employees
- the speed with which working groups were set up and plans were made for each area of activity
- the successful achievement of ambitious timetables – with time to spare in some cases
- the enthusiasm, commitment, effort and co-operative spirit of everyone at BBVA

The integration process was given an important boost in January 2000 by the rollout of the single BBVA brand. This helped the group to generate quickly an image that was strongly positioned in terms of identity and distinguishing characteristics. The BBVA integration process was carried out with rapidity and efficiency and concluded in February 2001.

Continued

Table 5.1   Continued

The integration of the group's retail businesses in Spain (BBV, Argentaria, Banca Catalana, Banco del Comercio and Banco de Alicante) led to the creation of a significant branch network under the BBVA banner.

The efficiency of the BBVA integration was recognised by top financial publications. In 2000 it was chosen World's Best Bank (Forbes) and Best Bank in Spain (The Banker). In 2001 it was Best Bank in Latin America (Forbes) and Best European Bank (Lafferty).

BBVA's international activities are already a hundred years old. Banco de Bilbao opened a branch in Paris in 1902 and a London branch in 1918. It was thus several decades ahead of other Spanish banks.

During the 1970s Banco de Bilbao, Banco de Vizcaya and Banco Exterior became international groups with branches and representative offices in the main capitals of Europe, the Americas and Asia. They also started to acquire local banks in these areas, mainly in Latin America.

In 1968 Banco Exterior had created BEX Panama and this has now become BBVA Panama after merging with BBV Panama in 2000.

Banco de Vizcaya acquired Banco Comercial de Mayagüez in Puerto Rico in 1979. This bank was founded in 1967 by a group of traders and manufacturers. After becoming BBV Puerto Rico, in 1992 it commenced a phase of growth through acquisitions, leading to the current BBVA Puerto Rico.

However in 1995 BBV started to develop an international expansion strategy that led to the construction of a large network in Latin America. This entailed important investments in capital, technology and human resources.

In 1995 it entered Peru following the privatisation of Banco Continental and Mexico through Probursa.

The origins of Banco Continental – known as 'the friendly bank' – go back to 1951. It combines concern for both customers and culture. Banca Asociada was added in 1970 with a state holding.

In 1996 BBV expanded its presence in Colombia through Banco Ganadero and in Argentina through Banco Francés.

Banco Ganadero was started in 1956 with the support of some local farmers. Its purpose is to support and encourage agricultural activity. In 1959 legislation (Ley 26) converted the bank into a mixed company with shares held by the government, private individuals and farmers.

Banco Francés (Río de La Plata) was set up in Buenos Aires in 1886. For more than a century it serviced large companies in Argentina. During the 1980s it extended its branch network throughout that country, adding SMEs and private individuals to its customers.

In 1997 BBVA entered Venezuela through Banco Provincial, which had been set up in 1953. At the beginning this bank focused its activities on the capital city and the central region. Today it is the most important and most solid financial institution in Venezuela. It has enjoyed this position of leadership since 1983.

Continued

Table 5.1   Continued

In 1998 a start was made in Chile through Banco BHIF.

The origin of this bank goes back to 1883 and the creation of Banco Hipotecario in Valparaíso. In 1976 it started to expand with the help of the three industrial groups that controlled the bank and it moved its headquarters to Santiago. In 1989 it merged with Banco Nacional and became Banco BHIF.

In Mexico, BBV Probursa merged with Bancomer in 2000 to create BBVA Bancomer – the leading bank in that country.

Bancomer was started in Mexico City in 1932 with the name Banco de Comercio. In 1977 it consolidated the entities in its merchant banking system to create Bancomer. Along with other Mexican banks it was nationalised in 1982 and in 1991 a group of local investors acquired a controlling interest.

Deployment of the common platform was completed in 2001 for all business areas and countries. The BBVA brand was thus applied to the group's subsidiaries in Latin America.

In 2004 the banks in Chile and Colombia changed their name to BBVA.

At the beginning of 2004, BBVA launched a bid to buy out all the minority interests in Bancomer. In line with the strengthening of the Group's position in the Mexican market, BBVA also acquired 100% of Hipotecaria Nacional, the country's largest private institution specialising in mortgage business.

The other area of international expansion was the Group's entry into the US market. During the second quarter of the year, the Group purchased Valley Bank, California through BBVA Bancomer. In September, BBVA continued its expansion in the US Hispanic market when it announced that it was buying Laredo National Bancshares in Texas.

In order to continue its the strategy with individuals and the SME market in the US, a specific business unit has been set up which will take charge of all the Group's businesses in this region, which includes BBVA Puerto Rico and the US banks.

In October 2005, BBVA purchased Granahorrar in Colombia; an acquisition that places BBVA at the head of the country's mortgage market, whilst also incorporating a broad customer base.

BBVA announced in May 2006 the acquisition of Forum, a company that specialises in financing vehicle purchases in Chile. In June the Group announced the purchase of Texas Regional Bancshares Inc. and State National Bancshares Inc., two important banks in Texas.

Source: BBVA's website.[2]

The unexpected death of Pedro de Toledo made it necessary for the Bank of Spain to stabilise the internal situation of the bank, and the Spain's central bank encouraged Sánchez Asiaín to retire, and replaced him with Emilio Ybarra from Banco de Bilbao. From that moment, Ybarra and Pedro Luis Uriarte, his COO or managing director – also from Banco Bilbao – steered the bank towards a customer-oriented culture. This culture targets specific products to specific customers, rather than revolving around the launch of multiple products.

Neither the merger with Argentaria nor the internationalisation process of the bank affected this culture, even when the sphere of business of the new Banco de Bilbao Vizcaya Argentaria (hereinafter BBVA) grew. On the contrary, this emphasis was maintained under the leadership of Francisco Gónzalez and José Ignacio Goirigolzarri, the current Chairman and CEO, since January 2000, and the President and COO (or presidential COO) since December 2001, respectively.

This chapter analyses how BBVA has come to be one of the top twenty banks in the world, in terms of stock capitalisation, by sticking closely to a business model with a PA (profit arithmetic) style approach. Faced with the same business environment, the leaders of most Spanish retail banks have tended to focus on short-term cash-flow generation. Despite the existence of major differences in the banks' approach, their basic model is founded on three pillars – a penchant for size and growth in pursuit of size, operational efficiency and IT systems.

After looking at BBVA's organisation structure and business areas in the light of its strategic approach, we will review the bank's business model. This will be done, firstly, to explain how the actions of this bank fit with the PA model and secondly, to analyse the business model's three main axes, as described in chapter 3, and thirdly, to consider the possibility of replicating this model.

BBVA's business model

Organisational structure

The organisational structure of BBVA appears to reflect the bank's strategic thinking, (see Figure 5.1 *Organisational Chart as at May 2007*). At BBVA the work of the CEO and the COO seems to be both combined and divided; one of the strategic components of Spanish banks (as considered in Chapter 3). Thus, Francisco González, Chairman and CEO, centres his attention on functional areas, such as the general secretariat, legal, tax, audit and compliance, image and communications, and so on.

The operational areas are managed by José Ignacio Goirigolzarri, the president and COO (or presidential COO in the words of the bank's managers), although he does so under the supervision of the chairman.

From the chart we can see that (1) the business units are separated into the geographic areas covered (Spain and Portugal, Mexico, USA, and South America) as well as into the functional areas (Chief

Financial Officer, Risk, and Global Business Area), and (2) IT systems report directly to the President and COO, forming part of an umbrella unit (HR, IT & Operations), reflecting the importance placed on IT systems.

The last point is confirmed by the explanation provided on the bank's website on its philosophy of the organisation of business areas:

BBVA is divided into three kinds of areas and units: Business, Support and the Chairman's Office. The first two are the direct responsibility of the president (COO) and the third comes under the chairman (CEO). The business units are defined as 'value-creation centres' with direct responsibility for market approach, growth and their own income statement. This is part of the empowerment plan for business units and part of BBVA's corporate culture. (BBVA website on its business areas)[3]

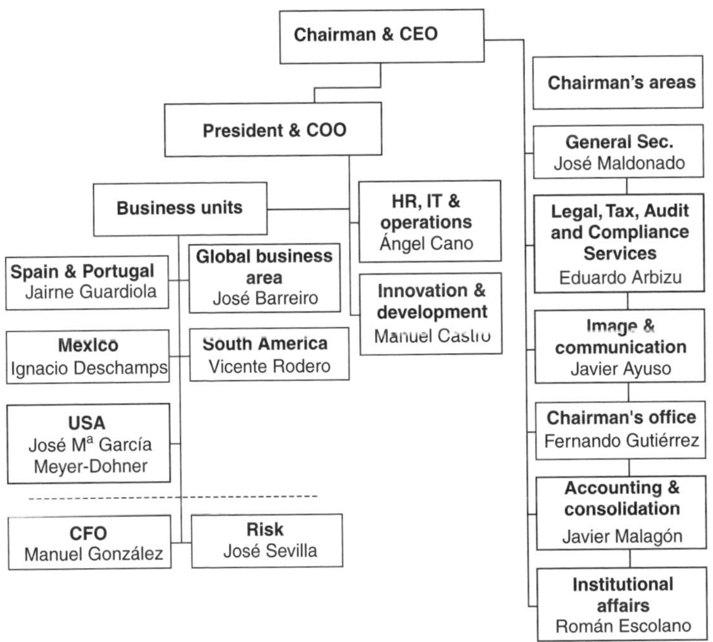

Figure 5.1   Organisational chart
Source: BBVA website.[4]

BBVA's business areas

The bank expounds its thinking underlying the definition of business areas (See Table 5.2.):

The purpose of this structure is to help the Group develop on three fronts:

1. To facilitate the creation of business units that are more capable of operating and taking decisions in an autonomous manner. They are responsible for their own growth strategy within the strategic parameters set by the Group.
2. To boost Customer Outreach. Transformation and innovation are the tools that will provide more people in more markets, with more appropriate and more profitable solutions.
3. To create a management structure that allows every unit to maximise the advantages of being part of a global group with a first-class brand and highly diversified risk, soundly based, profitable and efficient. (BBVA website (http://www.bbva.com) accessed in May 1st 2007.)

Table 5.2   Business areas

Business areas of the BBVA group

Business areas

Business in Spain and Portugal comprises the retail banking business and company & business banking (CBB) in these countries. It covers all business with private individuals, small and mid-size enterprises (SMEs), other companies and institutions, consumer finance, insurance (Seguros Europa) and BBVA Portugal.

Business in Spain and Portugal includes:

- Commercial banking and company & business banking
- Innovation and business development
- Consumer finance
- Insurance Europe
- BBVA Portugal
- Transformation and productivity

Global Businesses is an area of great importance from the point of view of growth and expansion in new parts of the world and for new Group activities at international level. It comprises all market and global customer activities in Europe, the Americas and Asia, as well as business and real estate projects, and investment banking.

This area includes:

- Global markets and distribution
- Asset management and private banking

Continued

Table 5.2   Continued

- Global customers Europe
- Global customers in the Americas
- Asia
- Business and real estate projects
- Investment banking

Mexico is one of the Group's main areas of growth.

South America covers the activity and results of the Group's subsidiaries in this region and their subsidiary undertakings, including pension-fund managers, insurance companies and the international private banking business.

USA. BBVA's franchise in the USA consists of five businesses: 1. Banking business in Texas (Laredo National, Texas Regional and State National) with a leadership position in commercial banking and superior ability to develop business with private individuals, SMEs and other companies. 2. BBVA Bancomer USA, a banking franchise in California for first-generation immigrants, based on money transfers (remittances), and financial and non-financial services and products. 3. BBVA Puerto Rico, a franchise with an important range of mortgages and consumer finance, serving private individuals and SMEs. 4. Bancomer Transfer Services (BTS), the leading provider of US-Mexico money transfers, with around 40% market share. It is extending its reach to cover the rest of Latin America, China, India and the Philippines. 5. BBVA Finanzia USA, a company specialising in consumer finance and credit cards.

The Finance, the Risk and the Innovation & Development areas are different to the business units above but they are part of this section because they contribute directly to the creation of value for the Group.

Support areas
HR, IT & Operations comprises the human resources unit; technology & operations; transformation & productivity; purchasing, buildings and services; and corporate security. These units are the drivers of change, transformation and improvement in the Group's efficiency and service quality.

Chairman's area
The units under the Chairman's Area are responsible for developing the corporate governance model, supervising internal control and managing the Group's intangible assets. They are:

- General Secretary
- Chairman's office
- Legal services, tax advice, auditing and compliance
- General inspection
- Image & communication
- The BBVA Foundation
- Institutional affairs

Source: BBVA's website.[5]

The 'world-view' of management that lies behind BBVA's business model

The worldview embraced by the management of BBVA points to a Profit-Arithmetic approach. Analysis throughout this section confirms that the bank shows many of the characteristics of a PA approach, such as basing their management decisions on their 'sense of business', their clear understanding of what levers to pull to generate profits, and their prioritisation of a few performance indicators which are more short-term operation-oriented rather than long-term vision-oriented.[6]

A more in-depth analysis on the cognitive approaches of Spanish banks' top executives is included in Annex 1.[7] One of the findings in it points to the possibility that perhaps BBVA's focus is on growth and earning, while Santander's is on internationalisation and income. Nevertheless, circumstantial evidence suggests that BBVA is oriented towards the customer and profitability, while Santander towards product and growth. Some industry experts interviewed by the authors assert that the portfolio mix of BBVA reckons on a wider base including retail, trade finance and project finance, whereas Santander centres more on just retail.

As shown in Figure 5.2, *BBVA's conception of change in the business environment*, BBVA (2005: 4) stresses that the world is changing at high speed, essentially on the two fronts of increased competition and technology/information. As shown in the bank's presentation,

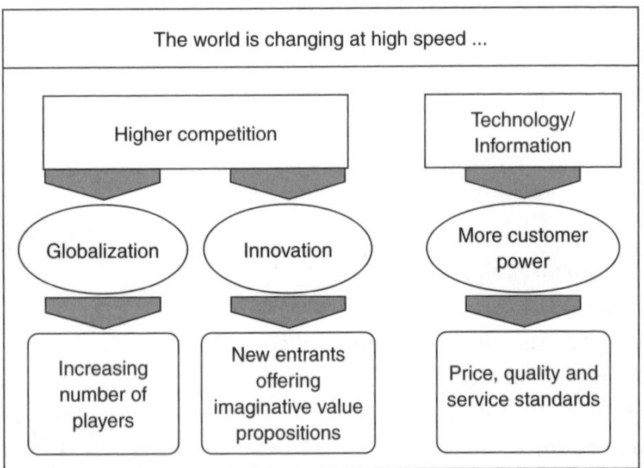

Figure 5.2   BBVA's conception of the change in business environment
Source: BBVA (2005: 4).

globalisation, innovation, and more customer power result from this change. This in turn leads to a greater number of players, new entrants offering imaginative value propositions, and increased levels of price, quality, and service.

This rapid change in the business environment has given rise to concerns about (1) the scarcity of growth, (2) perception of higher risk, and (3) the need to reduce costs and improve asset quality (BBVA, 2005b: 5). In the face of these concerns BBVA pursues profitable growth coinciding with the generic business model leaning on a penchant for size and growth for size.

On the one hand, growth is sought by concentrating on high-growth markets with excellent economic prospects, and, on the other, by operational efficiency and low risk profile across the group comprising a tested model to drive efficiency, asset quality, and diversification in geographic and business portfolio (BBVA, 2005b: 6).

Likewise BBVA (2005) underlines a shift of wealth towards emerging economies. In terms of GDP growth Asian countries stand out with 7.3 per cent between 2004 and 2005, followed by Latin America (5.2 per cent). Japan and Euro-zone grew only by 2.4 per cent and 1.6 per cent, respectively (BBVA, 2005a: 5).

For BBVA (2005) it follows that in this situation of rapid, continual change only the best prepared in the banking industry will be able to create value for their shareholders. This requires that there be ongoing and continuous transformation in the banks, much in the same vein as Japanese automobile manufacturers' *kaizen* movement.[8] This idea is backed up by the expressions and words used during our interview surveys with current executives of BBVA who time and again used phrases such as 'industrialisation', 'working like the Romans', and 'factory management', by which they express the idea that bank operations are like an industrial or factory production process subject to continuous, day-to-day improvements, rather than cerebral, vision-based activities.

Value creation is determined by two factors: corporate positioning and the business model (BBVA, 2005a: 10) as illustrated in the following Figure 5.3.

The first of these two factors, corporate positioning, is determined by market potential and the position within that market. Decisions should be taken strategically since they are critical in the profitability and risk profile (BBVA, 2005a: 11). This positioning in turn affects the business portfolio. The second factor, the business model, lends the basic support necessary to achieve competitive advantage.

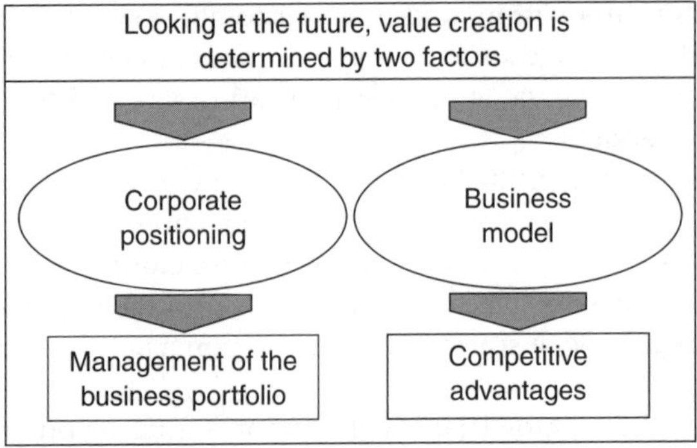

Figure 5.3   BBVA's value creation factors
Source: BBVA (2005: 10).

Altogether therefore, we may conclude that the creation of value for shareholders is the basic objective for BBVA's management. But how is this shareholder value creation turned into more manageable indicators? Perhaps by monitoring Key Performance Indicators (Gary, 2002) or Key Variables (Anthony et al., 1989: 500–501) that 'need to be watched especially closely, because they indicate factors that determine the success of the business.' Growth, profitability, and efficiency appear to be the set of indicators of choice, for their ease of understanding and relative simplicity in monitoring.

Growth, profitability, and efficiency

BBVA's president and COO, José Ignacio Goirigolzarri's speech at the Merrill Lynch European Banking & Insurance Conference in London on 5th October 2006 nicely summarises in its title where BBVA's strategy is heading:[9] 'Risk, return and growth: getting the balance right'. These are key variables for the Spanish bank.

In fact, in another presentation BBVA (2005c: 4) states its competitive position as based on profitability, efficiency, and EPS (earning per share) growth in line with its 2002 strategy plan. BBVA (2005b: 4) also lists profitable growth as the first element of its strategy. The bank boasted the 1st position in terms of ROE in the Eurozone in the first half of 2005, with 35.6 per cent compared with the European bank average of 19.8 per cent; the 2nd position in terms of efficiency, with an efficiency ratio 46.7 against the European average of 60.4; and the 1st position in terms of asset quality measured by the NPL (non-performing liabilities) ratio standing at 0.95 against European a average of 3.9 (BBVA, 2005a: 8).

The following Figure 5.4 *Circular And Perpetual Cause-Effect Relationships* explains the working of BBVA's strategy much in line with the triad of components explained in Chapter 3: (1) IT systems with open and modular product architecture, (2) penchant for size and growth for size, and (3) operational efficiency.

In pursuing the creation of shareholder value monitored through the three indicators, Goirigolzarri (2006: 7) accounts for the excellent performance of BBVA on the basis of three strategic fronts: (1) corporate positioning, (2) business model, and (3) capital discipline. The three as a whole lead to value creation based on 'a virtuous circle of top-line growth and bottom-line profitability'.

We will first describe the corporate positioning and then the business model and capital discipline, before going on to contrast these concepts with the analysis we conducted on Santander in the previous chapter.

Corporate positioning

The change in corporate positioning is reflected in the composition of the business portfolio as shown in Table 5.3: BBVA's business portfolio shift between 2002 and 2006. The bank's wholesale business grew by 7 per cent, from 14 per cent to 21 per cent in contrast with the reduction in Industrial holding- and corporate centre-led businesses from 27 per cent to 21 per cent. The retail business in Spain gained two percentage points from 23 per cent in 2002. Goirigolzarri (2006: 8) summed up the situation as the allocation of more capital to high-growth businesses.

The process used by BBVA to change the business portfolio is composed of three steps as shown in Figure 5.5: *BBVA's Approach To The Management Of Their Business Portfolio.* Therefore the future portfolio is shaped on the basis of the preferred framework, an area in which the

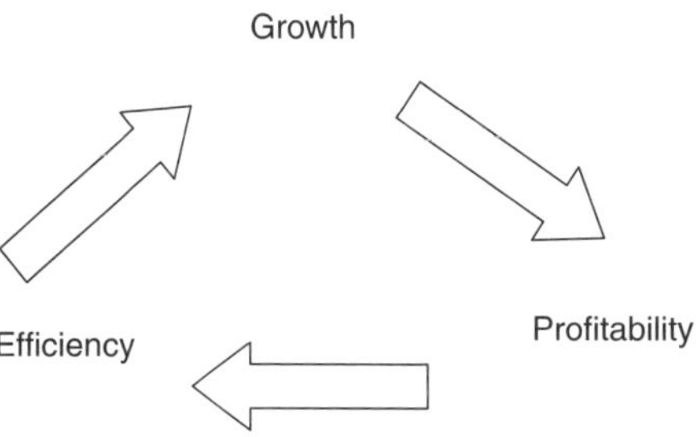

Figure 5.4   Cause-effect relationships

Table 5.3 BBVA's business portfolio shift between 2002 and 2006

	2002(%)	2006(%)
Industrial holding and corp. centre	27	21
Retail Spain	23	25
Rest of America	23	15
Wholesale business	14	21
Mexico	23	21
USA	n.a.	7

Source: Goirigolzarri (2006: 8).

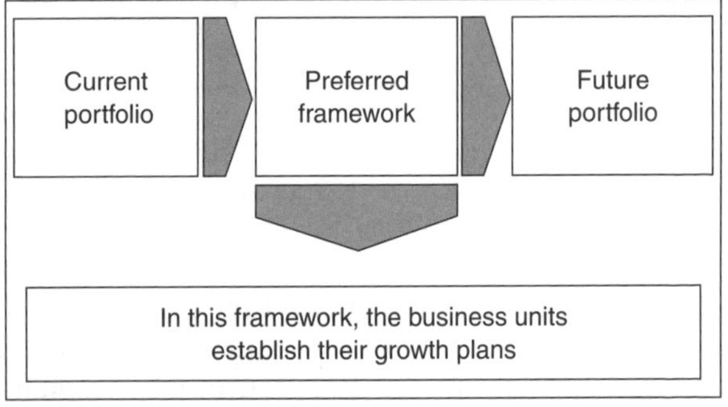

Figure 5.5 BBVA's approach to the management of their business portfolio
Source: BBVA (2005a: 12).

business units hold a lot of sway in the establishment of their growth plans (BBVA, 2005a: 12).

Lastly, there is no denying the fact that BBVA's home market has offered a base for the bank's strength and growth. BBVA's presence in the Spanish market is solid because 8.5 per cent of all bank offices in Spain belong to BBVA, 10.8 per cent of total private deposits are in the hands of BBVA, 11.1 per cent of all private loans are BBVA's, and so on (BBVA, 2005a: 15). It also holds the leading position regarding financing SMEs and micro-businesses (those with fewer than 5 employees) with respectively, 45.3 per cent and 45.4 per cent market-share in these segments, according to FRS 2003 and 2004 data cited by BBVA (2005a: 16).

Table 5.4   Spain's GDP year-on-year growth in percentage

	2003	2004	2005	2006e
Spain	2.9	3.1	3.4	3.2
EMU	0.7	1.7	1.4	2.2

Source: BBVA Economic Research cited by BBVA (2005a: 18).

Spain has shown a strong increase in employment (five million jobs created between 1994 and 2004) and GDP per capita, while the number of households has also grown exponentially; 2.6 million in ten years (1991–2001), with 3.3 million more estimated to be created over the next ten years.) (BBVA, 2005a: 17).

As a result Spain is one of the most dynamic economies in Europe, as evidenced by its GDP growth (See Table 5.4 *Spain's GDP Growth*.)

Overall, in the retail banking business, BBVA has two regions where it can leverage its retail experience in Spain: Mexico and USA. In the wholesale businesses the bank may go for a global franchise (BBVA, 2005c: 14).

Internationalisation, first in Latin America, later in Europe, and ultimately in the US, works on cultural links and the accumulation of knowledge and resources gained from experience. Indeed, immigrants from Latin America constitute the basis upon which entry to the US market is founded. Since their standard of living generally increases in the second generation, BBVA will have effortlessly positioned itself through capturing the first generation.

The components of BBVA's business model and corporate discipline

BBVA's business model comprises components revolving around the pursuit of operational efficiency measured by efficiency ratio, quest for profitability, and a penchant for size and growth for size.[10]

Operational efficiency and risk management

Goirigolzarri (2006: 9) suggests that the core management skills are (1) risk management, (2) efficiency, and (3) retail network management; all of which contribute to high profitability. The first addresses the question of risk profile with low NPL ratio and high coverage; the second is reflected in the efficiency ratio, bringing down the cost of operations; and the third seeks the increase of average sales by the sales force. (See Figure 5.6 *BBVA's Conceptual Representation Of The Three Core Management Skills*.)

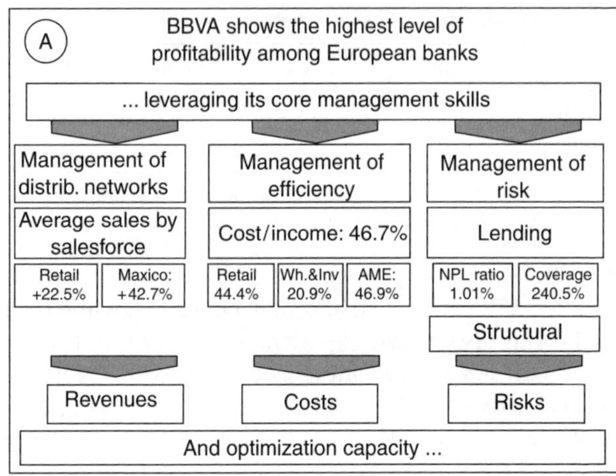

Figure 5.6   BBVA's conceptual representation of the three core management skills
Source: BBVA (2005a: 31).

According to Goirigolzarri (2006: 10) the asset portfolio of BBVA is distributed as follows: 83.1 per cent in Europe and the rest being in the US and Latin America, of which only 4.2 per cent are below investment grade,[11] a credit designation given municipal securities that is below investment grade. 46 per cent of this lending is collateralised.

Goirigolzarri (2006: 10) maintains that BBVA would suffer minimum impact in case of change in the global credit-risk cycle and cites a Merrill Lynch study estimating the impact of such a cycle change on BBVA Group's pre-tax profits as –1.1 per cent in contrast to the European bank average of –6.7 per cent.

NPLs at BBVA improved from 0.91 in December 2001 to 0.55 in December 2004 (BBVA, 2005b: 33). This is streets ahead of other banks' and savings banks' as shown in Table 5.5, *NPL Ratios In Spain And The Americas*. The coverage ratio was 228 per cent (BBVA, 2005b: 34),[12] which improved to 275 per cent (Goirigolzarri, 2006).

The efficiency ratio,[13] according to Goirigolzarri (2006: 11), experienced ten points improvement from 54.0 in 2002 to 44.3 in the first half of 2006 when the Euro Zone banks achieved an average of 56.3.

In terms of BBVA's retail management capabilities, the network productivity in retail banking in Spain and Mexico improved year-on-year by 34 per cent and 42 per cent in 2005, respectively thanks to improvements in processes and organisation (Goirigolzarri, 2006: 12).

Table 5.5   NPL ratios in Spain (*)

	December 2001	December 2002	December 2003	December 2004
Average Spanish banks	1.00	0.96	0.83	0.69
Savings banks	0.90	0.86	0.75	0.62
BBVA	0.91	0.83	0.72	0.55

(*) Pre-dating IFRS (International Financial Reporting Standards).

Source: (BBVA, 2005b: 33).

Quest for profitability

BBVA (2005c: 4) states its competitive position as being based on profitability, efficiency, and EPS (earning per share) growth, depicted in its 2002 strategy plan. The bank (2005b: 4) also lists profitable growth as the first element of its strategy.

BBVA boasted the top position in ROE (return on equity) in the Eurozone in the first half of 2005 with 35.6 per cent compared to the European banks' average of 19.8 per cent; the 2nd position in efficiency with 46.7 against the European average of 60.4; and the lead position in asset quality measured by the NPL ratio, standing at 0.95 against the European average of 3.9 (BBVA, 2005a: 8). ROE in the first half-year of 2006 was 35.8 per cent, a slight improvement on the 35.6 per cent in the first half-year period of the previous year.

High profitability ensures shareholder remuneration and self-financing growth (Goirigolzarri, 2006: 13). The remuneration of shareholders can come from various sources, such as an increase in share price, payment of dividends, etc, all of which contribute to both the actual profitability and expectation of future profitability. With the exception of the acquisition of Compass in the US, none of the mergers in which BBVA was involved diluted capital. This contrasts with Santander's pro-growth strategy which is able to accept dilutive mergers and acquisitions in the short term if the opportunity arises.

BBVA (2005a: 9) cites a case of value creation recognised by core brokers: In December 2003 the target price per share was €9.50, which grew to become €15.50 in the second half of 2005.

The increase in the weight of small businesses is considered to improve profitability as shown in Figure 5.7 *SMEs, business growth and profitability*.

Penchant for size and growth for size

Even if the geographical expansion through mergers and acquisitions has been a tool to expanded BBVA's business scope, this bank has

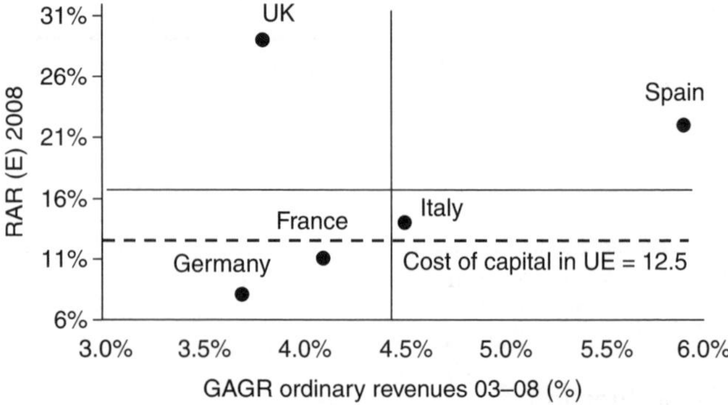

Figure 5.7   SMEs, business growth and profitability

Source: Mercer Oliver Wyman publication cited by Goirigolzarri (2006: 17).

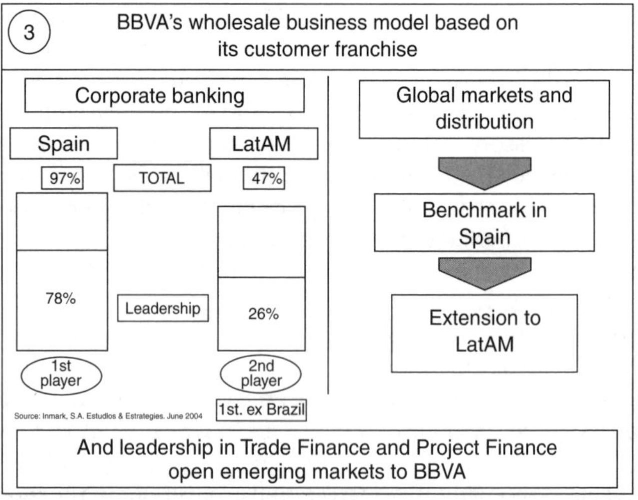

Figure 5.8   BBVA's wholesale business model

Source: BBVA (2005a, 26).

consistently preferred to focus primarily on profitability and its core business; on organic rather than inorganic growth.

Thus, instead of centring its business on retail banking as a whole, it aims at achieving a balance between retail and wholesale banking on the basis of organic, international growth. (See Figure 5.8 *BBVA's wholesale business model.*)

The Spanish market provides opportunities because of the change in the business mix (See Table 5.6.). As shown in Table 5.7 *Business Mix*, the weight of the mortgage business is steadily declining, having dropped from 25.3 per cent in the first quarter of 2005 to 19.9 per cent in the second quarter of 2006. On the other hand, work with small businesses has increased from 20.8 per cent in the first quarter of 2005 to 23.7 per cent in the second quarter of 2006.

Recently, Goirigolzarri (2006) noted how he foresees potential for growth in consumer loans, since the loans per capita are still low in Spain compared with other European countries and the USA. Whereas in 2005 in Spain the consumer loan per capita amount was US$1,051, it was US$6,230 in the US and US$4,136 in the UK.

As shown in Figure 5.9 the immigrant market in Spain also promises potential growth since a 26 per cent growth is expected in the non-Spanish population of the country between 2005 and 2008. BBVA already offers basic banking needs to this group such as Dinero Express and more developed products targeting over 400,000 clients (Goirigolzarri, 2006: 19).[14]

Last but not least, on May 25, 2007, BBVA decided to increase the scope of its activity entering all areas of the retail sector (Expansión, May 25, 2007). In doing so, BBVA will compete with supermarkets offering

Table 5.6 Growth in different activities

Operating profit	1st Quarter 2004 (*)	1st Quarter 2005 (*)	Year-on-year growth in percentage
Retail banking	586	654	11.5
Wholesale banking	156	174	12.0
The Americas	547	629	15.0
Of which Mexico	298	358	20.2

Source: (BBVA, 2005b: 15–18).

Table 5.7 BBVA's business mix (in per cent)

	1q2005	2q2005	3q2005	4q2005	1q2006	2q2006
Small businesses	20.8	20.7	23.9	23.1	24.3	23.7
Mortgages	25.3	24.5	23.7	22.7	21.8	19.9
Consumer + cards	12.0	13.0	12.7	13.9	14.1	18.6

Source: Goirigolzarri (2006: 16).

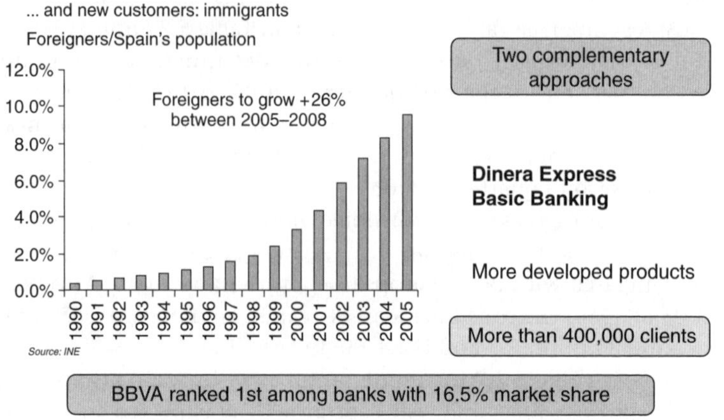

Figure 5.9   Immigrant market
Source: Goirigolzarri (2006 : 19).

banking services, yet the aim of this policy is more than ever a banking target because the fundamental target is to decrease the efficiency ratio by 10% by 2010.

BBVA sets as its objective self-financing and growth for which capital management discipline is regarded as fundamental (BBVA, 2005a: 34). The core capital is set to be around 6 per cent, whereas the pay-out is kept at approximately 50 per cent, so as to meet two objectives: (1) self-financing growth and (2) shareholders' remuneration (BBVA, 2005a: 34). As to the latter concept the dividend per share was 10.3 per cent in 2002/2003, 15.1 per cent in 2003/2004, and 15.0 per cent in the first dividend payment in 2005.

Internationalisation

Although the expansion in Latin America experienced some delays despite Spanish firms being more pro-active, the penetration and expansion throughout the whole continent were carried out in less than five years, which enabled BBVA to reach a critical size and prepare the acquisition of Bancomer in 2000. (See Figure 5.10 *Internationalisation Process In Latin America*.)

In terms of geographical focus, Latin America, and especially Mexico, is one of BBVA's main targets, since the region is shifting towards more economic pragmatism and continuity (Goirigolzarri, 2006: 21–22). Vitalino Nafría, BBVA's Managing Director responsible for the

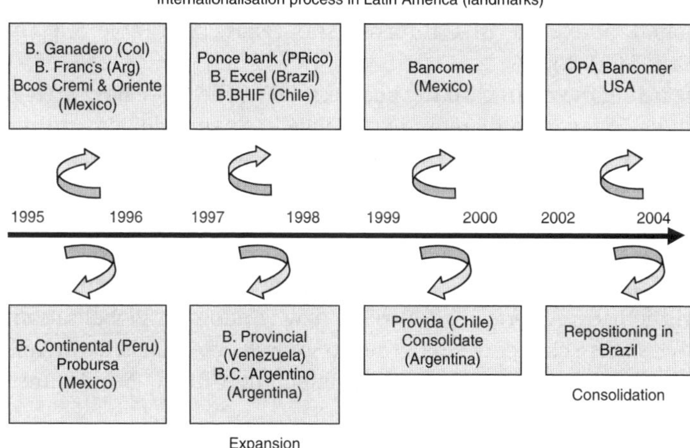

Figure 5.10   Internationalisation process in Latin America
Source: Nafría (2004: 40).

Americas, lists a number of reasons for investment in Latin America; (1) population growth, (2) potential for economic growth, (3) market maturity, (4) good potential for profit margins, and (5) the replicability of experience and products developed in Spain, a similar culture and with the same language (Nafría, 2004: 14).

In addition, the loan/GDP ratio is still low in Latin America, ranging from Chile's 56 to Venezuela's 13 passing through Peru's and Mexico's 19, signifying a great potential for consumer finance and credit cards, mortgages and finance for SMEs (Goirigolzarri, 2006: 23).

BBVA is especially drawn to Mexico (1) because it estimates that Bancomer has the potential to capture some 45,000 SME clients; a huge increase on the current 25,000, and (2) because the Spanish-speaking country receives 38 per cent of Texan exports, and Texas is the 8th largest economy in the world in terms of GDP (Goirigolzarri, 2006: 26–29).

On the other side of the frontier, BBVA covets the US market. The bank is attracted by the demographics of the US Hispanic market, comprising some 43 million people, representing 13 per cent of the total US population, and reckoned to grow to 73 million by 2030. This large section of American society has a growing purchasing power estimated to reach the US average by 2008 (BBVA, 2005a: 22). Mexico, again, may serve as a stepping stone to enter the US market since 66 per cent of all Hispanic Americans are originally from Mexico, concentrated, above all, in California and Texas. (See Table 5.8 *The US Hispanic Market.*)

Regarding the retail banking business, BBVA therefore has two regions in which to leverage its retail experience in Spain; Mexico and the US Hispanic market, while in the wholesale businesses its strategy is to go for a global franchise, as shown in Figure 5.11.

The quest for new customer segments led BBVA to position itself in Asia as a player in project and trade finance. Currently, the new growth engines are USA and Asia. China's rapidly increasing import of commodities has given the Latin American countries a new window for globalisation. For BBVA, it spells a chance to strengthen its growth potential in Latin America and further contemplate its development in China. (See Figure 5.12 *Business in China.*)

Table 5.8   The US Hispanic market

Hispanic population needs		BBVA's proposal
Money transfers (Lower income segment strategy)	Product focus on remittances and telephony	BTS
Basic products	Immigrants bank: cross selling	• BFS • Valley Bank
Better lifestyle	General market: 2nd generation and SMEs	Laredo National Bancshares

Source: (BBVA, 2005b: 23).

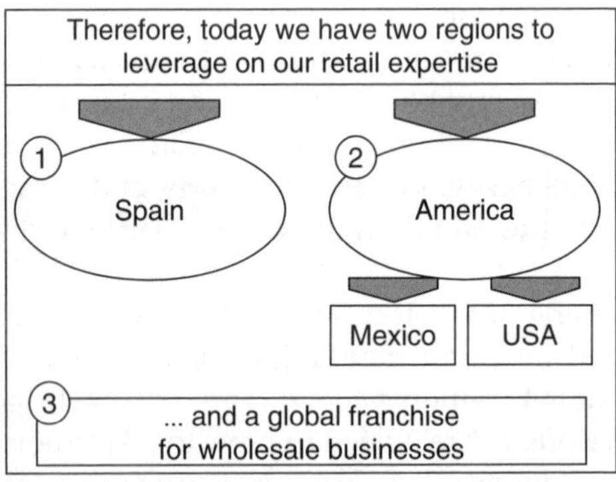

Figure 5.11   BBVA's retail and wholesale business strategy
Source: (BBVA, 2005a: 14).

Rank	Institution	# of Deals	Market Share %
1	BBVA	99	21.76
2	Deutsche Bank	74	16.26
3	Citigroup	64	14.07
4	ABN amro	61	13.41
5	Societé Generate	56	12.31
6	Standard Chartered	45	9.89
7	ING	34	7.47
8	Natexis	31	6.81
9	West LB	28	6.15
10	HSBC	27	5.93
		455	

Figure 5.12   Business in China
Source: BBVA (2005a: 27).

IT systems and processes[15]

In reference to their expansion in Latin America, Francisco González, BBVA's chairman and CEO, stresses the relevance of a business model centred on the brand, new technologies, the substitution of back office personnel by automatic processes, internet, and latest-generation software (González, 2002: 130–131). From this statement we may deduce that BBVA abides by the rules of the game in the international banking arena – giving prominence the use of IT systems. It is unsurprising that an executive of Francisco González' professional background takes this approach, as the bank's website informs: 'Francisco González (...) began his professional career in 1964 as programmer in an IT company. His ambition to transform 21st-century banking with the support of new technology dates back to this time' (BBVA's website).[16]

Indeed, the part played by IT systems in the development and growth of BBVA has been critical. The IT systems carry out three essential value-creation roles: (1) increased operational efficiency, (2) production and/or distribution of services leading to organic growth, and (3) the stimulation of inorganic growth. The labour saved by automation can be reassigned to sales functions.

The first role is supported by the automation of manual processes and on-line versus batch treatment of data input. 90 per cent of data entry is handled on-line. The data entered on an individual client when they sign up for a product will be automatically registered in the client database and can be called up for the provision of other products and services. This role is a strong driver in the reduction of operation costs.

The second role relates to production and distribution of services. As shown in Figure 5.13: *IT Systems And The Front Office*, a customer is attended by a sales person at a branch then, based on the personal data defining his segmentation, he is offered a particular set of products or services. The selection of the set of services is done by the IT system. The sales person in the branch has only to key-in the customer's name. These products, which may include mortgages, loans, credit cards, etc, are handled by specific applications or combinations of applications. Obviously the assortment of products to be offered becomes more varied and more adapted to the needs of the customer, where there are more products on offer. A larger portfolio of products to offer is usually linked to economies of scale, since the bank achieves more synergies arising between customer demand and the combination of products available. Sales people are not required to have much specialist expertise, although they are encouraged to suggest ideas (and they do) for the development of new applications to satisfy customer demand not covered by existing ones. This brings about organic growth.

The third role concerns inorganic growth. BBVA's growth owes a great deal to their acquisitions of other banks where, in many cases, the difference in the level of IT systems has been one of the economic justifications for the merger. The achievement of operational efficiency through the application of BBVA's *Altamira* platform in Latin America made the

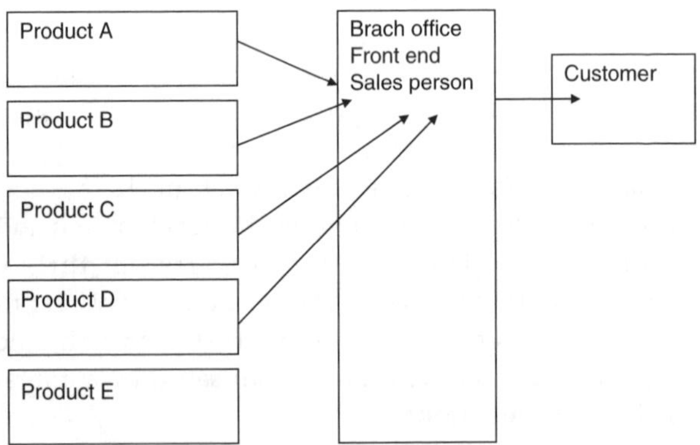

Figure 5.13   IT systems and front office work

Source: authors.

acquisitions worthwhile.[17] Since the merger between Banco Bilbao and Banco Vizcaya where an attempt was made to develop a new IT system from the two existing ones, BBVA has learnt that, rather than installing new systems from scratch, it is more judicious to make use of the existing system and adapt it to their own.

Network productivity in retail banking is another advantage, exemplified by the fact that in 2004–2005 BBVA enjoyed an increase in network productivity in Spain and Mexico, thanks to improvements in processes and organisation (Goirigolzarri, 2006: 12).

However, this function was not taken advantage of by the majority of competing Spanish banks. Banks in the lower leagues are now, perhaps, too late to grasp the opportunity to expand in Latin America given that the market is already too saturated for newcomers to really benefit from the acquisitions of local banks.

Of the large Spanish banks, we believe that only BBVA and Santander have been able to benefit from inorganic growth outside Spain by means of acquisitions in Latin America. Indeed, this was where these banks first achieved their world-class competitive edge over the others.

Firstly, their IT systems and open and modular product architecture (see Chapter 3) make it easy to replicate the success of similar products across borders.

Secondly, products and financial services developed in Spain may be relatively easily transplanted to a Chilean operation, for example. The open and modular nature of product design implies easy interfacing with existing systems and allows them to fit smoothly into the platform used in Chile. Local regulations may present a hindrance to automatic transplant, but the use of a more or less standardised interface means that any adaptation can be done by local IT staff.

Thirdly, thanks to the common ground provided by Altamira, the IT platform used in Latin America, and its being designed to be easily scalable, BBVA can use different IT development systems for different countries, thus avoiding excessive development of unnecessarily sophisticated specifications and its attendant higher costs.

Fourthly, the IT systems developed by BBVA are customer-focused, an idea which dates back to the 1980s. The advantage of customer-focused systems lies in the facilities for CRM (customer relations management) and the flexibility to combine this with product applications. This works in a different way to the silo system where each line of business is independent, with its own customer database, making it difficult to combine products in line with customer needs.

The silo system facilitates the sell-off of business units, since the synergies between them hardly exist at all and their disposal is unlikely to affect the running of the remaining IT systems. The systems used by the Spanish banks, on the contrary, hinder this possibility since the business units are not stand-alone. The focus on customers and a centralised customer database dissuade the separation and sale of business units. Moreover, as seen above, synergies may grow as the scope of offer increases.

Conclusion

In this chapter we reviewed the strategic approach of BBVA and its application. The bank has widely published its view on this, as comprising the belief that it delivers solid, improving results, strong fundamentals such as revenue, earnings, assets, liabilities, growth, etc., and value creation, as a consequence of a sound strategy based on (i) corporate positioning guaranteeing growth, (ii) a business model delivering excellent ROE, and (iii) capital discipline leading to competitive financial cost structure, all of which results in value creation, and the strong adherence to a business model based on core management skills involving (i) risk management, (ii) efficiency, and (iii) retail network management.

We analysed these principles in Chapter 3 and looked at the PA approach as taken by the CEO/COO and the group of leading executives, as well as the three key components – operational efficiency, IT systems, and a penchant for size and growth for size.

We may conclude that BBVA's business model, with more or less variation from the generic business model advanced in Chapter 3, coincides with the generic model, despite more stress on retail, wholesale and corporate banking, and the orientation towards customer-specific products.

6
Conclusions and Discussions

Research questions revisited

At the beginning of the book we put forward the posit that Spanish retail banks have a clear business model focused on cash flow generation, largely through operational efficiency supported by the strategic use of IT systems. The changing regulatory environment was considered to be the catalyst for the development of such a model, particularly the introduction of competition in a traditionally closed circle of 'gentlemen bankers'.

However, the existence of that regulatory environment *per se* does not explain why some banks fared better than others, since all of them faced the *same* changes in the *same* regulatory environment.

The existence of a clear-sighted CEO, together with his staff and COOs, was one answer. With their individual ways of thinking, each CEO brought about change and adaptation to their bank. It does not exclude, however, the possibility of a mutual learning process taking place among some of those banks that have emerged as world-class competitors.

We also posited that the model's characteristics coincide with the Profit-Arithmetic (PA) approach, identified by Kase et al. (2005). This approach recognised that top CEOs generally display certain characteristics that include (1) the prioritisation of short-term cash generation in preference to the pursuit of a long-term vision, (2) the pursuit of excellence in day-to-day operations, (3) the consideration of the future as a continuation of the present, and (4) a general no-nonsense approach to business.

The business environment surrounding the retail banking industry supports the PA approach, because (1) the pace of technological change in the industry, while fast, is not radically discontinuous, (2) the key factor for success consists of maintaining or improving the interest spread by cutting costs faster than the fall in the rate of interest received, (3) and this takes advantage of the cost structure by transplanting the same low-cost business model to the new acquisitions abroad, using centralised IT systems and introducing a modular and open product architecture. All of this is achieved not by some grand, long-term, and vision-based strategic design, but rather by relentless pursuit of operational excellence (Kase, Sáez, & Riquelme, 2005).

In the light of lengthy analysis of these assumptions, we are now in a position to devote further discussion to questions relating to the sustainability and 'replicability' of the model, and its limitations in terms of time and space.

Discussions

1. Does the existence of a specific model make such a difference?
2. Why did the regulatory environment favour the emergence of excellent banks in Spain?
3. Why did some Spanish banks do well and others not so well? Is the positioning or the resources more important?
4. How long can the generic model continue to be the source of excellence? What circumstances may put it in jeopardy?
5. Will the model variations between the two representative banks (i.e., Santander and BBVA) diverge or converge in future? Why?
6. Can banks of other countries imitate the model? Should they? What elements facilitate the transplantation of the model? What elements impede it from being replicated?

Does the existence of a specific model make so much difference?

This is the central point of this book, and relates to the nature of strategy as debated by Mintzberg (1990a; 1990b; 1991; 1996), Ansoff (1991), and Goold (1996). The moot point concerned whether strategy can or ought to be designed, and whether it is the only way.

In several articles and books, Mintzberg distinguished *intended*, *realised*, and *emergent* strategies, and held that there are three different modes of strategy-making, namely, by visionary entrepreneurs, by strategic planning professionals, and by lower echelons of management (Mintzberg, 1973, 1990a, 1994; Mintzberg, Pascale, Goold, & Rumelt, 1996; Mintzberg, Quinn, & Ghoshal, 1995; Mintzberg & Waters, 1985).

Grant (2004: 24–27) addresses this question and argues (1) that 'for most organisations, strategy making is a combination of design and emergence', and (2) that 'strategy-making as an iterative process involving experimentation and feedback is not necessarily an argument against the rational, systematic design of strategy'.

Grant (2004: 26) further holds that:

> The view that strategic management in a turbulent environment is to be achieved through a combination of rational, top-down planning and decentralised emergence, is supported by the findings of complexity theory. Rapid adaptation to changing environmental conditions is typically achieved through the seemingly chaotic process of decentralised responses, where the overall effectiveness of this adaptation is maintained through moderate levels of adaptive tension and simple rules that foster co-ordination…Jack Welch's management of General Electric embodied simple directives…together with strong performance incentives, which corresponds closely to the implications of complexity thinking.

We subscribe to this interpretation of Grant's and conclude that, in the current turbulent environment facing the financial industry in general, and the retail banking in particular, the best fit and therefore the triggers for differentiation are 1) rational top-down planning or strategic orientation in the pursuit of size via growth and 2) simple rules, such as measuring operational efficiency by using the efficiency ratio as a key performance indicator binding the behaviour of the entire organisation.

Why did the regulatory environment favour the emergence of excellent banks in Spain?

The essence of the question consists of (1) why the deregulation process did not produce a similar effect in other countries and, (2) why in Spain?

To address the first point we would need to have done comparative studies in other countries where a similar deregulatory process has taken place, and which thus stimulated an improvement in the banks' management. France, Germany, Italy, and the UK, among others, ought to provide evidence for or against the idea that the deregulation process fosters the emergence of excellent banks, if in all countries their banks' performance had improved and gained world-class status. As this has not been the case, then the deregulation process alone clearly does not provide the necessary conditions for the emergence of such banks. Circumstantial evidence seems to support this last conclusion, namely, that a move towards deregulation is in itself not sufficient for banks to become best-of-class entities.

Why then, did this phenomenon occur in Spain, a country considered until very recently to be marginal in the European context (Vilar, 1977)? And why did it happen in Spain, but not in more-or-less comparable countries such as Italy and Portugal?

The explanation may partly be found in the fact that Spanish banks such as Santander and BBVA started their internationalisation around the same time as other Spanish firms, especially in the electricity and communications industries (the telecommunications company Telefónica, in particular) (Kase & Kinoshita, 2001).

This fact may indicate that there was an air of innovation and growth in Spain, which facilitated the ambitions of innovatively-minded entrepreneurs. There may also have been a group-learning effect, as they learnt from each others' examples. However, this appears to be only a part of the story – a necessary condition but, on its own, not sufficient.

Without doubt, the existence of outstanding business people such as Toledo, Sánchez Asiaín, Botín, Ybarra, Uriarte, Sáenz, and Goirigolzarri is also a major and essential ingredient, as we have repeatedly mentioned in the foregoing chapters. After all, value creation is realised from the top down (Collis & Montgomery, 1998; Goold, Campbell, & Alexander, 1994), and the study of strategy necessarily includes a study of top executives (Valero y Vicente & Lucas Tomás, 2005).

The personality, or *ad hominem*, argument is actually the cornerstone of our book. The cognitive processes of an organisation's CEO are the basic units of analysis, according to Kase et al. (2005). Our assumption is that the way that the CEOs express their ideas reflects their strategic thinking, and this is what we presume to have been the basic driving force of the change in Spain's retail banking industry.

Why the key 'change masters' at the top level happened to appear at a certain time and in a specific country will perhaps be impossible to explain. That many of these bankers studied at the same university (the Jesuit-run Deusto University or La Comercial de Deusto in Bilbao), and that they therefore hail mainly from the Basque country, might offer some explanation. Be that as it may, the elucidation of this point seems to lie beyond the purpose of this book. Suffice it to say, though, that the personalities or change masters are a necessary condition for the appearance of these world-class banks.

Why did some Spanish banks do well and others not so well? Is positioning more important than resources, or vice versa?

The foregoing discussion opens the way to this question. The deregulation process paved the way for the establishment of some world-class banks in Spain, whereas in other countries the same phenomenon did not occur, at least not as widely. We argued that deregulation, by creating a stiffer competitive environment, might have offered a more fertile ground for the growth of competitive banks. However, in the face of such a competitive environment some banks adapted better than others.

To explain why Spain produced best-of-class retail banks where other countries have failed, we have observed above that the CEOs' personalities are the essential ingredients. We assume that the same argument applies to why some Spanish banks fare better than others. Banco Popular (at least until recently) and Bankinter employ strategies more focused on the maximum profitability of each transaction and customer by providing personalised services, and they have traditionally shied away from the pursuit of size and, as a consequence, growth for the sake of size. These two banks therefore have (or had) a Proto-Image of the Firm (PIF) approach as defined by Kase et al. (2005).

By contrast, our theory throughout the book has been that the outstanding Spanish retail banks are of PA approach, more clearly inclined to cash flow generation by focussing on day-to-day operational efficiency supported by excellent IT systems as well as a penchant for growth.

The discrepancy in these strategic approaches, namely PA or PIF, may be explained away by the historical background and predominant corporate culture and shared values. But it is also true that the personality of the CEO, and his '*querencia*' or homing instinct, are key when deciding on the strategic orientation and direction of his entity.

That is not to say that Banco Popular and Bankinter have not been doing well in terms of their yearly performance. On the contrary – as of December 31st 2005 the net profit of these banks were €606 million and €161 million respectively,representing 38.8 per cent and 24.8 per cent profitability on ordinary margin.

However, in the current competition arena, the size issue looms large, with an approach prioritising the maximisation of profits from each transaction or customer, which is to say that selective focus on qualitative transactions may not provide the best fit for long-term manoeuvrability, although it may not mean that such an approach is actually an intentional choice.[4]

The Spanish economics daily, Expansión, points out that, out of 8,505 banking organisations existing in 2007 in Europe, over 700, or 8 per cent, may disappear in two years' time because of mergers with other, larger entities (Expansión, 2007a: 30). The same newspaper cites an expert from Deloitte, Touche & Tohmatsu, who holds that one of the reasons for these mergers comes from the difference in efficiency ratio. Currently many Spanish banks boast a ratio of around 50 per cent, against the European average of 60 per cent.

Overall, therefore the difference in performance and long-term perspective is derived first from the existence of CEOs with a given strategic penchant, and second from the focus on the use of PA approach focused on the use of the business model as described in Chapter 3.

Accordingly we may conclude that one particular resource, in the form of the CEO's thought processes, is a major factor in the bank's success, yet does not detract from the bank's focus on strategic positioning. Our viewpoint is that the positioning is sought and attained because of the PA approach advocated, and propelled by the CEOs.

How long can the *generic* model continue to be a source of excellence? What circumstance may put it in jeopardy?

The fundamental working of the model described and analysed in Chapter 3 sheds light on the permanence, or otherwise, of the model's validity. The discernment among the temporary and permanent elements – both internal and external – that favour the excellence of the model ought to help us in answering this question.

The working of the model depends both on each component and on the systemic working of the components as a whole. First, let us scrutinise each component, as regards the permanence of its validity.

Scrutiny of each component part of the business model

Regulatory environment, CEOs, COOs and management teams

Regarding the regulatory environment, we have observed the dual trends of 1) strengthening various measures to secure the stability of banks' financial health, and 2) enhancing competition in favour of the banks' customers. We expect these two trends to continue in the foreseeable future. The question here, therefore, was whether Spanish banks can retain their ability to adapt to measures that the monetary authorities may adopt. Our assumption was that this ability emanates from the CEOs, and this leads us to the next component part: the CEOs.

Whether the CEOs, together with their staff and COOs, can continue to adapt their banks to changes in the sector AND keep their organisations performing so well largely hinges on the profile of those leaders; that is, whether they can 'renew' themselves and identify and coach future generations of leaders to replace them. Our guess is that there is no discernible trend or pattern in this. Whether and new CEO's approach be PA or PIF is *per se* immaterial, bearing in mind that the approach and its success hinge on its fit with the environment. If it changes, then probably the approach will have to vary as well. CEO figures are similar to artists. Artists such as Picasso and Velázquez are not born periodically – rather they are a product of their time, education, and happy chance. What we can conjecture, though, is that if Spain has produced excellent business leaders in the recent past, it is likely to continue producing them in the future.

Operational efficiency, IT systems, and penchant for size

How will the three components of the model (the pursuit of operational efficiency, the strategic use of IT systems with open and modular product architecture, and the penchant for size and growth for size) react to changes in the surrounding environment?

Operational efficiency, mainly consisting of a reduction in operational costs and general overheads, is valid whenever cost efficiency is the key for success. There could be several obstacles, though. Firstly, BBVA's presidential COO, José Ignacio Goirigolzarri,has pointed out that the reduction of cost can not be eternal because the day will come when you cannot reduce it any more and, therefore, it will be necessary to look at the income side as well. Another threat to the operational efficiency may come from changes in the nature of the retail banking business. The sources of financial resources may change from taking deposits through the network of branches to other totally different modes, such as internet banking, or the resources may end up 'marching to a different tune'. Products such as home mortgages and consumer financing may lose their appeal in favour of other products. Thirdly, the 'universal banking' to which many banks tend to gravitate may impair the validation of the current business model. Investment banking is a different creature with different dynamics and ways of operating. Spanish banks have so far been adept at striking a balance between their excellence as retail banks and as other financial businesses.

The strategic significance of IT systems may change depending on several circumstances. Firstly, the levelling-out of the IT differences between banks may reduce the competitive advantage in terms of operational ratios, if we accept that these ratios are greatly influenced by the IT systems used. To this, our comments are twofold.

In the first place, the use of IT systems is a function of the strategic role to which the bank management assigns it. In other words, IT systems do not work wonders by themselves. Their performance is not a consequence of the mechanical application of the systems. Instead, the performance depends upon the whole systemic and strategic context.

A failure to understand this key point is exemplified by the system breakdown that took place at the time of the merger of three Japanese banks (Dai-Ichi Kangyo, Fuji, and Industrial Bank of Japan – IBJ) to create Mizuho Financial Group in 2002. The newly born Mizuho Bank, belonging to the Mizuho Financial Group, started trading on April 1st 2002 and immediately faced a failure in its ATMs and bank transfers (which numbered as many as 2.5 million transactions by April 5th). The failure lasted for over a month. In view of the gravity of the situation, the Financial Services Agency sent its inspectors to the bank on May 8th. The holding company's President was summoned to the Diet. The root cause of the system failure was found to lie in the management's misjudgement in choosing to combine the systems inherited from all three banks by means of three sets of RCs (relay computers) instead of scrapping two systems and concentrating on one. Nakao (n.d.) maintains that the misjudgement is rooted in the power struggle among the three merging banks for dominance in the new bank; system selection was obviously used as an indicator of power gain. Another reason for such a 'botch-job' is attributable to management indifference or even ignorance of the key role played by IT systems (Nakao, n.d.).

In the second place, the benefit of IT systems is not limited to their innate mechanical excellence. That Spanish banks were capable of making the most of them was not only attributable to factors such as the excellence of their systems and the favourable environment where there were IT consultancies such as Andersen Consulting (now Accenture) with thousands of professional staff in Spain, but also to the conviction on the part of the banks' management that the banking industry is like a factory production line, where every component at every stage must work in harmony.

The last of the three strategic components of the business model described in Chapter 3 refers to the penchant for size, and growth for size. We now raise two questions, and comment on them.

Firstly, why do they go after size and growth? The driving forces to pursue growth are usually economies of scale, economies of scope, positive appreciation of growth at the financial markets, the chance for staff promotion, management's social reputation, market power,monopoly or oligopoly benefits, and so on, all of which are a mixture of operational and strategic reasons, and provide management and staff motivation.

At Santander and BBVA, the business paradigm – the way they view and judge the management situation – takes it for granted that growth is a given and is to be rigorously pursued.It implies a kind of no-questions-asked attitude. Accordingly, unless a radical and discontinuous management change takes place at these banks, size and growth for size will continue to be their basic tenets for the foreseeable future.

Secondly, do size and growth for size continue to be success factors for the long-term financial and economic health of the banks? Obviously the wave of consolidation among European banks referred to previously predicts it, or at least the banks see it that way. At the time of writing, Santander, in a consortium with the Royal Bank of Scotland and Fortis, was launching a take-over bid for the Dutch Bank ABN. Santander intends to spend over €20,000 million taking over ABN's Italian and Brazilian operations (Expansión, 2007b: 22). Banco Espírito Santo's Eva Hernández, cited by Expansión (2007), considers that the operation is a logical one, as it would create great synergies with Santander's Brazilian operations. Therefore we may venture to suggest that size, and competition for growth in pursuit of size through mergers and acquisitions, rather than organic growth, may dictate the rules of the game in the foreseeable future.

Systemic scrutiny

The basic functioning scheme of the model consists of (1) open and modular product architecture,(2) whose handling is facilitated by IT systems, (3) by which the operational efficiency is also pursued, measured in terms of efficiency ratio as a Key Performance Indicator (KPI)of the staff, (4) which is transferred to overseas operations in the form of mature, tried and tested products, (5) driven by a penchant for size. Then (6) the growth effect thanks to mergers and acquisitions (usually justified because of the difference in efficiency ratios between the acquiring bank and the acquired one), improved by the transference of the business model, is replicated again from (1) through (6) in an upward, spiralling cycle of growth.

Potential causes of failure of this cycle may come from various directions. The change in product architecture from open and modular to closed and integral may impair the entire system. IT systems may continue to be relevant but to a lesser extent. Operational efficiency may also carry differing weight over time. This may take place if the bank's business domain is modified; for example, to focus more on investment banking.

Market dominance may become less attractive if the life-cycle of the whole retail banking industry enters the maturity-to-decline stage. At such a stage the prioritisation of profit for profit's sake will become the key to prosperity, or perhaps even the key to for survival. We, however, think that such a cataclysmic change will be a long time coming.

Will the model variations between the two representative banks (i.e., Santander and BBVA) diverge or converge in future? Why?

Approaching this question of convergence or divergence raises two further issues, specifically: (1) whether the difference in business models between Santander and BBVA is of an essential character, i.e., they differ from each other radically and fundamentally, and (2) whether sticking to the different models may cause the downfall of either of them and thus convergence into one model is unavoidable for survival.

Firstly, we have based the theoretical framework of this book on the assumption that there could be a basic and generic business model as an *ideal type* among the leading banks in Spain, and, throughout Chapters 3, 4, and 5, we have elaborated at length on this point. On the basis of such an assumption we have provided an explanation of the variations of both group's model, although the variations are basically within the same generic model. We have also maintained that the differences stem from corporate values and historical background. While Santander shows the characteristics of being led by its 'owner', BBVA functions more collectively.Secondly, our assessment of both bank's model makes us believe that, in the foreseeable future, the divergence will continue due to a number of factors, including cultural *'querencia'* or 'homing instinct', the top executives' track records, and success being achieved by both of them and not requiring radical change for either of them.

As an interesting aside, it should be noted that some of Santander's top executives came from Banco de Vizcaya, whose merger with Banco de Bilbao led them to leave the new bank. It is likely, therefore, that there may be more to the differences in business model than meets the eye.

Can banks of other countries imitate the model? Should they? What elements facilitate the replication of the model? What elements impede it from being replicated?

Circumstantial evidence and a cursory glance at the way some other European banks operate suggest that there are some whose business model is similar, in that they regard the importance of size, operational efficiency, IT systems, and so on, much in line with Spanish banks. The difference between them and Santander and BBVA, lies in the fact that Spanish banks operate the business model in a systematic way; they are more efficient and effective because they created the model and thus it is well assimilated into their behaviour. In trying to imitate it, other banks will collide with 'path-dependency' where 'resources cannot be instantaneously acquired, but rather must be built over time' (Collis & Montgomery, 1997: 33). Trying to leapfrog path-dependency will give rise to adverse 'time compression dis-economics'. The only way to circumvent it is to acquire the whole organisation and absorb it.

But even where another bank absorbs the entire organisation with the business model, finding fit remains a gigantic task. Many factors may get in the way, including corporate culture, management credibility, and personal preferment.

Therefore, we may suspect almost-insurmountable hurdles if a bank with a different model tries to implant the Spanish banks' business model to the letter. For example, if Japanese banks tried to copy it, they would certainly need to change their way of doing business. We reasonably suspect that the Japanese tend to design their product architecture on the basis of closed and integral type. In other words they tend to stress the personalised, labour-intensive side of products and services. If so, the use of IT systems that maximise 'waste' by eliminating services that can be taken care of by systems will be not be optimised. Annex 2b, however, describes the case of a local bank in Japan (Suruga Bank) that managed to independently create a system with similarities to the Spanish model, although it is true to say that it took years for the bank's president to finally and satisfactorily bring about change in his organisation.

The illustration of Japan's Suruga Bank elucidates the question of what elements help or hinder the implant or replication of the business model, since, as described in Annex 2B, the basic force of change is the determination and decision of the CEO. If the top executive adopts the business model only half-heartedly, his staff will almost certainly sense this lack of commitment and the attempt will be doomed to failure.

Suggestions for future research

Our research, based on in-depth interview surveys with bank executives and financial experts, serves as grounds for future confirmatory research. We took it for granted that the business model that resulted in excellent performance was developed by the Spanish banks themselves. Their business approach follows, as mentioned many times in this book, the typology of behaviour identified by Kase et al. (2005) as a PA approach.

As shown in Annex 1, Content Analysis, the Japanese banks 'pull in different directions' where strategic approach is concerned. They may be classified as PIF type. Although for years their performance was awful, and their ranking in the world league fell spectacularly, they seem to be now recuperating and regaining the lost positions. It is clear, however, that their interest will be always centred on the domestic market, which is large enough to provide them with sufficient profit and growth potential.

Future research ought to focus on these two different approaches and to elucidate which of the two is more universal and less constrained for expansion outside, since until now our attention was focused on retail banking. Does a PA approach provide more prosperity than PIF when other banking businesses, such as investment banking or corporate banking, are concerned? And if so, why?

The 'replicability' of the business model has been discussed above, but certainly it requires more in-depth comparative studies within different country contexts.

Another interesting issue to research is whether its country culture can constrain the expansion of the Spanish model. Concretely, Santander and BBVA are entering the US markets by different methods. Both of them have minimised risks by first entering the Latin American markets, where the language and culture are more similar to Spain's. The rest of the European market offered low-risk opportunities too, after these banks had gained experience in internationalisation in Latin America, since European countries offer more or less similar cultures, despite the language differences.

In the case of Santander, they have now entered the UK market by taking over Abbey National, and are in the middle of learning how to operate in an Anglo-Saxon environment. It is obvious that, on their horizon, the US market looms large. BBVA had a similar learning process and is penetrating the US market through Florida, many of whose inhabitants are of Hispanic origin. Thus, culturally and even linguistically, the risk may be kept to a minimum. However, can both banks finally wean themselves off their national heritage?

Given that the world cannot ignore emerging markets, especially China and India, the assessment of the validity of Spanish banks' business models in these markets will be of great relevance.

Annex 1 – Content Analysis of Bank CEOs' Speeches

The questions to address

The questions we address here concern the distinctiveness of the Spanish banks' business model and strategy. In other words:

Q1 Is the Spanish banks' business model different from the models and strategy characterising banks from other countries?

Q2 Does the business model vary from one bank to another in Spain? Does each bank have a significantly different model and strategy or can the banks be grouped together and classified as one business model and strategy-based entity?

Analytical tool

For the identification and establishment of the Spanish retail banks' business model, four exploratory and seventeen in-depth interview surveys were conducted with banks' CEOs, COOs, senior management, banking experts, and academics during 2005, 2006, and 2007, as well as documentary review of academic journals and economic papers.

To confirm the findings from these interviews and documentary surveys from a more objective perspective, content analysis of several bank executives' speeches was carried out, as content analysis is used to 'make valid inferences about the material contained in the text, properties of the speaker, etc.' (Leximancer, 2005). It allows us to non-invasively analyse groups of individuals by comparison. It is 'a research technique for making replicable and valid inferences from texts to the contexts of their use' (Krippendorff, 1980:18). The analysis, when conducted with the help of computer applications such as Leximancer,[1] is based on the Grounded Theory approach (Glasser & Strauss, 1967) and the important themes or concepts in the text analysed appear from the text alone, independent of the observer (Smith, Grech, & Horberry, 2002). Computer-aided content analysis boasts two forms of reliability, namely stability and reproducibility. Stability refers to the consistent re-coding of the same information in the same way, whereas reproducibility refers to the consistency of classification (Leximancer, 2005).

In the light of the difficulty that researchers frequently experience in accessing first-hand empirical data, the non-invasive nature of the content analysis is a great advantage. *Narrative analysis* (Franzosi, 1998; Jameson, 2000), another non-invasive way to conduct research, lags behind in stability and reproducibility aspects.

Before proceeding to the next section we ought to define the basic term *concepts*, as employed in the Leximancer application we used. Concepts are 'collection of words that generally travel together throughout the text' (Leximancer, 2005:24). Words are weighted according to how often they occur in sentences which contain the compared concept. They are weighted in such a way that the presence of each word in a sentence provides the accumulated evidence for the presence of a concept. A sentence is marked as containing a concept if the accumulated evidence is above a set threshold.

Sampling data

In consideration of the purpose of this book in analysing best-practice Spanish banks with 'excellent' performances, we chose Santander, Banco Bilbao Vizcaya Argentaria (BBVA), and Banco Sabadell on the one hand, and three top-ranking Japanese banks, on the other. We did not include the Bank of Tokyo Mitsubishi UFJ, due to the fact that this bank was created in 2006 as a consequence of a merger of three component banks and thus did not issue any annual report at the time of this analysis.

Japanese banks were chosen for the comparative analysis because anecdotal evidence and the general impression we have attest to their strategy being more of a value-laden, Proto-image of the Firm (PIF) approach, different from the Profit-Arithmetic (PA) approach observed among Spanish banks. Another reason for the selection of Japanese banks is the depth of information we have access to.

The following Table A1.1 compares their relative positions in the world's top 50 banks, except for Banco Sabadell.[2]

Santander ranks 13th over Sumitomo Mitsui (15th), The Bank of Tokyo Mitsubishi UFJ (16th), and Mizuho (22nd) in terms of assets. BBVA figures 38th. From this we can observe that (1) the two banks from Spain carry a similar weight to the giants from Japan and (2) in a relatively small country like Spain (See Table A1.2 *World GDP By Country*) the banks seem to have had a phenomenal growth.

Data sources

For this analysis the published annual reports were used. They were downloaded from the banks' Web pages. The language of these reports

Table A1.1 Top 50 Banks in the world

Current rank	Previous rank	Bank	Assets US$m	+ or – (local curr) (%)	Captial US$m	Balance sheet
1	(1)	Barclays PLC, London, UK	*1,586,879	71.76	2,786.27	31.12.05
2	(2)	UBS AG, Zürich, Switzerland	*1,563,282	18.60	660.9	31.12.05
3	(4)	BNP Paribas SA, Paris, France	*1,483,934	38.87	11,442.56	31.12.05
4	(3)	The Royal Bank of Scotland Group plc, Edinburgh, UK	*1,300,124	29.80	9,409.44	31.12.05
5	(6)	Crédit Agriccle SA, Paris, France	*1,251,997	30.19	20,665.25	31.12.05
6	(5)	Deutsche Bank AG, Frankfurt am Main, Germany	*1,170,277	18.10	1,674.92	31.12.05
7	(7)	Bank of America NA, Charlotte, USA	*1,082,243	–	2,836.40	31.12.05
8	(8)	ABN AMRO Holding NV, Amsterdam, Netherlands	*1,038,929	21.08	1,260.91	31.12.05
9	(9)	Credit Suisse Group, Zürich, Switzerland	*1,016,050	22.91	473.48	31.12.05
10	(10)	JPMorgan Chase Bank National Association, New York	*1,013,985	4.82	1,785.00	31.12.05
11	(–)	Société Générale, Paris La Défense, France	*1,000,728	–	640.48	31.12.05
12	(11)	ING Bank NV, Amsterdam, Netherlands Banco Santander Central Hispano SA, Santander,	*983,764	34.51	619.25	31.12.05
13	(–)	Spain	*954,361	–	3,688.54	31.12.05

Continued

Table A1.1 Continued

Current rank	Previous rank	Bank	Assets US$m	+ or – (local curr) (%)	Captial US$m	Balance sheet
14	(12)	UniCredito Italiano SpA, Milan, Italy	*928,285	–	5,704.46	31.12.05
15	(13)	Sumitomo Mitsui Banking Corporation, Tokyo, Japan	*916,710	– 2.37	6,253.69	31.03.05
16	(14)	The Bank of Tokyo-Mitsubishi UFJ Ltd, Tokyo, Japan	*865,663	8.22	9,375.77	31.03.05
17	(17)	Caisse Nationale des Caisses d'Epargne et de Prevo	*739,311	42.88	8,014.14	31.12.04
18	(18)	Citibank NA, New York, USA	*706,497	1.72	751	31.12.05
19	(22)	Fortis Bank NV/SA, Brussels, Belgium Industrial & Commercial Bank of China Limited,	*700,515	22.32	3,670.49	31.12.05
20	(19)	Beijing, China	675,395	6.68	19,412.07	31.12.04
21	(20)	HSBC Bank plc, London, UK	*663,385	32.12	1,368.24	31.12.05
22	(21)	Mizuho Bank Ltd, Tokyo, Japan	663,014	0.96	6,112.76	31.03.05
23	(23)	Rabobank Nederland, Utrecht, Netherlands	*597,115	4.69	–	31.12.05
24	(32)	Agricultural Bank of China, Beijing, China	*591,190	18.87	–	31.12.05
25	(24)	Bank of Scotland, Edinburgh, UK	*586,543	25.23	1,555.00	31.12.04
26	(25)	The Norinchukin Bank, Tokyo, Japan Bayerische Hypo-und Vereinsbank AG, Munich	582,567	0.47	11,520.19	31.03.05

27	(26)	Germany	*582,122	5.59%	2,656.29	31.12.05
28	(–)	Calyon, Paris La D˘fense, France	*567,724	–	7,876.86	31.12.05
29	(27)	Dresdner Bank Group, Frankfurt am Main, Germany	*544,199	–	1,772.82	31.12.05
30	(28)	Lloyds TSB Group plc, London, UK	*531,767	8.91	2,437.77	31.12.05
31	(29)	Mizuho Corporate Bank Ltd, Tokyo, Japan	526,193	−6.62	10,071.61	31.03.05
32	(30)	Commerzbank AG, Frankfurt am Main, Germany	*524 724	4.70	2,011.09	31.12.05
33	(31)	Bank of China Limited, Beijing, China	*515 972	7.30	22,520.39	31.12.04
34	(37)	Landesbank Baden-Wp rttemberg, Stuttgart, Germany DZ BANK AG Deutsche Zentral-	*477,606	3.66	5,855.49	31.12.05
35	(33)	Genossenschaftsbank, Frankfurt am Main, Germany	*473,730	12.74	3,395.85	31.12.05
36	(34)	Wachovia Bank NA, Charlotte, USA	*472 143	–	455	31.12.05
37	(35)	China Construction Bank Corporation, Beijing, China	471,792	9.86	23,467.65	31.12.04
38	(36)	Banco Bilbao Vizcaya Argentaria SA, Madrid, Spain	*462,833	19.11	1,959.80	31.12.05
39	(39)	National Westminster Bank Plc, London, UK	*447,387	32.14	2,880.69	31.12.05
40	(41)	Wells Fargo Bank NA, San Francisco, USA	*403,258	–	520	31.12.05

Continued

Table A1.1 Continued

Current rank	Previous rank	Bank	Assets US$m	+ or – (local curr) (%)	Captial US$m	Balance sheet
41	(38)	Bayerische Landesbank, Munich, Germany Kreditanstalt fz r Wederaufbau (KfW), Frankfurt am	*402,046	2.33	5,775.85	31.12.05
42	(42)	Main, Germany	401,411	3.81	3,892.43	31.12.05
43	(43)	Royal Bank of Canada, Montr˘al, Canada	*398,981	10.16	6,687.63	31.10.05
44	(44)	Danske Bank A/S, Copenhagen, Denmark	*384,604	18.49	11,775.60	31.12.05
45	(45)	Nordea Group, Stockholm, Sweden	*383,993	16.24	1,264.45	31.12.05
46	(49)	Abbey National plc, London, UK Banque F˘d˘tative du Cr˘dit Mutuel, Strasbourg	*355,423	12.07	254.08	31.12.05
47	(46)	France The Hongkong and Shanghai Banking Corporation	*352,516	15.66	1,535.74	31.12.05
48	(48)	Limited, Hong Kong, Hong Kong	*344,687	7.47	2,901.14	31.12.05
49	(51)	Banca Intesa SpA, Milan, Italy	*322,641	–0.94	4,241.57	31.12.05
50	(52)	National Australia Bank Ltd, Melbourne, Australia	*320,418	2.01	8,771.29	30.09.05

Notes

* Figures are consolidated.

* These bank rankings are compiled from balance sheet information included on Bankersalmanac.com available.

Table A1.2   World GDP by country

1	United States	12,485,725
2	Japan	4,571,314
3	Germany	2,797,343
4	People's Republic of China	2,224,811
5	United Kingdom	2,201,473
6	France	2,105,864
7	Italy	1,766,160
8	Canada	1,130,208
9	Spain	1,126,565
10	South Korea	793,070
11	Brazil	792,683
12	India	775,410
13	Mexico	768,437

Source: International Monetary Fund, World Economic outlook database, April 2006

is English to homogenise the language originally used (Japanese and Spanish) and, in order to avoid personal bias in translating them, we used the English version prepared by each bank.

Data material

For the analysis of the text the focus was centred on the Chairmans' and Managing Directors' speeches included in these annual reports. Where there are two figures leading the strategy of a bank we included both the speech of the Chairman and the CEO. Santander is a case in point; Emilio Botín, Chairman, and Alfredo Sáenz, Managing Director and CEO, are both cited and analysed.

Journalistic articles, interviews, etc., were taken into account for overall judgement but not for this specific analysis.

CEO's speeches typically run three to four pages in the annual reports.

Analysed period

The period covered spans from 2003 to 2005. For Spain the period represents a normal growth period, but Japan during this time saw its banks recovering from the debacle that followed the burst of the speculation-based real estate economic bubble.

Sample banks

From Spain, Santander, Banco Bilbao Vizcaya Argentaria (BBVA), and Banco Sabadell were included for the analysis. The selection criteria were that (1) from the judgemental viewpoint they stand out as representative examples of Spanish bank behaviour in the retail business, (2) their strategy is considered to relate to the PA approach (*quod vide*), (3) their coverage is national and local and has less local bias, and (4) in terms of the assets owned by the banks in Spain at the end of 2006 these three banks represented 65 per cent of the total financial system in Spain. Savings banks, such as La Caixa and Caja de Madrid, though a major presence in Spain, were excluded in the light of their being not-for-profit and, as such, their behaviour may not be comparable to that of other for-profit banking entities in the world.

From Japan we chose Mizuho, Resona and Sumitomo Mitsui banking groups. The Bank of Tokyo Mitsubishi UFJ was excluded as mentioned above. These three banks represent 25 per cent of the total assets of Japan's banks.

Tools and steps for analysis

Leximancer version 2.21 served as the principal tool for the content analysis. This application allows us to carry out data-mining on the chosen texts to find out concepts and words frequently used, their interconnection structure and their co-occurrence to draw up a map (Leximancer, 2005).

Leximancer also makes it possible for us to conduct 'Discriminant' Analysis (DA) on the output produced by the application.

SPSS version 14 for Windows was made use of to run DA on these outputs.

In carrying out the analysis, words such as 'million', 'billion', 'continue', etc., were either merged or eliminated using the Concept Editing command.

Q$_1$ Do Spanish banks differentiate themselves from the banks of other countries, such as Japan, regarding their business approach?

We addressed ourselves to answering the first of the two questions by comparing the speeches of Presidents and CEOs included in the annual reports of the sample six banks for the period mentioned before, namely, 2003 to 2005. Our theory is that the verbal expressions reflect the difference in the cognitive process in strategy.

For this purpose the Concept Profiling command functioned as the primary means to discover new concepts. Thus segregation between various document categories was obtained on the basis of the *folder tags* function, which created concept classes for each folder containing different speech files of different CEOs for different years from different banks.

Sentences for Context Block were kept at three, considered to be normal by the manual (Leximancer, 2005:44). Word Classification and Name Classification Threshold were left at their default values of 2.4 and 4.5.

The analysis was then run for the entire process from Preprocess Text, Automatic Concept Identification, Concept Editing, Thesaurus Learning and Locate Concept Occurrences through to Mapping. In the last Mapping stage we used the Concept Statistics command to plot the frequency, by bank, of thirty concepts generated by the application (See Table A1.3 *Frequency Of Concepts By Bank*, which shows some of the concepts used).

Word linkage summarises the following relations (Table A1.4):

Table A1.3   Frequency of concepts by bank (partial)

	Activity	Areas	Assets	Banking	Banks	Businesses
BBVA	0.0655	0.1179	0.02183	0.0655	0.04803	0.09606
Mizuho	0	0.04411	0.1029	0.25	0.08823	0.07352
Resona	0	0.0153	0.0153	0.07653	0.1326	0.0153
Sabadell	0	0	0.1162	0.06976	0	0.06976
Santander	0.03181	0.05909	0.01363	0.109	0.06818	0.05
Sumitomo Mitsui	0	0.009722	0.1111	0.2361	0.01388	0.25

Table A1.4   Agglomeration schedule

	Cluster combined			Stage cluster first appears		
Stage	Cluster 1	Cluster 2	Coefficients	Cluster 1	Cluster 2	Next stage
1	1	4	.037	0	0	2
2	1	5	.080	1	0	3
3	1	3	.251	2	0	4
4	1	6	.502	3	0	5
5	1	2	1.077	4	0	0

The vertical icicles group different banks as shown Figure A1.1.

And, finally, the 'Dendrogram' produced points for the grouping of all three Spanish banks as a cluster to which Resona adheres, followed by Sumitomo Mitsui (See Figure A1.2.) The last to join the cluster is Mizuho.

We may therefore conclude that the Spanish banks point to a similar conceptual mapping, which probably signifies that their strategic

Vertical Icicle

Number of clusters	Case										
	2: Mizuko		6: Sumitomo Mitsui		3: Resona		5: Santander		4: Sabadell		1: BBVA
1	X	X	X	X	X	X	X	X	X	X	X
2	X		X	X	X	X	X	X	X	X	X
3	X		X		X	X	X	X	X	X	X
4	X		X		X		X	X	X	X	X
5	X		X		X		X		X	X	X

Figure A1.1   Vertical Icicle

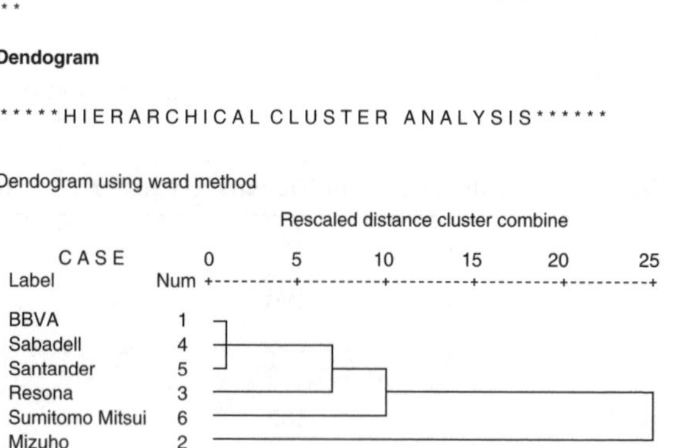

Figure A1.2   Dendogram

orientation marks a sharp contrast to that of Japanese banks. The latter do not seem to have common features among them, with each one having a different orientation.

For the confirmation of this point we ran the 'Canonical Discriminant' analysis using the data output processed by Leximancer, comparing the 2003–2005 speeches of respective CEOs of the chosen Spanish and Japanese banks.

As shown in Table A1.5, the Eigenvalue was .658 with Chi-square being 441.886 at p < .001. Therefore H_0: there is no difference between the two groups (Spanish and Japanese banks) is rejected.

The classification results are set out below in Table A1.6. In line with the cluster analysis the predicted membership of Group 1, the Spanish group, carries a higher percentage (91.0%) than that of the Japanese group (62.1%), since the latter's membership seems to be 'fuzzier'.

Conclusion

Accordingly the first question on the distinctiveness of Spanish banks' business model or strategy was affirmatively answered. We will now proceed to analyse the data in search of an answer to the second question concerning the similarity or disparity of the business model among the three Spanish banks: Is there one model or three different models?

Table A1.5   Summary of canonical discriminant functions eigenvalues

Eigenvalues				
Function	Eigenvalue	% of Variance	Cumulative %	Canonical correlation
1	.658[a]	100.0	100.0	.630

Note: [a] First 1 canonical discriminant functions were used in the analysis.

Wilks' Lambda				
Test of function(s)	Wilks' Lambda	Chi-square	df	Siq.
1	.603	414.886	28	.000

Table A1.6   Classification results[a]

	1 Spain 2 Japan	Predicted group membership		Total
		1	2	
Original Count	1	454	45	499
	2	128	210	336
%	1	91.0	9.0	100.0
	2	37.9	62.1	100.0

Note: [a] 79.3% of original grouped cases correctly classified.

Q$_2$ Similarity or disparity of business model among Spanish banks

To answer this question we analysed the speeches by the CEOs of three Spanish banks, namely BBVA, Santader, and Banco de Sabadell, published in the annual reports for 2003, 2004, and 2005. As with the previous analysis, in the case of Santander the speeches of Emilio Botín, Chairman, and Alfredo Sáenz, CEO, were both used.

First the content analysis was conducted on these materials using Leximancer. Instead of merging three yearly speeches of each of the speakers into one file, we used the 'folder tags' command (Leximancer, 2005:39–40).

Secondly, based on the output produced by the Leximancer application (highresdata.txt), we further conducted Discriminant analysis, in which 'a dependent variable (DV) is treated as categorical (e.g., Sex = female, male) and of variables (IVs) to predict the DV' (Meyer, 1993:389). Its goal is to predict group membership (Ishimura, 2001:158).

Thirdly, Factor Analysis was conducted on the basis of the same Leximancer output, (1) to discern if there are common factors among the 'concepts', and, based on the factors thus discovered, (2) to establish the differentiation between BBVA, Santander, and Sabadell.

Content analysis

How are the concepts positioned in relation to each other in each bank? For a visual analysis we used Leximancer analysis outputs.

Santander

In Santander's case, after 3000 iterations to facilitate the learning process, Leximancer produced the following Figure A1.3.

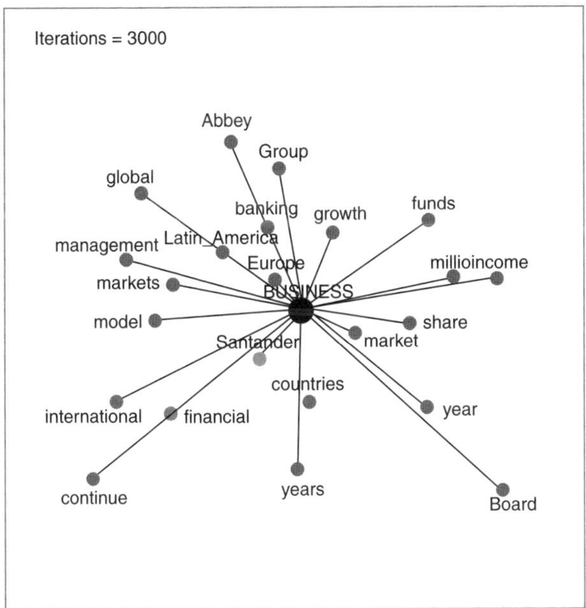

Figure A1.3   Conceptual map of Santander's top management (1)

This conceptual map with themes at 33 per cent is shown in Figure A1.4 below.

In this Figure we can see the User Defined Concepts, PA (profit-arithmetic) and PIF (proto-image of the firm), which were inserted into this analysis. Graphically it is obvious that PA occupies a central position in relation to other concepts. However, it must be borne in mind that the content of PA and PIF is a combination of various other concepts and words, which may risk being rather arbitrary due to the fact that we did not necessarily find the typical ingredients of PA and PIF in annual report speeches and, accordingly, a compromise was struck between the availability of ingredient concepts and words, and their similarity with what we usually understand as PA and PIF.

For the sake of simplifying the relationship between the five most frequent concepts and the others, we manually drew up the following Figure A1.5 based on data from 2005. The numbers signify the number of times those five most frequent concepts were mentioned, and the numbers on the connecting lines are the frequency of their mention in relation to each other concept.

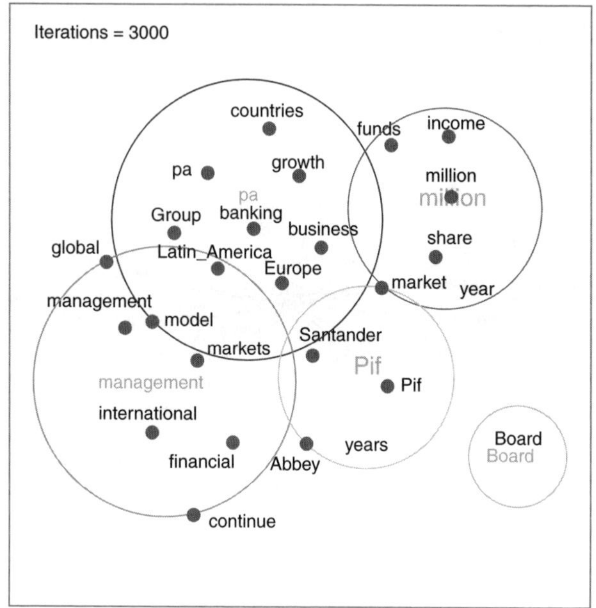

Figure A1.4   Conceptual map of Santander's top management (2)

As can be seen, the terms *Group* (Santander), *Abbey International*, *share* (market share), *business*, *income*, and *model* all stand out in the graph.

It is interesting to note also that concepts related to geographic regions, as well as business model ('model'), market share ('share'), etc., are also located nearby.

Similarly, the Leximancer summary analysis of the texts read as follows:

Leximancer Document Summary
File: data/./santander ceo 2003.pdf Document: S1 Summary Sample: In Latin America, the Group manages €12,000 million in pension plans (8 million unit holders), with growth in all countries, and a further €12,000 million in mutual funds. (TG_SANTANDER_CEO_2003_TG) The performance in Brazil and Puerto Rico in local currency terms was very positive. (TG_SANTANDER_CEO_2003_TG)

File: data/./Santander ceo 2004.pdf Document: S1 Summary Sample: A large European bank We are Europe's largest bank, with 5,900 branches in 15 countries. (TG_SANTANDER_CEO_2004_TG) In

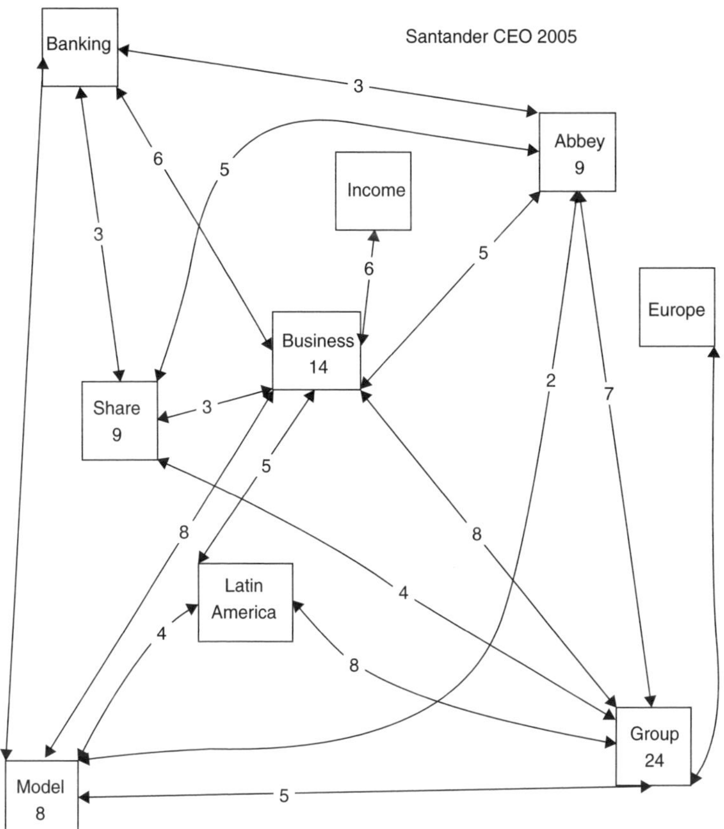

Figure A1.5   The relationship between the five most frequent concepts and the others at (Santander) (*) Numbers: frequency of mention between two concepts

Source: The authors.

Spain, the Santander Central Hispano branch network is the leader, driven by its dynamism and innovation. (TG_SANTANDER_CEO_2004_TG) Banesto, which has an innovative, solid and efficient banking model, is taking market share in lending, year after year, from commercial and savings banks. (TG_SANTANDER_CEO_2004_TG)

File: data/./santander ceo 2005.pdf Document: S1 Summary Sample: In Latin America, retail banking took a qualitative leap forward with clear gains in market share and improved business management, laying the foundations for sustainable growth in the future. (TG_SANTANDER_CEO_2005_TG) The region's US$2,208 million of attributable income, mostly generated by retail banking, gives the Group, over and above its quantitative value, tremendous potential for growth and diversification. (TG_SANTANDER_CEO_2005_TG) Our investment in the US bank Sovereign directs the Group's financial resources towards retail banking, diversifying our revenues in a market which is known to us and where we have had very positive experiences in the past. (TG_SANTANDER_CEO_2005_TG)

Overall here again references related to regions, countries, and markets stand out, and all seem to point to the bank's desire to grow and to internationalise.

BBVA

The following Figure A1.6 shows the Leximancer analysis on the three-year period speeches by BBVA's chairman. More concepts were generated compared to the analysis of Santander. Words such as earnings, customers, areas, etc., are frequent.

The conceptual map with themes at 58 per cent is as shown in the following Figure A1.7. Growth, business, model, etc., are positioned

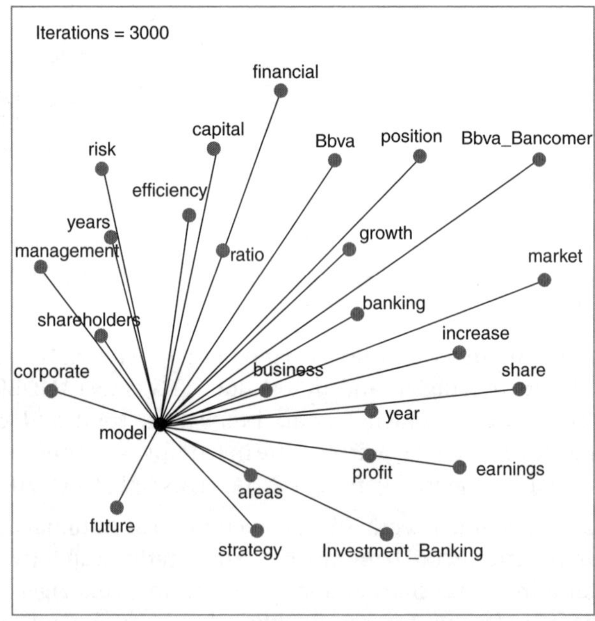

Figure A1.6   Conceptual map of BBVA's top management (1)

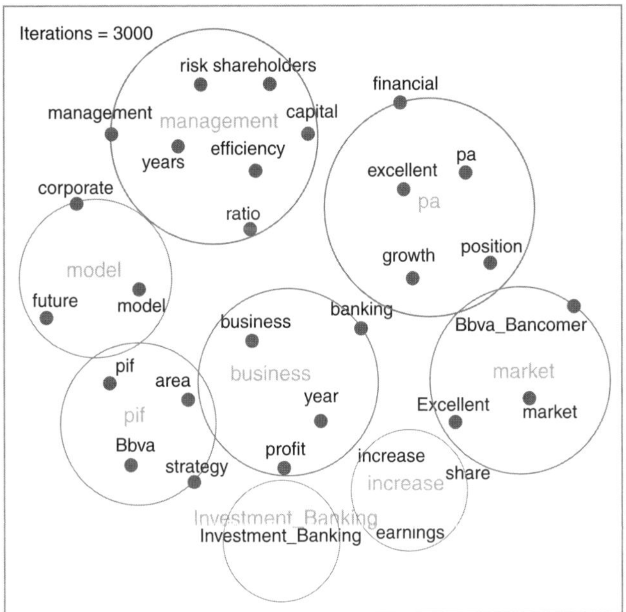

Figure A1.7   Conceptual map of BBVA's top management (2)

in the centre of the map. Qualifying words such as *Excellent* also stand out.

Here again in an effort to simplify the relationship representation we drew up the following Figure A1.8 for the year 2005. The main concepts are the five most frequently mentioned ones. BBVA and growth concepts form a loop including profit and earnings. Another feature characterising this representation is high frequency in absolute terms of each concept.

The summary automatically produced by Leximancer reads as follows:

Leximancer Document Summary
File: data/./bbva letter ceo 2003.pdf Document: S1 Summary Sample: Dear shareholder: 2003 was an excellent year for BBVA as shown by the Group's net attributable profit, which grew by 29.5 per cent to €2,227 million. (TG_BBVA_LETTER_CEO_2003_TG) However, even more significant was the high quality of BBVA's income statement, with a gradual improvement in more recurrent earnings throughout

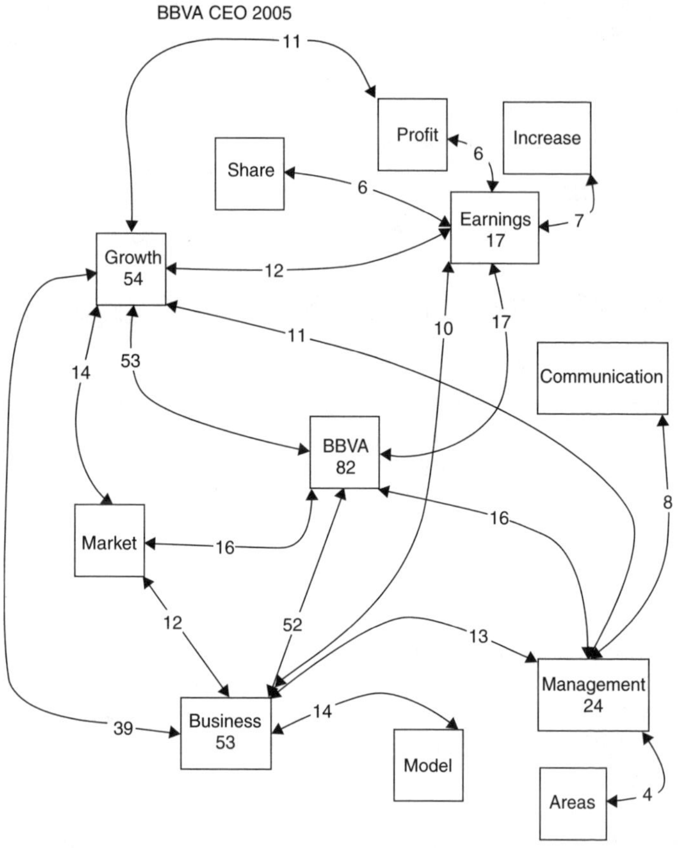

Figure A1.8   The relationship between the five most frequent concepts and the others at (BBVA) (*) Numbers: frequency of mention between two concepts

Source: The authors.

the year based on the clear progress made in our three core business: Retail Banking in Spain and Portugal, Wholesale and Investment Banking and America. (TG_BBVA_LETTER_CEO_2003_TG) The BBVA share price rose by 20.1 per cent in the year, which is higher than the 15.7per cent gain in the Euro Stoxx 50 Index. (TG_BBVA_LETTER_CEO_2003_TG)

File: data/./bbva letter ceo 2004.pdf Document: S1 Summary Sample: With regard to Retail Banking Spain and Portugal, we are launching an expansion programme in the branch network, concentrating on new areas of urban development, with young population growth, and we are going to dedicate a major effort to the segment of businesses and SME's, in which we are already clear leaders, and in which there is considerable potential. (TG_BBVA_LETTER_CEO_2004_TG) In Wholesale Banking, 2005 is to be the year in which our customer franchise model is deployed in Latin America, and we are going to reinforce such activities as project finance, which are essential for opening new markets, especially those in Asia. (TG_BBVA_LETTER_CEO_2004_TG) In The Americas, we are going to focus on credit expansion, particularly in Mexico, with highly ambitious goals in consumer lending and mortgages. (TG_BBVA_LETTER_CEO_2004_TG)

File: data/./bbva letter ceo 2005.pdf Document: S1 Summary Sample: BBVA: an excellent risk profile The Group has managed to combine growth with efficient risk management, which BBVA considers to be a core competency for providing investors with stable and ongoing value creation. (TG_BBVA_LETTER_CEO_2005_TG) The result of this accomplished management has been that at year-end 2005, the BBVA Group's non-performing loans (NPL) ratio has recorded its lowest ever level of 0.94 per cent, with the NPL coverage rate soaring to a record high of 252 per cent. It should furthermore be remembered that 95 per cent of the Group' assets are located in investment grade countries, and that BBVA adopts a hands-on approach to structural risk management (exchange (TG_BBVA_LETTER_CEO_2005_TG) Such factors lie behind the high score BBVA has been awarded by the main rating agencies: AA≠ by Standard & Poor's and Fitch, and Aa2 by Moody's. (TG_BBVA_LETTER_CEO_2005_TG)

Again, references to geographical regions, as well as types of business stand out as being the central topics.

Banco de Sabadell

We ran 1000 iterations on Banco Sabadell, since they did not produce any different positioning of concepts. In view of the lack of the concept 'Model' in the analysed map, we used 'Business' as the main one to see the relative positioning of other concepts and word. The concepts produced are fewer than BBVA, similar to Santander's case. The output is as shown in Figure A1.9.

In the map with themes at 34 per cent of theme size, it is interesting to observe concepts such as 'Profitability' and 'Growth'. Overall the Spanish banks differ from the Japanese in that the latter tend to emphasise customer service, quality of services, and other similarly qualitative or 'soft' words, while the Spanish usually focus more on

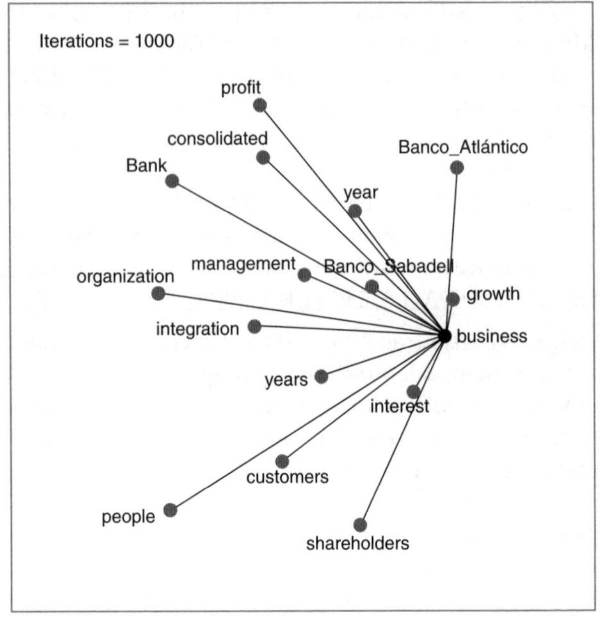

Figure A1. 9   Conceptual map of Sabadell's CEO

quantitative or 'hard' words such as profit, earnings, results, efficiency, and so on.

The automatically-produced document summary of the speeches by Banco Sabadell's CEO reads as follows:

Leximancer Document Summary
File: data/./sabadell ceo 2003.doc Document: S1 Summary Sample: It also includes annual reports on Corporate Governance and Corporate Social Responsibility, as well as the annual report of the Audit and Control Committee. (TG_SABADELL_CEO_2003_TG) Banco Sabadell is a stronger and more competitive organization now than it was a year ago. (TG_SABADELL_CEO_2003_TG) It has made resolute strides towards achieving its goals of business growth and consolidation; and it has successfully updated and strengthened the values that underpin its solid business culture, a culture that reflects a way of being and of doing things in which adherence to ethical principles, rigour in decision making, and upholding our corporate good name are fundamental values which (TG_SABADELL_CEO_2003_TG)

File: data/./sabadell ceo 2004.doc Document: S1 Summary Sample: In a separate volume you will also find the annual report on Corporate Governance, the annual report of the Audit and Control Committee, and the report on Corporate Social Responsibility. (TG_SABADELL_CEO_2004_TG) As I mentioned in last year's report, our priority then was to move ahead rapidly with the integration of Banco Atl·ntico to be able to start the new year as a single organization. (TG_SABADELL_CEO_2004_TG) The task of integration has been performed efficiently and in record time, a milestone development in Europe's banking industry. (TG_SABADELL_CEO_2004_TG)

File: data/./sabadell ceo 2005.PDF Document: S1 Summary Sample: In it you will, as usual, find full and detailed information about the audited consolidated balance sheet and profit and loss account, and details of the many internal and external actions and initiatives put in hand by the Bank and by Group subsidiaries and associates throughout the year 2005. (TG_SABADELL_CEO_2005_TG) You will also find the annual report of the Audit and Control Committee, and annual reports on Corporate Governance and Corporate Social Responsibility. (TG_SABADELL_CEO_2005_TG) The year 2006 marks the end of the first five years of trading in Banco Sabadell shares on the stock market. (TG_SABADELL_CEO_2005_TG)

What distinguishes Banco Sabadell's speeches are the references to Corporate Social Responsibility (CSR) and corporate governance. Growth and business are also referred to, but with less emphasis.[3]

Discriminant analysis

The concepts contained in the analysed file were as per the following Table A1.7 *Analysis Case Processing Summary.*

Table A1.7   Analysis case processing summary

Unweighted cases		N	Per cent
Valid		486	100.0
Excluded	Missing or out-of-range group codes	0	.0
	At least one missing discriminating variable	0	.0
	Both missing or out-of-range group codes and at least one missing discriminating variable	0	.0
	Total	0	.0
Total		486	100.0

As shown in the following Table A1.8 the functions 1 through 2 indicate at p < .001 level the significant difference rejecting H_0: thus, there is no difference among the three groups.

The standardised Discriminant function in the following Table A1.9 points to concepts such as Growth and Income as important concepts contributing to the differentiation of the groups.

Table A1.8   Eigenvalue

			Eigenvalues		
Function	**Eigenvalue**	**% of Variance**	**Cumulative %**	**Canonical correlation**
1	.226[a]	87.8	87.8	.431
2	.032[a]	12.2	100.0	.175

Note: [a] First 2 canonical discriminant functions were used in the analysis.

	Wilks' Lambda			
Test of function(s)	**Wilks'Lambda**	**Chi-square**	**df**	**Sig.**
1 through 2	.790	111.671	42	.000
2	.969	14.700	20	.793

Table A1.9   Standardized canonical discriminant function coefficients

	Function	
	1	**2**
Banking	−.208	−.032
Business	−.008	−.332
Capital	.259	.240
Corporate	.008	−.103
Customers	.102	.038
Earnings	.138	.113
Efficiency	.167	−.102

Continued

Table A1.9   Continued

	Function	
	1	2
Financial	.036	.273
Future	.199	−.429
Global	−.275	−.048
Growth	.469	−.007
Income	−.476	.187
Increase	.445	.379
International	−.249	.181
Management	.181	−.023
Market	−.088	.264
Model	−.053	.589
Position	.165	.282
Share	−.080	−.131
shareholders	.265	−.147

Classification function coefficients are shown in Table A1.10.

Fisher's classification function coefficients are shown in Table A1.11.

Factor analysis (FA)[4]

Once the Content Analysis and Factor Analysis were conducted (which demonstrated the existence of the differences between the three Spanish banks), we proceeded to carry out Factor Analysis in order to find the common 'factors' existing among the 'concepts' identified by Leximancer, and to further elucidate the differentiation among the banks by ranking them using those factors (Ishimura, 2001: 128–157).

The basic data for the analysis were generated by Leximancer using the speeches of the CEOs of the Spanish banks contained in the banks' annual reports between 2003 and 2005. The 'concept statistics', a function of Leximancer, thus listed the identified 'concepts' and words frequently mentioned by the CEOs and by bank.

FA generated two Factors among which 100 per cent of the variance was explained as shown in Table A1.12 *Total Variance*.

The following Table A1.13 shows the Component Matrix:

The 'Concepts' are mentioned in upper case, whereas frequent words appear in lower case. Factor 1 seems to point to Growth- and Earnings-related concepts and words because of the positive values such as EARNINGS (.999), GROWTH (.905), POSITION (.957), management (.998), etc. Factor 2 emphasises Internationalisation- and Income-related

Table A1.10   Classification function coefficients

	1 BBVA	2 Sabadell	3 Santander
	1	2	3
Banking	−.331	−7.623E−02	.404
Business	1.964	2.410	2.018
Capital	1.050	7.091E−02	−.155
Corporate	.443	.706	.432
Customers	.109	−7.726E−02	−.279
Earnings	.873	.515	.397
Efficiency	.822	.897	.336
Employees	.916	−2.882E−03	.932
Financial	.667	3.103E−02	.496
Future	1.197	2.032	.564
Global	−.421	−3.750E−02	.652
Growth	1.060	.828	8.986E−02
Income	−1.725E−02	−2.890E−02	1.367
Increase	.962	−.329	−.718
International	.331	.111	1.270
Management	.550	.467	4.987E−02
Market	.241	−9.059E−02	.403
Model	−4.312E−02	−1.132	1.839E−02
Position	.658	−9.487E−02	5.419E−02
Share	.447	.747	.695
shareholders	1.082	1.178	.264
(Constant)	−2.613	−2.421	−2.132

Note: Fisher's linear discriminant functions.

Table A1.11   Classification results[a]

	1 BBVA 2 Sabadell 3 Sartander	Predicted group membership			
		1	2	3	Total
Original Count	1	84	64	76	224
	2	10	15	18	43
	3	29	44	146	219
%	1	37.5	28.6	33.9	100.0
	2	23.3	34.9	41.9	100.0
	3	13.2	20.1	66.7	100.0

Note: [a] 50.4% of original grouped cases correctly classified.

Table A1.12   Total variance explained

Component	Initial eigenvalues			Extraction sums of squared loadings		
	Total	% of Variance	Cumulative %	Total	% of Variance	Cumulative %
1	14.307	57.228	57.228	14.307	57.228	57.228
2	10.693	42.772	100.000	10.693	42.772	100.000
3	3.792E–15	1.517E–14	100.000			
4	1.991E–15	7.962E–15	100.000			
5	1.265E–15	5.061E–15	100.000			
6	6.451E–16	2.580E–15	100.000			
7	4.614E–16	1.846E–15	100.000			
8	3.983E–16	1.593E–15	100.000			
9	3.444E–16	1.377E–15	100.000			
10	2.373E–16	9.490E–16	100.000			
11	2.034E–16	8.135E–16	100.000			
12	1.941E–16	7.766E–16	100.000			
13	1.187E–16	4.747E–16	100.000			
14	5.183E–17	2.073E–16	100.000			
15	3.864E–17	1.546E–16	100.000			
16	–1.053E–16	–4.211E–16	100.000			
17	–2.043E–16	–8.170E–16	100.000			
18	–2.095E–16	–8.380E–16	100.000			
19	–2.474E–16	–9.894E–16	100.000			
20	–3.703E–16	–1.481E–15	100.000			
21	–4.585E–16	–1.834E–15	100.000			
22	–4.954E–16	–1.982E–15	100.000			
23	–6.713E–16	–2.685E–15	100.000			
24	–9.856E–16	–3.942E–15	100.000			
25	–3.862E–15	–1.545E–14	100.000			

Note: Extraction method: Principal Component Analysis.

concepts and words such as BANKING (.607), BUSINESS (.895), GLOBAL (.864), international (.960), etc.

The classification of the banks according to these factors is as shown in Table A1.14.

The value demonstrated by BBVA regarding Factor 1 (Growth and Earning) is significantly higher than Santander's and Sabadell's, while regarding Factor 2 (Internationalisation and Income) Santander showed more interest than BBVA and Sabadell.

Table A1.13   Component matrix[a]

	Component	
	1	**2**
Banking	−.717	−.697
Business	.446	.895
Businesses	.796	−.605
Capital	.991	−.132
Corporate	.472	−.881
Customers	.997	7.395E−02
Earnings	.999	4.248E−02
Efficiency	.979	.203
Employees	.483	.876
Financial	.617	.787
Future	.348	−.937
Global	−.504	−.864
Group	.616	.788
Growth	.905	−.425
Income	−.628	.779
Increase	.982	.187
International	−.279	.960
Management	.998	−5.776E−02
Market	.765	.644
Markets	.555	.832
Model	.195	.981
Position	.957	.288
Ratio	.852	.524
Share	.981	−.194
Shareholders	.803	−.596

Note: Extraction method: Principal Component Analysis.

[a] 2 components extracted.

Table A1.14   Factors

	Factor 1	**Factor 2**
BBVA	1.09571	.36434
Sabadell	−.23233	−1.13109
Santander	−.86339	.76674

This can be interpreted as meaning that BBVA's focus is on growth and earning, while Santander's is on internationalisation and income.

Sabadell's Factor 1 and Factor 2 values are negative, which may also signify that its focus is rather fuzzy on these scores, at least when compared with BBVA and Santander. It may also mean that, given its smaller size compared to the other two giants, Sabadell has arrived rather late in the race for internationalisation and growth.

In summary, FA suggests that the three Spanish banks do differ from each other in line with the results of the discriminant analysis we referred to previously.

Conclusion

To answer the question of whether there is one management model or different ones, we ran both content analysis and statistical analysis on the basis of the Leximancer and SPSS applications and discovered that Discriminant Analysis (DA) pointed to the existence of a significant difference between the analysed Spanish banks: BBVA, Santander, and Banco Sabadell. The membership of each category could be predicted. Factor Analysis (FA), too, confirms the existence of difference.

To discern the differences of the three banks' models we analysed the conceptual maps and automatically produced summaries.

The number of concepts produced, and the relative positioning of these concepts and words, differ among the three banks, but the intuitive comprehension of the difference, nonetheless, is not easy to grasp.

In combination, the answers to the two questions coincide with the opinion expressed by an important banker to the effect that whether there is one identifiable business model or several among the mainstream Spanish banks depends on the degree of abstraction.[5] Viewed from outside Spain there seems to be just one model, but a closer observation reveals differences.

In Chapters 2 and 3 we dedicated more space to the business models prevailing in the Spanish banks and thus built up a construct to provide a comprehensive explanation of them, and our description was based on more judgemental or subjective criteria.

Annex 2A – Japanese Banks: A Contrast to Spanish Banks

In the preceding annex we conducted Content Analysis of the speeches of the Spanish retail banks and compared them with those of their Japanese counterparts.

Our conclusions therein gave grounds for believing that, whereas the Spanish banks form a cluster in their strategic approaches, therefore suggesting the existence of similar business models, the Japanese banks do not share a common approach.

This annex attempts to provide circumstantial evidence that these banks lack a clear-cut strategic approach due to historical reasons, such as the over-protection of the monetary authorities of the country (in particular, the so-called 'Convoy System' whereby risk was spread evenly as all banks pursued similar actions under the supervision of the Ministry of Finance). This over-protection thwarted any real creativity in designing a business model that would have enabled them to compete in the world arena.

Annex 2b, however, offers the case of Suruga Bank as an example of a bank that has managed to carve out its own strategic niche despite the *Convoy System*. Curiously enough, Suruga Bank's business model carries quite a striking resemblance to the general business model found among the excellent Spanish banks, namely, the pursuit of operational efficiency and the strategic use of IT systems.

Historical backdrop

In contrast to the 'buoyancy' in the Spanish banks in the last two decades thanks to their successful growth, the banking industry in Japan was overcast with doom and gloom. The feeling was summed up by a Japanese author in no ambiguous tone: 'The fact of the matter is that the Japanese financial institutions were defeated in the war of finances. They sustained damage so severe that it is impossible not to admit it' Yasuda (2006: 3).

Yasuda (2006) maintains that the Japanese banking industry helped the Japanese economy to enjoy growth for fifty years after WWII, and managed to exert an influence on the world financial market by the

1980s, but such influence was brought about by the Ministry of Finance's 'convoy system' and was not something won on its own merits.

Due to the regulators' mishandling of the banking crisis after the burst of the real-estate bubble in the Japanese economy in the 1990s, the Japanese banks underwent a lengthy and severe readjustment period for almost fifteen years, during which time they had to face non-performing debts amounting up to ¥39 trillion in 2001, equivalent to 8 per cent of their total lending (Yasuda, 2006). (Regarding the crisis that affected the banking industry in Japan see Table A2A.1 *Financial Data Of The Japanese Banking Industry Between 1990 And 2005*.)

The banks' net worth, net of Government money injection, fell from a peak of ¥32 trillion to ¥10 trillion in 2001, signifying a 70 per cent loss (Yasuda, 2006). By the fiscal year ended March 2005, however, the major banks, or city banks as they are known, managed to halve the ratio of the non-performing debts thanks to Finance Minister Takenaka's programme for financial revival (Nozaki, 2006: 68).

How are they faring now? In terms of absolute profit figures, larger banks such as the Bank of Tokyo-Mitsubishi UFJ (MUFJ), Mizuho, and Sumitomo Mitsui Banking Corporation (SMBC) are doing well, with operational profits in the financial year ending March 2006 amounting to ¥1.3 trillion, ¥0.77 trillion, and ¥0.96 trillion, respectively.[1] (See Table A2A.2 *Comparison Of The Top Three Japanese Banks*.)

Compared with the US's Citigroup, Bank of America, or the UK's HSBC, however, the Japanese banks ROA (return on assets) lag behind. The foreign competitors' 1 per cent-strong returns dwarf those of the Japanese banks (which are less than half).

Table A2A.1   Financial data of the Japanese banking industry between 1990 and 2005 (in trillions of yen)

	Total assets	Lending	Shareholders' equity	Market capitalisation
1990	943	476	28.6	147
1995	846	539	32.3	82.3
2000	769	494	33.1	36.6
2005	751	419	10.4	38.1

Source: Yasuda (2006: 9) based on Japanese Banking Association and Tokyo Stock Market's monthly bulletin.

Table A2A.2   Comparison of the top three Japanese banks as of FY 2006 ended in March (*) (in ¥ trillion)

Bank	Total assets	Operational profit	Unrealised profits on securities	Employees	Branches	Impaired loans rate (%)	Efficiency ratio (%)
MUFJ	187.0	1.307	2.953	38,730	783	2.07	53.3
Mizuho	149.6	0.769	2.150	25,689	440	1.41	54.7
SMBC	107.0	0.966	1.343	20,332	426	1.70	40.8

Note: (*) Total assets are on the consolidated base, the number of branches includes overseas branches.

Source: Nihon Keizai Shimbun (2007: 136).

Why is the profitability of the Japanese banks low?

The question to raise is, then, why? Kawamoto (2000; 2004) asserts that the Japanese banks did not have to worry about their profitability until the 1980s in an industry strictly controlled by the Government, which might have changed in the 1980s thanks to the deregulation taking place, but, unfortunately, it coincided with Japan's economic boom in the 1990s, with the result that creativity was severely hampered and the elimination and shedding of low return businesses did not take place on account of the ease of achieving high profits during the said economic boom.

Kawamoto (2000) list the following reasons for the low return on assets experienced by the Japanese banks:

1. Low profitability from the traditional banking businesses
2. Unreasonably low return
3. Insufficient risk-return management
4. Wrong pricing of commissions and service fees
5. Wrong cross-shareholding
6. Insufficient management of securities in portfolio

Low profitability from the traditional banking businesses

At the beginning of the 1990s Kawamoto (2000) estimated the Japanese banks' bad loans at ¥30 to 40 trillion but, due to the banks' delay in employing drastic measures, the amount bloated to ¥80 trillion by

1998, which forced the government to inject ¥60 trillion into the industry.

In the meantime the banks increased their lending in the mortgage market by 43 per cent between 1994 and 1998. The lending rate was linked to the rate granted by the Government Housing Loan Corporation, which tended to keep it lower as a matter of policy.

Lending to large enterprises, for its part, did not provide too much profitability since its rate was linked to the base rate, which likewise was low (Kawamoto, 2000: 35).

Similarly, on the basis of the international comparison of ROE and lending/GDP prepared by the Bank of Japan's International Bureau, Kawamoto (2000: 37) deduces that, despite the fall in the return on equity, the weight of the banks' lending on GDP increased. This may be interpreted as the banks' reticence to reduce their size.

Unreasonably low margin

At the time of her writing Kawamoto (2000) estimated Japanese banks' five-year spread average at 1.11 per cent, a third of the US's 3.57 per cent and half Germany's 2.04 per cent.

Kawamoto (2000) is not sure if this is due to the pressure from borrowers, the media, political lobbies, etc., competitive reasons for not losing customers, or the fact that, at many banks, nearly fifty per cent of their shareholders' equity as of the fiscal year ended March 1999 corresponded to the government subsidy, which might have created an atmosphere hostile to a rise in interest rates.

Nozaki (2006: 69) does not think that the low margin derives from the 'excessive' number of banks in Japan. For him it is a consequence of various circumstances combined. Firstly, many banks tend to concede special political preferential treatment to some customers under the pretext that it would facilitate the relationship and help to strengthen their business transactions. Secondly, many of these banks still cultivate the habit of considering growth as the priority, for which growth in volume is prioritised to the detriment of the profitability of each operation.

This profit profile of Japanese banks runs counter to the high-risk high-return axiom. Kametani (2007) points out that the risk tends to concentrate on banks discharging the role of main banks with which 'a firm has a strong relationship with its primary bank (the main bank) and the main bank has extensive shareholdings in the client firm, serving as a major source of short- and long-term financing and, in many instances, having a representative on the firm's board of directors' (Peek & Rosengren, 2003).

Insufficient risk-return management

Kawamoto (2000: 42) assumes that the lending behaviour of Japanese banks does not follow the high-risk high-return axiom. As graphically represented below, the interest rate behaves rather independently of the risk, experiencing discontinuity at certain point, followed by a high return area, which is usually covered by financial entities other than banks (See Figure A2A.1).

Kawamoto (2000) attributes this behaviour to the absence of an adequate risk-return assessment system at the Japanese banks. As a consequence, larger banks concentrate on low return businesses such as large enterprises or foreign operations. Kawamoto (2000) argues that the Japanese banks are inclined to consider consumer loans as a business for unsophisticated credit entities, and are not equipped with a database of individual consumers comparable to those owned by consumer credit companies.

The lack of a risk-return assessment system also surfaced in the credit crunch: the banks tended to withdraw credit from small- and medium-sized enterprises (SMEs) around 1997 to 1999. Pressured by the capital adequacy requirement the banks were forced to compress their lending. In the absence of a risk-return assessment they seemed to focus on SMEs.

Wrong pricing of commissions and service fees

Kawamoto (2000: 45) points out that, as of end-September 1998, each household had on average 22 bank accounts with 2.7 banks, though 90 per cent of the bank accounts in Japan had less than half million yen deposit and the average balance was as low as ¥45,699.

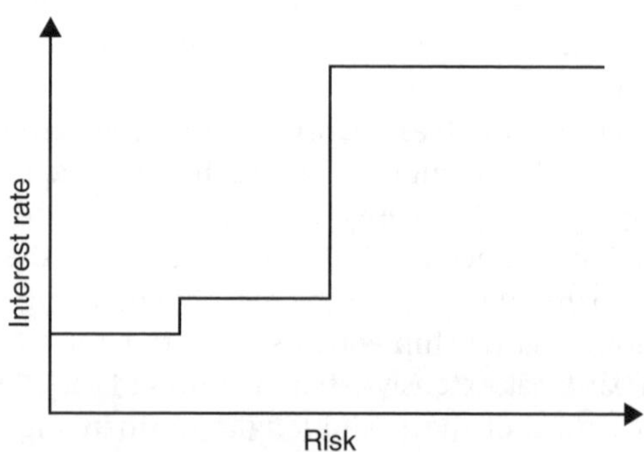

Figure A2A.1   The interest rate behaviour vis-à-vis risk

The cost of maintenance of the inactive accounts is huge for the banks. Kawamoto (2000) proposes the imposition of account maintenance fees, which, according to her, will provoke the closure of 70 per cent of them.

The other side of the coin is that the banks' fees are not systematically charged. Japanese banks started to charge fees for services such as the collection of letters of exchange, collection of bills, the issuance of transaction details, etc. However, many banks do not discriminate services and charge similar amounts compared to other competing banks.

Local tax collection services, the payment of water provision, the payment of civil servants' salaries, and other public sector-related services remain uncharged more often than not.

Kawamoto (2000: 51) suspects that this custom of not charging service fees to the public sector entities is predicated on the argument that the banks can handle the funds flowing in as the payment of salaries and can compensate for the possible service fees, and she is critical of such a practice as it may disfigure and disguise the cost/benefit relationship.

Wrong cross-shareholding

The 1980s is characterised by the strong presence of the Japanese banks in the world bank ranking. The appreciation of the yen against the dollar helped to increase the overseas assets owned by the Japanese banks – 'Japan money' – which was used to acquire foreign banks.

The Japanese banks figured in the top of the ratings by leading rating agencies.

Kawamoto (2000: 52) ascribes the good ratings to the belief that the Japanese Government would never let banks go bankrupt, as well as to the fact that these banks had unrealised book values thanks to the possession of the shares of their group companies estimated at their acquisition prices. In the 1998 BIS rule the Japanese monetary authorities managed to include the possibility that 45 per cent of the unrealised book value can be computed to the banks' net worth.

The tragedy struck because of this. Kawamoto (2000) reckons that, as of 1992, the Japanese banks held in total a 'buffer' in excess of the non-performing debts for the amount of ¥30–40 trillion, because, apart from provisions for insolvency and the shareholders' equity, the banks were thought to own the unrealised capital gains in shares and land estimated at ¥22.2 trillion and ¥10 trillion, respectively.

The belief that they were well supplied for, on the one hand, led to retarding actions on the part of banks' management, and, on the other, resulted in the bloating of non-performing debts, the amount of which doubled by 1998 to ¥87 trillion, owing to the mounting economic recession and worsened by the phenomenal fall in share prices, which turned the unrealised capital gain into unrealised capital loss (Kawamoto, 2000: 32–33).

Kawamoto's (2000) criticism is levelled against the shareholding of group companies by the banks not only because of the laxity in management that the unrealised capital gain may engender and the fluctuation risk it may subject the banks to, but also because of the low return it is bound to spell.

As the fiscal year to March 1999 ended, the Japanese banks in total held ¥43 trillion worth of shares. The weighted return of the First Division of Tokyo stock market between 1990 and 1997 varied between 0.61 per cent and 0.99 per cent per annum, improving to 1.03 per cent in 1998. Kawamoto (2000: 57–58) holds that, overall, the return of the investment folio is very low (if not blatantly negative) if the capital gain is not taken into account, which, under the circumstance, was nowhere to be seen.

Insufficient management of securities in portfolio

On account of the financing of the enterprise sector having traditionally been achieved by indirect finance, securities, with the exception of shares, in the banks' portfolio carried little weight. Kawamoto (2000) estimates them at 10.4 per cent for the entire banking sector and at 6.7 per cent for the city banks or banks deploying their activities throughout Japan. As a consequence the percentage of income derived from this account item is not too high, which otherwise could be a stable source of income (Kawamoto, 2000).

Annex 2B – Suruga Bank[1]

On 4th December 2003, Mitsuyoshi Okano, Suruga Bank's President and CEO, looked out of his car window at the streets overflowing with shoppers preparing for the holiday season. Okano was being driven to the Hotel Okura where, in a few hours' time, he would be the recipient of the third annual Porter Prize – a much-coveted award for Japanese firms demonstrating excellent performance through innovation in product, process or strategy. This year's prize was going to Suruga for their outstanding results in ROIC (return on invested capital) and ROS (return on sales) of 0.8 per cent and 25.9 per cent above the 5-year industry average, respectively.

For Okano this was at last the recognition from academics and practising managers, of his remarkable performance since having been appointed to the presidency of the bank in 1985. He found himself remembering the many difficulties and hardships he and his management team had had to overcome over the years and, while his car was stopped at a traffic light, one event in particular sprang to mind...

It was the summer of 2000. During one of Okano's unannounced visits to branch offices, he was absolutely incensed to find that some of the computers, specifically installed to improve customer service, were not even plugged in.

One year before, in August 1999, Suruga Bank had invested in the CRM system (Suruga Bank defines CRM as both Customer Relations Marketing and Credit Risk Management). The CRM system would allow the bank to integrate all the information on clients held by call centres, branches, etc., into a data-base, which would also include information such as the customers' ATM usage (automatic telling machines, also known as cash machines).

Branches would thus gain access to this customer data, enabling branch officials, while attending their customers, to be more efficient in their sales efforts; for example, by making use of information such as time deposits reaching maturity.

Suruga Bank was the first among the Japanese banks, even including the main city banks (i.e. major commercial banks, rather than regional – see Figure 4 later in this chapter), to introduce a CRM system. Okano saw it as a competitive edge over their competitors and decided its implementation should be a priority – it's easy to see why Okano was so angry to find the system was not being used.

The idea seemed to have been given the cold shoulder by the middle- and lower-management, despite the enthusiasm at the top level. This gives us an idea of how Information Technology is regarded in the banking industry in Japan; how reticent Japanese bankers can be regarding new technologies or new ways of doing business.

To break the impasse Okano decided to discuss with staff how to make the best of CRM for their business and how to optimise operations, and encouraged them to propose new ideas.

In the following pages we will examine why Okano needed to pursue this unusual strategy; a strategy that could set Suruga Bank apart in the competitive arena.

History

Suruga Bank was established by Kitaro Okano in Shizuoka Prefecture in 1895 as Nekata Bank, then the smallest bank in Japan, with ¥10,000 capital. The name was changed to Suruga Bank in 1912, by which time the capital had been increased to ¥600,000. As Chairman, Kitaro was the driving force of the bank until his death in 1965. (See Table A2B.1 for a summary of the bank's history and milestones.)

The bank's history has long been marked by the absorption of smaller regional banks, savings banks and credit unions. The Ministry of Finance tried to force Suruga Bank into a merger with Shizuoka Bank in 1943, within the context of the war-time economy, but Kitaro Okano managed to keep its independence.[2] The bank's last absorption was Atami Credit Union in 1991, by which time the nominal value of outstanding loans had grown from ¥2.5 million in 1912 to ¥1.8 trillion.

Shizuoka Prefecture, in which Suruga Bank is headquartered, sits right next to the Pacific Ocean on a passage from Tokyo to Osaka via Nagoya; the three most important metropolitan areas in Japan. The prefecture's population in the 2000 Census was just over 3.7 million, of which 1.86 million were male, and Shizuoka ranked 10th in terms of population in Japan. The combined area in which Suruga Bank operates (Shonan, a part of Kanagawa Prefecture plus Numazu and Shizuoka, both part of Shizuoka Prefecture) represents 10 per cent of Japan's GDP and population.

The savings per head in the prefecture amounted to ¥2,282,000 in 1984, on a par with Japan's average and ranking 24th in Japan, while the life insurance coverage per family was ¥18,170,000 in the same year,

Table A2B.1   Bank's history and milestones

1895	Established as Nekata Bank with ¥10,000 capital
1912	The name changed to Suruga Bank
1936	Japan's Association of Regional Banks established. Kitaro Okano appointed to its Board of Directors
1963	Listed in the Second Division of the Tokyo Stock Exchange
1965	Listed in the First Division of the Tokyo Stock Exchange
1973	On-line network implemented
1978	Card loan service launched as the first among regional banks
1985	Mitsuyoshi Okano appointed the bank's fifth president
1990	The spelling of the bank's name changed to the katakana characters instead of the Chinese ideograph
1991	Merger with Atami Credit Union. The capital increased to ¥30,043 million
1997	The access centre, internet home page, telephone banking, money mileage accounts opened
1998	JCB credit cards issued, as the first bank in Japan. Executive officer system introduced
1999	CRM for the management of the data base on customers implemented
2000	ISO 9002 for call centre business. 1S09001 as the first Japanese bank. 1S014001 for enviromnent management obtained
2001	Automatic credit evaluation system introduced
2003	Alliance on ATM with IY Bank started
2004	Bank card developed with ANA to add mileage on the basis of outstanding bank loans

Source: Suruga Bank IR Report 2003.

placing it among the top six prefectures. The prefecture was estimated as being among the top ten in economic strength.[3]

Thanks to this geographic and economic potential, the prefecture was ripe for competition among three regional banks (Suruga, Shimizu, and Shizuoka Banks) and fifteen credit unions, as well as city banks (except for the Bank of Tokyo, Saitama Bank, and Hokkaido Takushoku Bank which did not have branches in Shizuoka as of 1987).[4]

Suruga Bank's business developed both in Shizuoka and Kanagawa Prefectures. At the end of March 2003, 37 of its 120 domestic branches were based in Kanagawa Prefecture. This meant that the bank had to face competition from Shizuoka Bank and Yokohama Bank, in Shizuoka and Kanagawa Prefectures respectively. (See Figure A2B.1 *Location of Suruga Bank, Shizuoka Bank, and Yokohama Bank.*)

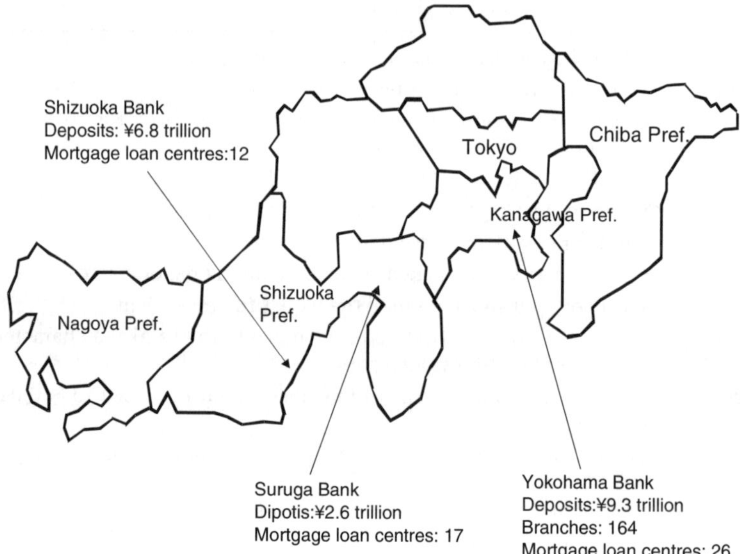

Figure A2B.1   Location of Suruga Bank, Shizuoka Bank, and Yokohama Bank
Source: Sizuoka, Suruga and Yokohama Bank IR Report 2003.

Competitive products

Highly profitable products offered by trust banks, such as loan trusts with payment of principal and interests at maturity, and by securities companies, such as mid-term government bond funds, were harming the competitiveness of city and regional banks. Due to regulations on competitive interests, however, competition among banks, credit unions, and so on, was fought on the basis of sacrificing margin and, as a result, everybody offered the same or similar products.

The launch of time deposits combined with long-term government bonds was a case in point. The product, first launched by Mitsubishi Bank on 16th April in 1983, consisted of automatically crediting the interest paid by government bonds directly to the deposit account. Suruga Bank hit the market with a similar product ten days later, and caused a stampede of regional banks launching similar or identical products. Shizuoka Bank, Shimizu Bank, Shizuoka Credit Union, Mishima Credit Union, among others, all entered the market between October and December 1983.

Suruga Bank responded by launching an ordinary deposit account combined with time deposits – every month the amount of the deposit

Table A2B.2   A comparison of Suruga, Yokohama and Shizuoka Banks

	Suruga Bank	Yokohama Bank	Shizuoka Bank
Impaired loan rate (%)	7.85	4.59	5.57
Outstanding loans	2,043,365	7,903,194	4,941,535
Of wich, lending to SMEs	1,898,272	6,414,090	3,440,771
Of which, Mortgage loans	1,159,000	1,746,551	1,105,034
Number of employees	1,591	3,057	3,292

Source: Kinyu Business February 2004.

exceeding a specific sum would be converted into time deposits.[5] As the interest rate was regulated by the Bank of Japan, the launch of highly-remunerated accounts signified an erosion of the banks' margins. Between 1980 and 1985, the ratio between interest paid and received increased from 0.629 to 0.643, a deterioration which was partly covered by the fall in the relative importance of interest income over the total income from 0.964 to 0.948 in the same period.

Against this backdrop, faced with bitter competition from Yokohama Bank in Kanagawa Prefecture and Shizuoka Bank in Shizuoka Prefecture, and despite the fact that both of were double the size of Suruga Bank and in a better position to survive an all-out war, Suruga Bank fought them head-on. (See Table A2B.2 for a comparison of these three banks). As a consequence, due to the negative spread between the interest received and paid, it was in crisis by the time it published its annual report in March, 1985.

Okano the reformer

Mitsuyoshi Okano was appointed the fifth president of the bank in 1985, when he was forty. Two things were clear from the start – it was essential for him to devise a strategy for survival, and also that fighting all-out against his larger competitors would spell disaster.[6] Ideally, the competition must be met in a market segment where Suruga Bank could pre-empt the others by breaking new ground, and where the first-mover advantage would be gained.

Suruga Bank was, then, a typical local bank whose staff was deeply steeped in the banking industry's culture, characterised by out-and-out conservatism: new measures or unprecedented actions were barely considered, the industry-accepted way of doing business was never called into question, and the pursuit of volume and size was the order of the day. It was a popular opinion among the staff in general that lending to individuals was somewhat elitist and outside of the core business, and that corporate lending was the business to be in. There was also the feeling among its staff that Suruga Bank would never be able to beat its larger competitors.

However, Okano possessed several characteristics that would work in his favour.[7] First and foremost in a culture placing so much importance on tradition, he was a direct descendent of the bank's founder. Second, he had an outsider's view, thanks to having worked for six years (between 1969 and 1975) for Fuji Bank, during which time he gained a wider perspective of banking thanks to a posting in London. Furthermore he had studied in the US, at Cornell College, after graduating from the pre-eminent Keio University.

It therefore comes as less of a surprise that Okano's blueprint for the future of the bank was based on the 'super regional banks' in the United States such as Banc One, US Bancorp, and similar, while no Japanese bank's model was included. After paying several visits to those banks in the US, it was brought home to Okano that the switch from wholesale or corporate lending to individual lending would be a strategy to pursue, but would require a drastic departure from the bank's existing culture.[8]

It took three years for Okano to steer the bank in the direction of lending to individual customers. He spent ten months visiting branch offices and talking with all branch staff under the age of thirty; the rationale being that the views and opinions of the ground-level staff tended to be quashed or distorted by branch management before they reached Okano. Therefore, he felt he had to go out to listen to them, and what became known as 'Junior Boards' (of which more later) were the solution.

Computerised databases should also be in place, he felt; not focused on accounting systems but providing information on individual clients. Likewise, Okano became aware that a PC-based network could provide better potential for flexibility and growth.

Strategic *volte-face*

Okano's strategic reorientation was launched on three key fronts: target client segmentation, an IT system suitable for CRM, and a change in corporate culture (see below for further discussion on these). Okano was adamant on one point, though: strategy would come from the top down.[9] It was he who mapped out the basic lines of strategy, but he nonetheless gave his staff a lot of encouragement to participate and cooperate, coming up with new ideas and suggestions along the way.

Target client segmentation

In the light of depressed demand from corporate clients, banks in Japan were eagerly seeking custom from individuals. Between 2001 and 2003 the lending to corporate clients by Japanese banks fell by ¥51 trillion, whereas those to household clients shot up by ¥5.8 trillion.[10] Those who worked for Tokyo's blue chip firms were relentlessly bombarded with advertisements for mortgages with low preferential interest rates.

To go head-to-head with large city banks (for the difference between commercial banks, see Table A2B.3, detailing the major categories of Japanese banks) and other regional banks would have been suicidal.

Table A2B.3   Major categories of Japanese banks (M&A – Mergers and Acquisitions)

Category	Name/service		
	City banks are those banks with head offices in large cities such as Tokyo or Osaka, deploying their operations throughout Japan. A quarter of the financial assets in the hands of financial institutions are handled by city banks.		
	5 Mega Bank Group	**Before M&A**	**After M&A**
Major commercial bank	Mizuho Financial Group	Dai-Ichi Kangyo Bank	Mizuho Bank
		Fuji Bank	Mizuho Corporate Bank
		Industrial Bank of Japan	–
	Mitsui-Sumitomo Financial Group	Sumitomo Bank	Mitsui Sumitomo Bank
		Sakura Bank	
	Mitsubishi-Tokyo Financial Group	Tokyo-Mitsubishi Bank	Tokyo Mitsubishi Bank
	UFJ Holdings	Sanwa Bank	UFJ Bank
		Tokai Bank	
	Resona Holdings	Daiwa Bank	Resona Bank
		Asahi Bank	Saitama Resona Bank

Continued

Table A2B.3   Continued

Regional bank	Regional banks operate in local regions. Their main business is transactions with their core regional customers who are either small- or medium-sized corporations or retail clients. Total cash in the hands of regional banks represents about 10% of the total held by financial institutions' in Japan. The number of regional banks was 64 as of February, 2004.
Second-tier regional bank	Second-tier regional banks number 50 in total. The difference between regional banks and second-tier regional banks is in their size. Their core functions and operations are the same.
Trust bank	A trust bank's main function is to offer financial management and trust service. Holding shares, land, or cash in trust for customers, a trust bank manages these asset items on their behalf. It focuses on long-term loans. As of February 2004 there were 8 trust banks.
Credit union	Not-for-profit financial institutions for small and medium sized enterprises, where the profits are re-invested for the benefit of the local region. Credit unions handle members' deposits, loans, discount of bills of exchange, and money transfers both inside and outside Japan. Members are residents, workers, and small and medium sized enterprises of the region. Loans are lent, in principle, to members but deposits may also be taken from non-members. As of February 9th, 2004 there were 307 credit unions in Japan.

Source: Financial Artist Academy. http://www.findai.com/cited by Globis Corporation (2003)

Typically, a war of attrition among banks offering similar products would have ensued, in which the survivors, if any, would have been those with sufficient size to endure the profit erosion for the longest.

In targeting retail lending to individual customers, Okano estimated that in the Tokyo metropolitan area, office workers working for companies listed in the stock market could not represent more than 12 per cent of the whole working population. The banks tended to focus on this 12 per cent, considered to be premium customers, to the exclusion of the remaining 88 per cent. Furthermore, out of that 12 per cent they restricted their attention to those who had many years' continuous service in the same company. In the light of growing professional mobility, such a restriction did not carry too much meaning.

He also thought that banks tended to push their standard range of products to customers instead of offering them '*a la carte*'; according to the selection customers wanted.

So it gradually dawned on Okano that the focus should be on the 88 per cent of the working population and on offering what customers might want to buy, not what banks wanted to sell.

He became aware that the industry's accepted wisdom was, more often than not, a mere fantasy created by and self-perpetuated among the industry 'specialists'. For example, it was accepted wisdom that customers preferred to be visited by bank officers to promote their business and collect deposits. In the bank's own survey of users of internet banking, it turned out that customers did not appreciate such visits, sometimes even considering them to be a nuisance.

Suruga Bank, therefore, targeted individual clients from whom other competitors shied away.[11] System engineers and professionals working for foreign multinationals are usually ignored by banks, on the grounds that they change jobs frequently and their incomes are, accordingly, unstable. The Government Housing Loan Corporation, for example, set a precedent by demanding that the loan applicant had to have been employed in the same place for at least two years.

Likewise, professional athletes were considered high risk. As such, unless they brought reliable guarantors, their request for mortgage loans was usually rejected by banks. Loans for the acquisition of flats for investment purposes were similarly rejected if solicited by ordinary 'salaried' office workers.[12] This client segment, however, enjoyed high levels of income and, due to rejection from other banks, tended to be agreeable to rather harsh loan conditions. These clients would agree to loans with high, variable interest rates, which would shield the bank from the exposure to interest rate risks, and avoid the battle over low interest rates. In 2003 Suruga Bank enjoyed a 1.59 per cent spread between lending and borrowing rates, as compared to the 0.78 per.cent average among local and regional banks.[13] (See Figure A2B.2 for the relative position of Suruga Bank.) In short, Suruga's success would not be wholly dependent on the sheer physical effort of its staff having to work long hours.

Some of the banking industry analysts were critical of Suruga Bank's strategy. They cautioned that clients rejected by other banks might have a high probability of defaulting on their loan payments. According to them,[14] seeking a high return in exchange for high risk might backfire. History seems to have contradicted the doomsayers, though; for in the financial year ending in March 2002, Suruga Bank's non-performing lending was ¥175 billion, out of which individuals' represented as low as ¥23 billion, or 1.8 per cent in contrast to the 20 per cent rate for lending to the corporate sector.[15]

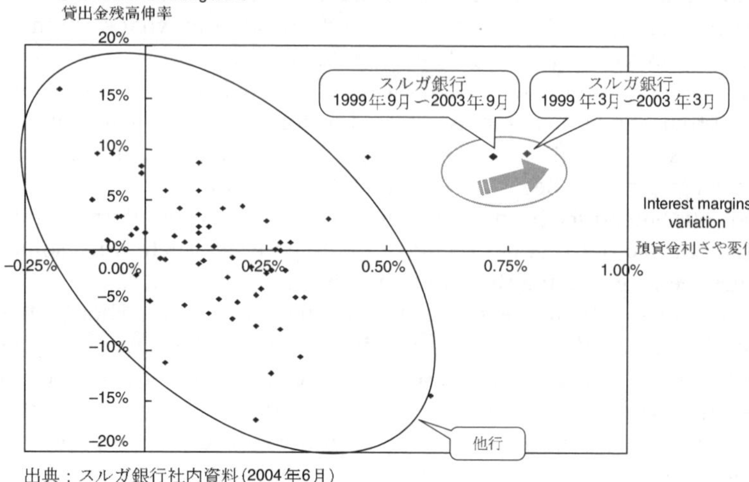

Figure A2B.2   Outstanding loan growth-interest margin matrix
Source: Suruga Bank Report (June, 2003).

In seeking clients, Suruga Bank contacted small- or medium-sized real-estate developers interested in finding a financial institution to provide loans to their clients. For the nature of their business, the time it took before a loan was granted was essential – clients visiting flats would usually make their purchase decision on the spur of the moment. With so much impulse-buying in this kind of business, the loan applications, if answered too late, would kill the developers' business chance. If Suruga Bank could provide a quick answer to loan applications, obviously these developers would then want to build up a mutually-beneficial and exclusive relationship with the bank. In return, the real-estate developers would see their clients provided with loans, facilitating the purchase decisions. Furthermore, as the business relationship continued and experience increased, the developers began to learn what kind of customers would typically be given loans by the bank. On the principle of give-and-take the developers would inform the bank before anybody else of their future housing projects. (See Table A2B.4 *New Mortgage Lending Per Year*.)

The usual arrangement in this regard was that banks would leave printed forms with real-estate developers, who would ask potential customers to provide them with necessary data such as marriage status,

Table A2B.4   New mortgage lending per year

		1993	1994	1995	1996	1997	1998	1999	2000	2001	2002
	Govt Housing	94,427	126,147	107,843	118,437	96,068	79,277	106,192	87,663	60,747	33,180
	Loan Corp City banks	40,341	48,274	90,018	70,650	69,965	69,518	66,695	64,479	70,268	74,290
Amount	Regional banks	22,470	26,130	54,304	37,399	36,455	36,186	36,583	39,306	50,353	55,922
	Second reg banks	10,655	12,740	24,120	17,269	16,292	15,190	14,955	15,257	18,067	17,134
	Credit unions	15,042	16,811	25,925	21,234	21,011	19,091	16,522	15,608	19,944	22,338

income and cash-flow streams. They then would fax the completed forms to Suruga Bank. A loan officer would enter the data and analyse the application. The decision on whether a loan might be granted or not would usually be given to the applicant within twenty-four hours. The only time the loan officer would see the applicant was when the customer came to Suruga Bank's office to sign the contract. In the case of other banks the response time tended to be significantly longer.

Another move, which may appear unorthodox for a regional bank headquartered outside Tokyo, was to focus its efforts on capturing clients in the Tokyo Metropolitan area.[16] Suruga opened branches for mortgage lending in places such as Tokyo's populous Shinjuku ward, the Nihonbashi business district, nearby Saitama City, and Chiba's Kashiwa City. Over 40 per cent of its mortgage loan specialists were based in the same area.

Suruga Bank adopted a flexible policy regarding the opening and closing of new branches in the metropolitan area. It would never try to get 100 per cent of the potential clients in a housing project. Once the clients with solvency were sought and netted from a project, the bank would rather close the office and would move onto another area or areas, shifting all the staff to the new branches.

This made good sense. In the banking industry, the growing trend was to view the location of access points (namely, branches and ATMs) as a product item itself, and a main one at that. Some banks such as Mitsubishi Tokyo FG entered into agreements with convenience stores in order to gain access points. The 'scrap-and-build' strategy was based on keeping branch locations 'fresh' and also on a high ROI (Return on Investment) from each branch, to shorten the payback from branches.[17] (See Appendix A2B.1 for more information on the current branch network and organisation chart.)

This moving-out of the community from where it was headquartered went counter to the accepted wisdom among regional banks. Their normal method was to prosper in close symbiosis with the local community. The FSA (Financial Services Agency) even defined the role of the regional banks as financiers of local economy, under the moniker of 'relationship banking'.[18]

In terms of product, too, Suruga Bank was unique. Indeed, some of its product innovations were mind-boggling. Take, for example, a mortgage where the loan amount was halved as a token of sympathy if the borrower was diagnosed as suffering from cancer; or a mortgage coupled with unemployment insurance that would pay the principal and interest for six months in case the borrower was unemployed.[19] Other unique products included mortgages for those suffering from liver problems, high blood pressure, and other ailments that normally disqualified a borrower from receiving the mandatory life insurance cover from life insurance companies. Time deposits linked to a lottery ticket was another product. In Japan, when a client opens an account, a small gift is given to customers. A young staff member suggested that, instead of a giveaway that people didn't really appreciate, a lottery ticket might be more attractive. It was a huge success. The product grew to be a ¥130 billion market, compared to the bank's initial target of ¥50 billion.

The focus on the aforementioned specific segment of individual clients was reflected in the lending breakdown in March, 2003: 63.9 per cent for individuals and 32 per cent for local SMEs (small and medium size enterprises) of Shizuoka Prefecture. (Suruga Bank's goal is to increase the proportion of individual customers to about 70 per cent).[20]

The focus on a particular segment of the market is unique in an environment like Japan's banking industry, in which everybody offers everything as a consequence of its strategic orientation. Following the strategy of another successful competitor is always the best way to minimise risk. The strategy initiator will have acquainted the market with the product or service. After the initial introductory stage, the success will depend more on operational effectiveness than strategic excellence. Long working hours and attention to minor details will become an important factor.

Customer relationship marketing and credit risk management (CRM)

The other successful factor in the focus on market segmentation is the handling of the data and information about clients. Despite Okano's initial frustration, the CRM system has since become one of the pillars on which Suruga Bank's success is based.

CRM was defined in two different but connected ways. Firstly, it was customer relationship marketing, since, to provide appropriate services, it was indispensable to know what, how and to whom services should be provided. Analysis of customer data was essential for this purpose.

The second definition was credit risk management. Banking was a business that inherently involved risks. Risk management by means of the assessment and scoring of customers was of vital importance. Loan applications must be handled in great volume and at a high speed.

As early as 1996, Okano started to consider the introduction of a CRM system. Newsletters published several articles on it. Training programmes were organised to familiarise the staff, including branch managers, with the system.[21] A video 'newsletter' was also used, in which Okano addressed himself to the staff emphasising the importance of the system. Model branches were chosen that excelled in the use of the CRM system. Okano visited them and personally interviewed the people in charge, which was included in subsequent video newsletters. This provided a great incentive for the active adoption of the system.

Okano was aware of the fact that system applications would affect and be influenced by the corporate culture, which meant that, for the implementation of the new system, the culture must be modified. Measures such as a performance-related salary system, and the use of a balanced score card for the evaluation of individual staff were adopted. Okano's conviction was that the CRM system would require a fair assessment of an individual's contribution, and that this should be reflected in their remuneration.[22]

The CRM system, by tracking each and every transaction and communication with clients, aims to precisely understand customer needs in order to increase their loyalty.[23]

Suruga Bank adopted CRM software developed by US-based EDS. The two entities jointly translated it into Japanese, which was customised later. The total implementation cost amounted to around ¥5 billion.[24] All the data on clients, which had been held on various media, were integrated into the data base in the CRM system, to which branches and departments had access through the so-called cell stations (PC terminals). Information on transactions, records on the use of call centres and ATMs, etc., could be viewed from these cell stations.[25]

The sales effort was also made easier, even for inexperienced part-time employees, since the system would provide them with such information as 'when and what kind of mail shots were made', 'if the mail shots were effective', etc.

The first milestone in adopting the CRM system was the introduction of MAP-C in April 1996. It helped classify the data by date and branch or business unit. Call Centre I was opened in July 1996 for telemarketing. Automatic loan assessment was put in place in November of the same year. MCIF (of which more later) was implemented in April 1997 for data mining, and Call Centre II was opened in October for telephone banking.

The last stage of CRM for the integration of channels and real-time management of data was reached in April 1999.

In addition to the foregoing, the advantages brought by an IT system including CRM were twofold – the lowering of client-relationship costs and the streamlining of the process, as well as the improvements in the service provided to clients.

First, let's look at how the bank achieved its low-cost positioning through the use of the CRM system. Even in the period between 1996 and 1999, at the initial stage of the CRM system implementation, Suruga Bank managed to increase lending to household clients by 11.8 per cent per year, double the average regional banks in the same period.[26]

Measured in terms of net operational profit per employee, Suruga Bank boasted ¥8.6 million in the April-September 1998 period, which far surpassed the comparable figures at Yokohama Bank and Shizuoka Bank by ¥4 million.[27] This productivity gain was attributed to the reduction of personnel during the same period and the implementation of IT systems. The closing down of branch offices, which would reduce the number from 139 in March 1996 to 121 in 1999, was compensated by the opening of ATMs and introduction of telephone banking services.

Suruga Bank focused therefore on the retail banking services, combined with the reduction of operational costs. Okano believed that money should be spent on systems to improve client services, instead of on the accounting systems. They therefore didn't invest in the accounting systems, running on an old mainframe (IBM 3090) – two generations too old – and written in Assembly language. This marked a difference with the city banks, which were investing tens of billions of yen in on-line accounting systems.[28] (For the conceptual representation of a CRM system, see Figure A2B.3.)

In relation to the second issue – easing the work process and improving client service – Suruga Bank set great store by MCIF (Marketing Customer Information File), considering database marketing as a key success factor in retail banking.

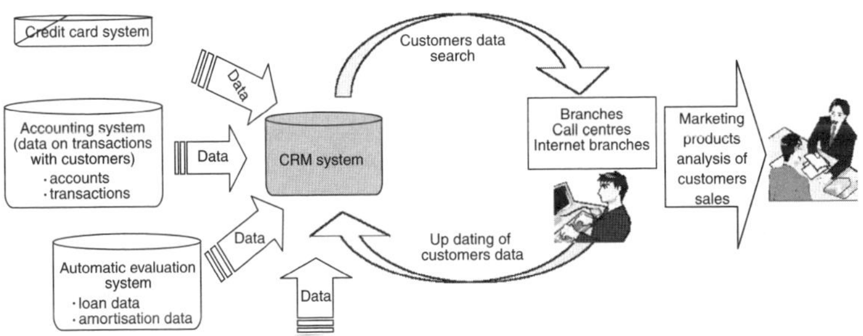

Figure A2B.3   Conceptual representation of CRM system

Source: Organised by Case writer, based on Nikkei Joho Strategy,1999(Hanazawa, 1999).

MCIF consists of approximately 2000 items on each client (including the client's characteristics, deposits, loans taken, past transactions, etc.). A project team spent half a year on the preparation, collecting data on 1.8 million clients. Retail marketing specialists were headhunted, and test runs were made in 1996, until MCIF was commissioned in April 1997.

To improve client information handling, the bank issued a new bank credit card through JCB – Japan Credit Bureau – in January 1998. It allowed Suruga Bank to access the database on card users managed by the association of card issuers. Applications for cards would provide detailed information on the applicants.

In the retail banking business Suruga Bank centred its attention on small lending through these bank cards, and so MCIF was a very useful tool for it. The data recorded on MCIF were analysed, using data-mining tools, to find common historical patterns among card users having been granted small loans. The patterns discovered would then be applied to other card-holders, who would then be classified into several segments. The one with the highest probability of using these card loans were then contacted, typically by direct mail shot, and this started to register high hit rates. In the fiscal year 1997 the Direct Mailing, or DM, hit rate averaged 1.4 per cent, but in the following year one DM campaign launched in November reached 3.8 per cent, doubling the previous record.[29]

However, card loan users might be potentially higher-risk clients because of their relatively young ages. Reliable risk assessment was a must to avoid loan defaults. Suruga Bank sieved 110,000 previous loan users with data mining tools in search of the characteristics that might highlight clients with a propensity to default.

An automatic credit assessment system resulted from this analysis.[30] It was put into service in November 1996. On the basis of the data on 25 items it would estimate the credit-worthiness of clients. Default rates dropped from 1–2 per cent to less than 0.1 per cent.

The benefit of the assessment system was not limited to default prevention. The increased speed of loan assessments was another advantage the system offered. If the loan amount was below ¥3 million, loan officers could answer yes or no in half an hour, even for first-time applicants.[31]

Culture reorientation and organisational change

Okano devolved the decision-making to lower management levels.[32] Contrary to a well-known saying in Japan ('the nail that sticks out gets hammered down'), he created an atmosphere of outspokenness by encouraging his staff to become just such a 'nail'. Young staff members were encouraged to challenge the accepted way of doing business. Okano stressed that his role was to offer the framework, while staff members were expected to actually try to change the organisation.

The Junior Boards were an example of Okano's effort to change the atmosphere. Each one of them comprised four to five young bankers (young in this case means below thirty-five years old). Three or four of these boards spent a year preparing a reform plan on new products and services, and presented their ideas to the Board of Directors.[33]

The Junior Boards are nowadays considered to be a spring-board for future promotion. Staff members who stand out with ground-breaking new ideas are marked out for a fast career track. Okano estimated that it took five years for the boards to get firmly established. Three quarters of the bank's total executives ('shikko yakuin') have been members of a junior board in the past.

Okano also lifted a tacit ban existing among banks regarding external hiring. He was convinced that, for a business such as banking, human resources were decisive elements for success. If the bank lacked people with certain skills, those with them should be brought in from outside. Not only would they bring these skills, but they would also bring new ways of thinking. The bank's staff was not allowed to teach the new employees the existing way of doing business. Okano's reasoning was that, on the contrary, existing staff should learn from the new employees.

The number of mid-career entrants in 2004 is estimated to be around an eighth of the total staff number (approximately 200 out of a total 1600).

Consultancy firms were frequently used to enhance the awareness of the staff that their way of doing business might be different from what customers really wanted. For example, in 1987 and 1988 a survey of customer satisfaction (CS) was performed. The result brought a shocking insight and since then a similar survey has been conducted every two or three years. A 'mystery shoppers' technique (in which anonymous surveyors paid a visit to branches and compared their level of service with that of other banks) was also used to periodically conduct a SWOT analysis of the bank. CS specialists of the bank also organised special sessions in which roles of customers and bank officers were played and video-taped for later analysis among the attendees. In Okano's opinion, such exercises efforts should be periodically repeated, otherwise the resulting awareness decreases with time.

Suruga Bank today

After a year of losses in 2001, Suruga Bank's performance picked up in 2002, mainly thanks to the strategy focus. Losses from marketable securities and non-performing debts were brought under control. Suruga Bank's mortgage loans increased to ¥2,995 trillion, representing 63.9 per cent at the end of FY 2002. The total interest spread stood at 0.72 per cent, a 22bp (base point) improvement from the previous year. The increase in mortgages contributed to a 1.5 per cent growth in the total loan amount. Overall, therefore, the new business model created by Okano started to provide competitive edge.[34] (See Annex 2 comparing the balance sheets and profit and loss accounts among Suruga, Yokohama, and Shizuoka Banks.)

At the end of September 2003 Suruga Bank's capital adequacy and Tier I ratios were 8.32 and 7.70 respectively. The corresponding ratios at Yokohama Bank were 10.32 and 7.00, whereas at Shizuoka Bank they stood at 12.42 and 11.01. When the ratio of impaired loans ('furyo saiken ritsu') was contemplated in the same period the contrast among Suruga, Yokohama, and Shizuoka became even clearer. Suruga stood at 7.85, three points higher than Yokohama Bank (4.59) and two points higher than Shizuoka (5.57).

The relative weaknesses of Suruga Bank in the balance sheet were compensated for, however, by its profit-generating capacity symbolised by its low ratio of expenses to gross profit, or overheads ratio (OHR – Keihi ritsu) standing at 55.59 per cent, compared with Shizuoka's 65.09 per cent. Yokohama stood out in this as well, with 41.76 per cent. Regarding the spread between interests received and paid on the total assets (so shikin rizaya) Suruga Bank boasted 0.75 as of September 2003 in contrast with Shizuoka's 0.33 (although Yokohama's was the best of the three with 0.87). The domestic loan-deposit margin grew from 1.05 per cent in September 2000 to 1.72 per cent in September 2003. The expense ratio, on the contrary, contracted from 1.55 per cent to 1.34 per cent in the same period.

In an interview with a financial newspaper in June 2003, Okano made it public that the Bank's target in the following three years would be to increase lending to individuals to 70 per cent, to triple consumer loans to ¥500 billion, and to improve its ROE from the current 6.4 per cent to 10 per cent.[35]

For the use of excess liquidity, treasury stocks or increased dividend payments would not be excluded. For Okano, however, this was not the priority concern. He expressed in the same interview his desire to concentrate on the minimisation of underperforming credits in the next two years before taking any decision in this regard.

Due to the increase in the proportion of individual lending and internet banking, Okano conjectured that regional placement would become less and less important. The bank's way of doing business would clearly deviate from the Financial Services Agency's 'Relationship Banking' based on symbiosis with the local or regional community. Okano was quoted as saying: 'In former times it was important to become a dominant player in your region; however, that became less important thanks to the appearance of Internet banking. The 'operational area' concept carries less weight nowadays than it did before. The administrative division into prefectures is meaningless except for administering government services. You operate where your clients are, not where your headquarters physically are.'[36]

From here to eternity

Lending to corporate clients surfaced as a problem on the occasion of the Ministry of Finance's inspection in 2002, which was conducted on regional banks in the light of the introduction of the 'pay-off' measurement (namely, deposit insurance coverage of up to ¥10 million in the case of a financial institution's failure) to be implemented in April 2002. Its default rate was estimated at 8.53 per cent at the end of March 2003. It seems to be under control for the time being, though. Some financial reports argued the possibility that corporate lending might deteriorate on the suspicion that the rate of impaired loans was still high at 18.6 per cent, which could be twice as high if loans of dubious quality were included.[37] In any event, Okano will have to find a solution to this.

Another issue that Okano must keep a close eye on is mortgage loans to individuals. Obviously the bank struck gold in them, and they are still contributing substantial profits to the bank, but any significant change in interest, continued economic depression, or any other environment change that may affect borrowers' income streams might negatively influence the solvency of the bank's loan assets. As a trend of insolvency, problems may surface eight to twelve years after mortgages are granted. Payment delays or default rate was estimated at 0.15 to 0.35 per cent in 2003, which was still at an acceptable level in view of Suruga Bank's charging about 1 per cent more to its clients.[38]

The growth of lending to individual customers has not yet peaked. The individual consumer market in Japan in 2003 was reckoned to be worth approximately ¥13 trillion, of which half may correspond to borrowers whose solvency deserves credit-worthiness. On the other hand, the overall mortgage loan market for individual borrowers in

Japan was ¥141 trillion in 1993, which grew to ¥183 trillion in 2003. Public-sector lenders, including the Government Housing Loan Corporation, had ¥61 trillion worth of outstanding loans in 1993 and ¥69.6 trillion in 2002. Regional banks' outstanding loans in this concept amounted to ¥14 trillion in 1993 and ¥26.5 trillion in 2003.

The downside of mortgage loans is that land price continues to fall, which makes evaluation difficult. The upside is that the demographic movement is heading towards the metropolitan areas; even the retirees tend to come back to this area. All these elements are positive factors, and help to push up the demand for housing.

In addition, another of Okano's concerns will be the training of future executives who can succeed him and his management team.

Once the dust settled after the Porter Prize excitement, Okano started to consider what new direction the bank should head in. At 59, he was still considered young in the Japanese gerontocracy (a society ruled by elders). He was not concerned about who should succeed him – time would tell. The dynamism he had created in the bank would lend itself to finding an appropriate successor.

His vision of the future of his bank points to converting Suruga Bank into an entity not narrowly defined as a bank but more broadly as a financial services provider, able to furnish customers with more 'concierge functions'. By this he means an entity that helps its customers to deal with the landmark events in their life, such as buying a house, planning for retirement, etc. Okano equates these 'concierge functions' with 'helping to make dreams come true' and to 'put a date to those dreams'.

The target segment will be the new affluent class, which has emerged as a consequence of the bipolarisation of the traditional middle class, characterised by having a small fortune, being highly educated, and anxious about their assets.

Appendix A2B.1

Appendix A2B.1   Branch offices and organisation chart

Branch offices	Shizuoka Prefecture	78
	Kanagawa Prefecture	37
	Tokyo	2
	Chiba Prefecture	1
	Saitama Prefecture	1
	Aichi Prefecture	1
	Total	120

Source: Suruga Bank Annual Report 2003.

Appendix A2B.2

Appendix A2B.2   Suruga's chart

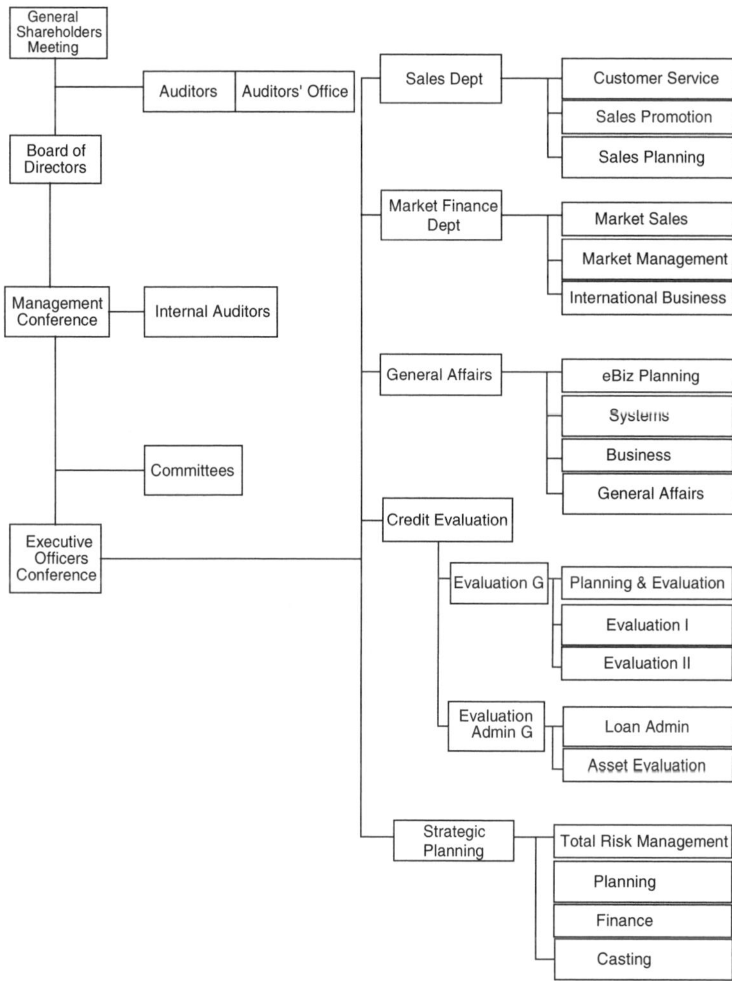

Source: Suruga Bank (as of April 2003).

Appendix A2B.3

Appendix A2B.3   Suruga, Yokohama, Shizuoka Bank, and Bank of Tokyo-Mitsubishi compared (FY 2002)

Balance Sheet	(In millions of yen)			
	Yokohama Bank	Shizuoka Bank	Suruga Bank	Bank of Tokyo Mitsubishi
Liabilities				
Deposits	9,364,106	6,881,028	2,672,629	52,095,330
Certificates of deposit	69,488	227,990	–	2,625,077
Securities	–	–	–	636,060
Call money	276	85,032	–	3,013,869
Sales 'gensaki'	–	–	–	2,828,308
Collateral for debt-credit transaction	–	32,095	–	1,996,214
Commercial papers	–	–	–	312,208
Liabilities for special transactions	4,167	3,895	–	1,455,493
Borrowed money	221,987	29,436	10,858	1,303,831
Foreign currencies	151	212	7	512,676
Short-term bonds	–	–	–	10,000
Bonds	45,999	182,120	–	3,188,379
Bonds with subscription warrant	60,000	–	–	50,528
Trust accounts	–	–	–	–
Other liabilities	113,721	91,281	16,622	2,166,328
Reserve for employees' bonus	–	–	619	12,531
Accrued severance costs	68	28,023	227	26,429
Other provisions	1,815	–	220	31
Provisions for special laws	0	1	0	799
Deferred tax	–	56	–	61,037
Deferred tax due to revaluation	22,536	–	–	133,453
Adjustment for consolidation	1,450	–	–	–
Agreed payments	303,666	119,962	11,370	4,518,715
Liabilities total	10,209,435	7,681,136	2,712,554	76,947,306
(Minority)				
Minority interests	6,135	8,750	387	330,812

Source: The Japanese Bankers Association.

Annex 3 – Banco Sabadell's Business Model

Santander and BBVA are the most eloquent examples of the 'Profit Arithmetic' (PA) approach in the Spanish retail banking industry. However, an analysis of Banco Sabadell as another national reference is also of interest in studying the emergence of Spanish banks in the competitive international banking arena. The case of Banco Sabadell serves as a case of 'triangulation' – that is, the application and combination of several research methodologies in the study of the same phenomenon – of why BBVA's and Santander's business models, explained in Chapter 3 as a construct or ideal type,[1 and 2] can be the source of competitive edge.

The first part of this annex reviews the restructuring and emergence of the Spanish banking industry as a world-class competitor, as well as the evolution of the European banking system. In the second part, the analysis of Banco Sabadell's CEO Josep Oliu illustrates how the bank grew on the crest of the second wave of mergers and acquisitions in Spain. Indeed, Santander and Royal Bank of Scotland's counterattack to Barclays' attempt to acquire ABN AMRO in April 2007 re-launched the debate in Europe on a massive concentration movement in the banking system, a system in which Spanish banks have facilities to operate thanks to their position concerning Basel II (L'Expansion, April 2007).

Organisational chart

Banco Sabadell's organisational chart, as shown below in Table A3.1, has several characteristics that can help us to understand the bank's strategic approach.

Firstly, it has a double-tier structure with the executive and management committees. It is probable that strategically-important decisions may collectively be taken by the Chairman/CEO, the managing director, the executive director, and the comptroller general. If so, it shows a clear variation from the CEO-COO tandem scheme at Santander and BBVA.

The management committee comprises thirteen executives from business areas and group or corporate services units. These latter units are Finance, Corporate Development, Organisation and Resources, Risk and Technology and Operations.

Table A3.1   Organisation chart

Executive Committee	
Chairman and CEO	José Oliu Creus*
Managing Director	Juan M. Nin Genova*
Executive Director	José Permanyer Cunillera
Comptroller General	José Luis Negro Rodríguez*
Specific Business Areas	
Commercial Banking	Jaume Puig Balsells*
Corporate Banking	Juan Antonio Alcaraz García*
Bancassurance	Ignacio Camí Casellas*
Treasury and Capital Markets	Rafael García Nauffal*
Asset Management	Cirus Andreu Cabot*
Marketing	Ramón Domènech Ibáñez
Regional and Brand Management	
Commercial Banking	
Barcelona	Antonio Sabaté Boza
Madrid and Canary Islands	Javier Vela Hernández
Northern Region	José A. Enjuanes Turmo
Levante and Balearic Islands	Jaime Matas Vallverdú
Andalusia	Juan Krauel Alonso
Catalonia	José Canalias Puig
Banco Herrero	Carlos J. Serrano Guerra
Solbank	Aleix Masachs Fatjó
ActivoBank	Cristina Moraes Sunyer
Corporate Banking	
Catalonia	Luis Buil Vall
Madrid	Blanca Montero Corominas
Levante	Cristóbal Peña López
Castilla and Galicia	Luis A. Requejo Bayón
Asturias and León	Herminio Huerta Cárcaba
Group Services	
Financial	Tomás Varela Muiña*
Corporate Development	Joan M. Grumé Sierra*
Organization and Resources	Juan-Cruz Alcalde Merino*
Risk	José Tarrés Busquets*
Technology and Operations	Miquel Montes Güell*
Audit	Nuria Lázaro Rubio
Communications	Joan Saborido Camps
Legal Department	María José García Beato
Quality, Compliance and CSR	Gonzalo Barettino Coloma

Note: * Member of the Management Committee.

Source: Banco Sabadell website (https://www.bancsabadell.com/en).

Second, IT does not seem to report directly to the corporate head. Its participation in general management issues seems indirect through the management committee (which, with so many committee members – thirteen – could sometimes be non-operational for quick decisions). Its position, as depicted in BBVA's website, is far removed from the top echelons. It may work with the Chairman and CEO and the executive committee, but this is not apparent from the information on the website.

Theory of the business

Oliu (2006), Banco Sabadell's Chairman and CEO, cites the severe deterioration of the traditional income sources as the motivation for Spanish banks to change and improve their business models. Pressures on interest rates, stiffer competition, sophistication of financial technology, and the change in the regulatory environment are the causes of such deterioration. Banco de España (2005: 12), Spain's central bank, reports that lending margins continue to narrow. Likewise, citing the central bank, Oliu (2006: 3) reports that between 1989 and 2004 the margin for intermediation on the average total assets ('ATM', *activo total medio*) shrank by 57 per cent in line with the 38 per cent fall in operational margin on ATM in the same period.

Readers interested in knowing whether Banco Sabadell's business model follows the dictates of the PA approach or not are referred to Annex 1 in which comparison is made with other Spanish banks as well as with the three large Japanese banks which hail from a business environment very different from Spain's.

Business model predicated on the two-tier structural changes

The basic tenet expounded here is that Banco Sabadell essentially follows the *generic* business model of successful Spanish retail banks, although with some variations. The nature of the CEO and management team, the priority given to IT systems, and the prioritisation of operational efficiency are the basic features that coincide with the model explained in Chapter 3.

For the Chairman and CEO of Banco Sabadell, there ought to be two levels of major structural changes to cope with income deterioration. In the first place, the adaptation of operational strategies bringing in new income sources, improving operational efficiency, and actively managing the capital equity structure.

In the second place, if the first level of changes prove insufficient, the 'consolidation process' must be attempted, based on mergers and acquisitions.

Operational strategy change

New sources of income include (1) business with SMEs (small and medium sized enterprises), (2) management of assets which led to a 225 per cent growth in investment funds managed by the bank between 1994 and 2004, as the funds grew from €68 billion to €220 billion according to INVERCO (la Asociación de Instituciones de Inversión Colectiva y Fondos de Pensiones) cited by Oliu (2006: 7), (3) *bancassurance* business , namely, the selling of insurance through the bank's distribution network so that it 'can offer banking, insurance, lending, and investment products to a customer'[3] at a single point of sale, and (4) service commissions.

Improvement of operational efficiency

The improvement measures split into commercial invigoration ('dinaminización') and the management of costs (Oliu, 2006: 8).

The first branch, the commercial invigoration, comprises (1) productivity increase, (2) focus on customer loyalty, and (3) specialised networks – *'redes especializadas'*.

The second branch relating to cost management implies (1) structural adjustments, (2) outsourcing of services, and (3) continual improvement of operational models. Citing Bankscope Database, Banco de España, and Roland Berger analysis, Oliu (2006: 8) compares the efficiency ratios among several European countries as shown in Table A3.2.

From this Table we see two distinct groups of countries; those that improved the ratio – France, Italy, and Spain – and those that saw their ratios deteriorate – Germany and the UK. Our working hypothesis

Table A3.2   Comparison of efficiency ratios

	1996(%)	2003(%)
Germany	65	71
France	73	67
Italy	76	67
Spain	61	54
UK	58	60

Source: Oliu (2006).

(which ought to be tested in another study, since it is beyond the scope of this book) is (1) that there can be similar business models within the two groups, (2) that the business models used by two groups are different, and (3) that in the case of France, Italy, and Spain, the use of IT systems and operational efficiency are prioritised and work in a systemic way, although with a note of caution about the French, and perhaps also Italian, systems regarding how up-to-date they may actually be.

The improvement in the three countries was remarkable. France improved six points, similar to Spain's seven points, whereas Italy improved by nine.

Our working hypothesis (which ought to be tested in another study, since it is beyond the scope of this book) is that the banking system exists as national or regional clusters. Inside this cluster, the information is processed on a constant basis and, in the case of the Spanish banks, it has enabled the main banks to improve their efficiencies ratios thanks to constant benchmarking of their practices.

Capital equity structure

Basel II is a treaty representing recommendations by bank supervisors and central bankers from the thirteen countries forming the Basel Committee on Banking Supervision ('the Committee'). This committee issues international standards for the measurement of the adequacy of a bank's capital.

The Committee (2004) issued Basel II in June 2004 with a minor revision in November 2005, followed by a Comprehensive version in June 2006 (The Basel Committee on Banking Supervision, 2004). The treaty aims to:

1. Ensure that capital allocation is more risk sensitive;
2. Separate operational risk from credit risk, and to qualify both;
3. Attempt to align economic and regulatory capital more closely, to reduce the scope for regulatory arbitrage.

To promote greater stability in the financial system, Basel II is founded on three pillars – (1) minimum capital requirements, (2) supervisory review, and (3) market discipline.

The first pillar provides a framework for risk sensitivity. It will have a larger impact on bank management than other two pillars (Picoult, 2006: 3). Its requirements are calculated for three major components of risk:[4] credit risk, operational risk and market risk. These risk components comprise concepts such as VaR (value at risk),[5] EL (loss function)[6] whose constituent elements are PD (probability of default), LGD (loss given default), and EAD (exposure at default).

Mainly on account of the first pillar, namely, the minimum capital requirements, Oliu (2006) predicts that there will be winners and losers in the banking industry in adapting Basel II.

Consolidation process

Oliu (2006: 10) opines that, at the level of domestic markets, the consolidation process is already under way. In France, BNP acquired Paribas, and Credit Lyonnais was absorbed by Credit Agricole. In the UK Royal Bank of Scotland took over NatWest and merged with Halifax. Lloyds TSB acquired Scottish Widows. Barclays carried out the purchase of Woolwich. In Germany Allianz acquired Dresdner Bank, while DZ Bank took on the management of Norisbank. In a similar vein BBV merged with Argentaria, and Banco Santander with BCH, becoming ultimately Santander. Banco Sabadell followed suit by acquiring Banco Atlántico.

However, in the Pan-European landscape the panorama differs. The consolidation process across borders is just beginning (Oliu, 2006). A few examples include the acquisition of Spain's Banco Zaragozano by UK's Barclays, Finland's Merita Bank merging with Sweden's Nordbanken, the acquisition of Portugal's BNC with Spain's Banco Popular, and the acquisition of Abbey National by Santander.

Nonetheless, Beaujean et al. (2005) points out that the value created by domestic consolidation strategies is no longer available. Härle (2005) substantiates this statement by affirming that large-scale domestic consolidation remains a possibility only in Germany and Italy, whereas the markets in Belgium, France or the Netherlands as well as the UK offer a high penetration of bank branches, whereby the banks in these countries will have to look beyond their borders to expand.

Obstacles to Europe-wide consolidation are barriers to transactions, namely, discrimination between domestic acquirers and acquirers from other EU member countries, and efficiency barriers that impede the harmonisation of retail products and services across borders (Härle, 2005).

Be that as it may, Oliu (2006) enumerates national champions or the entities that can become Pan-European entities. In Spain where there are 347 financial entities, Santander, BBVA, and La Caixa, a savings bank, may herald the Europe-wide consolidation. HSBC, Royal Bank of Scotland, and Barclays may trigger such consolidation from the UK (420 banking entities). France (933) counts on BNP Paribas, Credit Agricole, and Societé Generale. Italy (830) offers Intese BCI, Unicredito Italiano, and San Pedro IMI. The Netherlands' (483) ING, ABN Amro, and Rabobank may vie with these banks for European banking hegemony along with Germany's (2,222) Deutsche Bank, HVB, and Dresdner Bank and Belgium's (108) Fortis, Dexia and KBC Bank.

Oliu (2006: 12) is optimistic about the banks' Europe-wide consolidation process and alleges that the new rules of the game work in its favour. For him, firstly, the trend in the homogenisation of international accounting principles will enhance the transparency of accounting information and will enable better comparison of financial data among countries. Secondly, Basel II regulations aim at spreading risk by means of diversified investment portfolios among different countries. Thirdly, and most importantly, the existence of the difference in efficiency ratios estimated at 6 to 15 points among European banks, explained by the difference in the use of IT, alone can justify the process of consolidation.

Banco Sabadell's formal strategy

Oliu (2006: 14) sets great store by the growth process. The bank's CAGR (compounded annual growth rate) between 1995 and 2005 was 22 per cent, a consequence of the combination of organic expansion with the acquisitions of Banco Herrero in 2000 and Banco Atlántico in 2003.

Sabadell's recent growth history is shown in Table A3.3.

The bank's formal strategy consists of three-year framework plans (*planes directores trienales*). The period between 2002 and 2004 was aimed at growth and consolidation; specifically, the organic growth supplemented by the consolidation of Banco de Asturias, Banco Herrero and ActivoBank, as well as by the acquisition of Banco Atlántico (Oliu, 2006: 15).

The period 2005 to 2007 corresponds to ViC 07 which stands for value and growth (*valor y crecimiento*) on the basis of organic growth and the consolidation of Banco Atlántico acquisition (Oliu, 2006).

In terms of figures, the first three-year plan achieved an 87 per cent growth in loans, a 72 per cent growth in assets managed, a 51 per cent growth in net profit, a 27 per cent growth in equity, and a 73 per cent growth in market capitalisation (Oliu, 2006).

ViC 07, the second three-year plan, aims at a 42 per cent growth in loans, a 34 per cent growth in deposits, and a 34 per cent growth in off-balance resources as well as 45 per cent efficiency ratio and 16.5 per cent ROE (return on equity) (Oliu, 2006).

Table A3.3   Banco Sabadell's recent growth history

- 1975: Sabadell expanded beyond Catalonia by opening a branch in Madrid.
- 1978: Sabadell opened its first foreign branch, in London.
- 1988: Sabadell Group was formed.
- 1994: Banco del Bajío was established in León, Guanajuato, Mexico, and now is allied with Sabadell.
- 1995: Sabadell opened a representative office in Havana and a 50–50 joint venture – Financiera Iberoamericana – with Cuba's Grupo Nueva Banca.
- 1996: Sabadell acquired National Westminster Bank's operations in Spain and renamed them Solbank. Sabadell acquired Banco de Asturias.
- 1999: The Andorran government authorized the establishment of BancSabadell Andorra. It began operating in 2000.
- 2000: Sabadell established an alliance with Banco Comercial Portugués (BCP). BCP acquired 8.5% of Sabadell. Sabadell also entered into another alliance with La Caixa. La Caixa exchanged its shares in Banco Herrero for a 15% stake in Sabadell, making La Caixa Sabadell's largest shareholder and giving Sabadell 99% of Herrero. (Banco Herrero,founded in 1911 in Oviedo, had acquired Banca Masaveu in 1984 from the failed Rumasa group, which had acquired Masveu in 1982. Masavaeu, also based in Oviedo, was about 140 years old at the time.)
- 2003: Sabadell merged Banco Asturias into Banco Herrero. Sabadell acquired Banco Atlántico from Arab Banking Corporation. Sabadell also sold its Geneva subsidiary, BanSabadell Finance to EFG Private Bank, part of the EFG Banking Group, the 5th largest in Switzerland in terms of capitalization.
- 2004: The Banco Sabadell Group adopted SabadellAtlántico as the new brand name of the commercial bank for the whole of Spain.

Source: Banco Sabadell (http://www.bancsabadell.com/en/XTD/INDEX/?url=/en/GRUPO/HISTORIA).

Conclusion

The use of the 'triangulation' methodology provides some highlights concerning the past, present and future evolution of the Spanish and European banking systems.

Firstly, the analysis of Josep Oliu's speeches confirms their preference for inorganic growth in the Spanish banking industry and a continuous improvement in productivity, both of which go hand in hand. The combination of both factors, especially productivity, in an uncertain environment presages the emergence of PA-type leaders.

With the emergence of PA bank leaders, the positioning of Spanish retail banks has constantly improved in the last 20 years. For this reason it is worth studying the Spanish banking system in relation to its workings, strategic approaches, leadership figures, business environment, historical background, and so on, in search of the replicable and non-replicable components as compared with the radical restructuring in the banking industry that will be ushered in shortly as a consequence of the wave of mergers and acquisitions which has only just begun in Europe in particular and in the world in general.

The incipient internationalisation of Banco Sabadell, as well as the first wave of internationalisation undertaken by the two main Spanish banks, show that size may not be the only factor favouring expansion abroad. The presence of a distinctive business model, the ability to replicate one's business model in other markets, and superior IT systems are by far the most important elements for Spanish banks.

Annex 4 – Research Methodology

This book represents the culmination of a research process that started in the second half of 2005. It has its roots in the research of four in-depth case studies of outstanding Japanese transformational CEOs conducted between 2001 and 2003, later compiled as Kase, Sáez-Martínez, and Riquelme (2005). The cognitive approaches identified in that work form the basis of this book.

Defining the problem

In view of the varying performances, to say the least, of Spanish and Japanese banks, we began searching for an explanation. While the former have gone from strength to strength over the last ten to fifteen years, the latter have fallen from occupying eminent positions in the international marketplace, to modest positions constrained by the boundaries of their domestic market.

There could be reasons attributable variously to macroeconomics, the business environment, and organisational causes. However, founded on past behaviour patterns of Spanish and Japanese enterprises, we conjectured that an analysis of the strategic approach towards time-frame (short-term versus long-term), and the choice between an operational and strategic bent could shed some light.

The research: A three-stage process

With the above in mind, we conducted (1) four exploratory interviews with industry experts, in addition to four conversations with our academic colleagues at IESE Business School (one of whom was a Director General of one of the constituent banks that was integrated into the current BBVA) and bank experts, and (2) a documentary survey. Thus, we established the theory that the excellent performance of (some of) the Spanish retail banks springs from internal (the existence of clear-sighted and clear-minded CEOs and their teams) as well as external circumstances. For the former we presumed the existence of a specific cognitive process, which we define as Profit-Arithmetic approach. (See Figure A4.1 for the research process.)

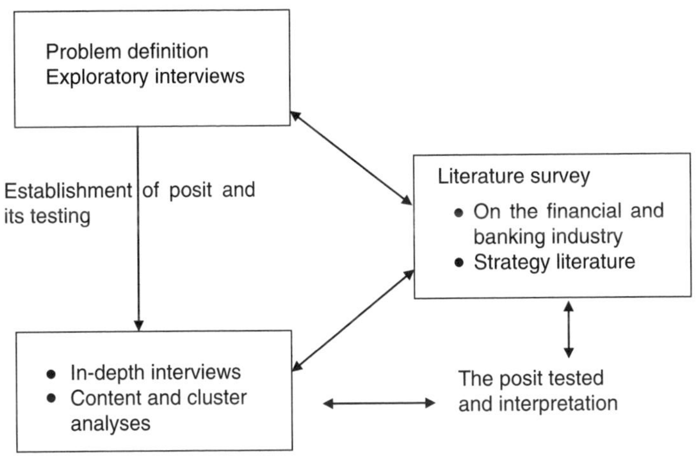

Figure A4.1 Research process

Once this theory was postulated, we next reviewed the existing literature in the fields of banking and strategy. Citations are mentioned at the end of each chapter.

Parallel to the literature survey which was ongoing throughout the duration of the research, we conducted the third and main stage of research: seven in-depth interviews with executives of Level 1 (CEOs and COOs of banks or financial institutions) and ten with those of Level 2 (directors or top executives working directly with the Level 1 executives). The interviews with Level 1 executives include the CEOs and the COOs of the leading Spanish banks.

The interview survey was conducted between December 2005 and May 2007, and the average duration of the interviews was 74.0 minutes, ranging from 45 to 310, with the median being 60 minutes.

We used an open-ended questionnaire, including questions such as 'do you think the Spanish banks have done well?', 'why do you think so?', 'in what field?', 'what explains the success?', 'why do you think the successful reasons adduced by you were not repeated in other institutions?' and so on.

In each case, we followed the *24 hour principle*; committing to writing the information and data we got within 24 hours of the interviews (Eisenhardt, 1989a, 1989b).

For further validation of the theoretical framework developed on the basis of the qualitative and subjective assessment of the findings, the content and cluster analyses of CEOs speeches published in the 2004–2006 annual reports of Santander, BBVA, and Banco Sabadell were carried out using the applications Leximancer Version 2.21 and SPSS Version 14, and was contrasted with the results obtained from the same analyses conducted on the speeches of the same period by the CEOs of Japanese banks (Mizuho, Sumitomo Mitsui, and Resona). The speeches of the Bank of Tokyo Mitsubishi UFJ were not taken into account because of the merger process having not yet been completed during the cited period.

A confirmatory mail survey was first considered but not implemented (1) because of the very low response rate we have had in our previous research on Spanish CEOs and their cognitive approach (the response rate was less than 1 per cent of 40-strong samples, despite the fact that our questionnaire was accompanied by personal calls to these CEOs), and (2) on account of the 'theory-building' and exploratory nature of this study.

To conclude, we should mention our confidentiality agreement with the interviewees, preventing us from disclosing their names, positions, and affiliations in detail.

Notes

1 Introduction and Overview of Book

1. Sources: International Monetary Fund, World Economic Outlook Database, September 2006. Data for the year 2005.
2. For the definition of 'value creation', see Chapter 3.
3. According to CECA (Spanish Confederation of savings banks: http://www.ceca.es/CECA-CORPORATIVO/en/caja_a.html), Spanish savings banks are characterised by

    (1) Regional identification
    - The Savings Banks were born with a clear regional vocation with the objective of attending to the needs of the families and businesses within their territories.
    - Today, the Spanish Savings Banks provide their services to 96.3% of the population with branches in their own towns and the other 3.7% in an itinerant manner.
    - At the present there are forty-six Savings Banks in Spain covering the entire national territory.

    (2) Management model
    - Differing from other credit entities, the Saving Banks combine their financial function with intense social activity. Both functions – financial and social – are inseparable parts on the same management model.
    - Thanks to their modern and efficient management, the Saving Banks have healthy profit and loss accounts that allow them to channel the financing of their numerous social projects, and

    (3) Mission
    The Saving Banks have been and continue to be Financial Institutions, with strong local roots, whose mission is extending financial service to large sectors of the population and distributing the profits obtained in the way of welfare work, with the purpose of contributing to the welfare and development of the society as a whole.

4. 'Interest spread is the difference between the average lending rate and the average borrowing rate for a bank or other financial institution.' (http://money terms.co.uk/interest-spread/).

2 The Great Leap of Spanish Banks, 1987–2005: A Profit–Arithmetic (PA) Approach

1. The information for this section was mainly drawn from (Canals, 1990, 1996; Caruana, 2004; Dermine, 1999; European Commission, 2004; Gómez Escorial, 2004; Lamfalussy, 2001; Lucas, 2006; Lucas & Palacios, 2006;

Palacios, 2004; Palacios, 2007; Palacios & Alvarez, 2003; Termes, 1991b, 1991a, 1995; Uriarte, 1994; Walter, 2004).

2. Acknowledgement must be expressed to Dr Juan Antonio Palacios who generously contributed to the drawing up of this chapter. Any value judgement is ours.

3. For many years it was common to refer to the banks that dominated the industry as the 'big seven'. In order of size (with minor changes over time) they were: Banesto, Central, Hispano, Bilbao, Vizcaya, Santander, and Popular.

4. There used to be six official institutions, but today only one, the ICO, has survived with very minimal activity.

5. For a more detailed description of the changes in the Spanish banking system between 1982 and 1995, see Termes (1995).

6. Ley de Bases de Ordenación del Crédito y de la Banca ('Law on Credit and Banking Arangements').

7. This rate, called tipo anual equivalente (TAE), is a standard procedure to calculate the internal rate of return of any credit or deposit, taking account of all commission applied.

8. The London reforms were widely known as the 'Big Bang'.

9. This Commission has a similar role to that of the SEC (Securities and Exchange Commission) in United States or the FSA (Financial Services Authority) in the United Kingdom.

10. A more complete description of the emergence of these markets can be found in Palacios [1995].

11. The monetary authorities would intervene, for example, in the determination of interest rates adjusting them in such a way that the weakest banks are guaranteed profitability. Administrative guidance (gyosei shido) was and is frequently applied. (See http://ja.wikipedia.org/wiki/護送船団).

12. Banca Catalana seemed such a huge problem to be dealt with that its shares were distributed between a group of the 14 major banks. These banks decided to appoint Banco de Vizcaya as responsible for clearing the mess for one year. In exchange for this, Vizcaya was granted an option to buy all the shares of Catalana at the end of this period, which it did.

13. Rumasa was a holding made up of banks and industrial firms. Most of the bank loans were granted to firms belonging to the holding. The Bank of Spain had little information about these undertakings and believed that the credit concentration of these banks could lead them to trouble. When it asked for more information and audited accounting statements it was flatly turned down. The reaction was fast and harsh from the government and the shares of the holding were expropriated on the 23rd February 1983. This extreme decision faced wide opposition and the disapproval of the banking industry. However, at the same time, the leading banks saw the risk that the 17 banks of the former group could be nationalised or sold to foreign investors and this led them to reluctantly assume the costs of the transaction.

14. Dermine (1999) provides a good summary of the evolution of banking in Europe during those years, and Walter (2004) an extensive survey of global mergers and acquisitions in the financial industry.

15. Initially, the Spanish government and Bank of Spain planned to merge Vizcaya and Central on the first hand and Banco Bilbao and Hispano the other hand.

16. Savings banks initially had to reinvest 80 per cent of their earnings in social causes. The regulation lift favoured their expansion, first in their province of origin and then in the rest of Spain.
17. With the exception of Banco Popular.
18. EU Member State Perspective Report: Spain (http://www.library.pitt.edu/subject_guides/westeuropean/wwwes/mspr-sp.html).
19. According to a study published by Wharton, economies of scale represent between 1 and 5 per cent of gain in the context of a merger between two banks at a national level (Berger & Humphrey, 1994).
20. 'Claudio Boada chaired Banco Hispano Americano (BHA) between 1985 and June 1990. Some months later José María Amusátegui, his successor would initiate merger talks with Banco Central, then headed by Alfonso Escámez' according to Libertadditigal website (http://www.libertaddigital.com/php3/noticia.php3?cpn=1276286176).
21. In the preceding years two mergers have taken place that resulted in BBV, Bilbao and Vizcaya, and BCH, Central and Hispano.
22. Because of secret accounts discovered to exist in some tax havens.
23. Popular was also the first Spanish bank to have its accounts audited, to disclose its results quarterly, and to provide its shareholders with ample and reliable information. These practices would later be adopted by all of its peers. Today, Popular maintains the same strategy it designed 40 years ago, that which made the bank widely recognised for its profitability and exceptional efficiency.
24. Five entities representing more than 70 per cent of loans and deposits.
25. On average, this share is substantially higher than similar statistics for Latin America. Only private banks have been taken into account to prepare this figure, which explains why some countries such as Germany and Spain have such low values, given that a very significant portion of their banking industry belongs to non-private banks, such as savings banks.
26. Rolf Breuer, Chairman of the Supervisory Board of Deutsche Bank, confirmed in early 2007 that the Bundesbank would oppose any attempt to takeover of Deutsche Bank by a foreign bank. In similar vein Chief Executive Josef Ackermann responded the concerns that Deutsch Bank could become a takeover target and said 'with € 60 billion in market capitalisation, they have reached critical mass', and that 'the bank wants to remain German, with German headquarters', according to Market Watch website (http://www.marketwatch.com/) accessed on May 28th 2007.
27. The main drawback of Santander Consumer in the short term is the incapacity to build up brand equity. Indeed, customers outside of Spain do not realise they have been conceived a loan by Santander.

3 Generic Business Model in Spanish Retail Banks

1. 'A concept, model, or schematic idea' (The American Heritage Dictionary, 3rd Edition).
2. 'In social science, mental construct derived from observable reality although not conforming to it in detail because of deliberate simplification and exaggeration. It is not ideal in the sense that it is excellent, nor is it an average; it

is rather a logical ideal used to order reality by selecting and accentuating certain elements.' (Encyclopaedia Britannica: http://web.archive.org/web/20001016212033/www.britannica.com/).

3. As to discussions on more general aspects of strategic issues involving the banking industry in general, see such works as (Canals, 1990, 1991, 1993, 1996a, 1996b, 1996c, 1997).

4. With the retail banking, we mainly refer to (a) (1) through (3) and especially, (a) (1), and certainly to the exclusion of (b), set out below:
   Bank types:

   (a) **retail banking**, dealing directly with
       (1) individuals and small businesses;
       (2) business banking, providing services to mid-market business;
       (3) corporate banking, directed at large business entities; and
   (b) **investment banking**, relating to activities on the financial markets.

5. (Porter, 1996).

6. If we look to the UK and its 'Big Bang' that took place on 27th October 1986, we see another example of where modifications to the regulatory framework played a huge role in changing the banking and financial sectors. The Economist (2006: 85) remarks that heavy-handed regulations in the US drove international finance out of Wall Street. Those banks 'found a ready home in London where the Bank of England monitored foreign banks with a feather-light touch.'

7. Gual (n.d.) attributes the steeper competition in the Spanish banking industry to (1) the increase in the competitiveness in the raising of financial resources for banks (el 'mercado de pasivo'), (2) the mergers among banks, (4) restrictions on credits, (5) the performance of the industry, etc.

8. Kumbhakar and Lozano-Vivas (2005) support the idea that the deregulation contributed to the improvement in TFP (Total Factor Productivity) in European savings and commercial banks. Kumbhakar et al (2001) found for 1986–1995 Spanish savings banks experimented productivity growth thanks to deregulation.

9. 'The Basel II Framework describes more comprehensive measures and a minimum standard for capital adequacy that national regulatory authorities are now working to implement through domestic law-making and adoption procedures. It seeks to improve on the existing rules by aligning capital requirements under the regulations more closely to the underlying risks that banks face. In addition, the Basel II Framework is intended to promote a more forward-looking approach to capital supervision, one that encourages banks to identify the risks they may face, today and in the future, and to develop or improve their ability to manage those risks. As a result, it is intended to be more flexible and better able to evolve with advances in markets and risk management practices.' (Bank for International Settlements: http://www.bis.org/publ/bcbsca.htm).

10. 'Solvency II, the EU-initiated project which aims at creating a more risk-related solvency model, is a key priority for CEA and we are dedicating significant resources to ensure that the industry provides input to the key decision-makers. Beyond imposing quantitative solvency requirements looking at insurance risks, Solvency II considers the overall management of

risks and the structure of insurance supervision. Solvency II will encompass every aspect of insurance operations.' (The European Insurance and Reinsurance Federation: http://www.cea.assur.org/cea/v2.0/uk/solvency/ solvency.php).

11. As to IAS (International Accounting Standard) evolution, see the home page of UK's Institute of Chartered Accountant: http://www.icaew.co.uk/library/ index.cfm?AUB=TB2I_35395.

12. Daft and Weick (1984) regard organizations as interpretation systems. There are four interpretation modes and each one is determined by management's beliefs about the environment, and organizational 'intrusiveness' – degree at which proactive interaction with the environment is enacted.

13. JI Goirigolzarri, BBVA's Presidential COO, reminisced the keen need they felt to integrate and improve IT systems when Banco de Bilbao and Banco de Vizcaya merged in 1988.

14. Maudos and Pérez (2003: 11) argue that 'a slight widening of the absolute price-cost margin has occurred since 1999, followed by an upturn since then. This is similar to what we can see in the evolution of the accounting margins (financial, ordinary and exploitation). Nevertheless, since the reduction of marginal cost has been higher than that of price, the Lerner index has increased in the period analysed. Thus, the widening of absolute margins is compatible with the increase in market-share (relative margin)' (author's translation).

15. Fernández de Guevara, Maudos, and Pérez (2002 :2) cite the European Central Bank's April 2000 report that non-interest income has been the most dynamic component of European banks' income and represented 41 per cent of the total as early as in 1998.

16. Interview with Alfredo Sáenz, Santander's CEO, on 3rd July 2006 at the bank's headquarters in Santander.

17. Interview with José Ignacio Goirgolzarri, BBVA's presidential COO, on 16th April 2007 at the bank's headquarters in Madrid.

18. Lleweyllyn (2003: 64–65) argues that even smaller banks may benefit from scale economies of technology if the technology is applied to bank processes rather than institutions, and outsourcing can be managed efficiently.

19. Canals (2000) extensively discusses the reasons why firms should or should not grow. He subscribes to Paul Romer's consideration that 'the key factor in growth is not capital or raw materials, but soft assets such as knowledge, instructions, or ways of rearranging things.' (Canals, 2000: 3). We sustain that the growth process of the Spanish banking industry has also implied the growth in this regard.

20. We draw mainly on Gómez (2007).

21. An interview with Accenture's Domingo Mirón on 3rd October 2006.

22. (Moreno & Avendaño, 2006).

23. (Datamonitor, 2002).

24. (Moreno & Avendaño, 2006).

25. (Moreno & Avendaño, 2006).

26. Pita and Sastre (n.d.: 87) assert that 'in the case of Spanish banking institutions, there appears to be an improvement in some measures of efficiency and productivity which seem to be related to investment in information and communication technologies.'

27. (Botín, 2002).

28. (González, 2002).
29. Interestingly, the concept of the modular type was developed early on by Spanish automobile executive, López de Arriortúa, at GM first (and in the rest of the automotive industry later) in the 1990s.
30. Other references in this field include (Clark, Chew, & Fujimoto, 1987; Clark & Fujimoto, 1990, 1991a, 1991b; Clark & Fujimoto, 1992; Fujimoto, 2003, 2004a, 2004b, 2005; Fujimoto & Nobeoka, 2004; Nobeoka & Fujimoto, 2004).
31. Other references in this field include (Clark et al., 1987; Clark & Fujimoto, 1990, 1991a, 1991b; Clark & Fujimoto, 1992; Fujimoto, 2003, 2004a, 2004b, 2005; Fujimoto & Nobeoka, 2004; Nobeoka & Fujimoto, 2004).
32. Refer to García-Lombardía, Kase, and Pin (2006: 52) regarding the nature of PIF in viewing the present from the ideal future, in contrast to that of PA which represents the future as a time continuing from the present.
33. For example, high planning influence combined with low control influence leads to strategic planning style, whereas low planning influence combined with high control influence leads to financial control style.
34. According to Investopedia, 'a ratio used to calculate a bank's efficiency. Not all banks calculate the efficiency ratio the same way. We've seen the ratio calculated in all of the following ways:

    1. Non-interest expense, divided by total revenue, less interest expense
    2. Non-interest expense, divided by net interest income before provision for loan losses
    3. Non-interest expense, divided into revenue
    4. Operating expenses, divided by fee income, plus tax equivalent net interest income.

    For all versions of the ratio, an increase means the company is losing a larger percentage of its income to expenses. The lower it is, the better for the bank and its shareholders.

    However the ratio is calculated, its purpose is to evaluate the overhead structure of a financial institution. Banking is no different from any other mature industry - the surviving companies are those that keep costs down. The efficiency ratio gives us a measure of how effectively a bank is operating. Efficiency is usually a decent measure of profitability. Also referred to as the 'overhead burden' or 'overhead efficiency ratio'. (http://www.investopedia. com/terms/e/efficiencyratio.asp).
35. Increase in shareholder value = Increase in the market capitalisation + Dividends paid during the year + Other payments to shareholders − Disbursement for capital increase − Convertible bonds converted.
36. Required profitability (Ke) = Long-term treasury bond profitability + risk premium. Risk premium is 'the return in excess of the risk-free rate of return that an investment is expected to yield. An asset's risk premium is a form of compensation for investors who tolerate the extra risk − compared to that of a risk-free asset − in a given investment'.
37. Shareholder value created = Market cap × (Shareholder profitability − Ke) = Market cap × Increase in the shareholders' value/Market cap − Ke = Increase in the shareholders value − Market cap × Ke.
38. You may read Income instead of Revenue.

4 Santander's Business Model

1. In a personal opinion of the authors', (many banks and savings banks from) the banking industry in Spain has been 'santanderised' in their strategic approach and business models: PA approach, operational efficiency, etc.
2. Refer to Chapter 3 Business Model.
3. This strategy was far from being the most common. Indeed, Deutsche Bank, Société Générale and BNP-Paribas have expanded their scope of activity from retail to investment banking with relatively less success compared with Santander that has struck a nice balance between the concentration on its core business (retail banking) and other businesses.
4. Apart from the interviews conducted by the authors with bank experts and Santander's management, the sources of information are: (Botín, 2002; Cacho, 1990; Canals, 1990, 1991, 1993; ESADE Business School, 2006; Euromoney, 2005; Expansión, 2007b; Fernández de Guevara, Maudos, & Pérez, 2002; Fernández & Carabrias, 2006; Gallifa & Pérez, 2002; García-Lombardía, Kase, & Pin, 2006; Ghemawat, Ballarín, & Campa, 2005; Gómez Escorial, 2004; Guillen, 2006; Maudos & Pérez, 2003; Mirón, 2006; Moreno & Avendaño, 2006; Observatorio de Corporaciones Transnacionales, 2006; Planellas, 2006a, 2006b; Sáenz, 2005; Santander, 2003, 2004a, 2004b, 2005a, 2006a, 2006b; Saracho, 2006; Termes, 1991a, 1991b; Universia-Knowledge@ Wharton, 2005 ; Van Rooyen & Chiavarini, 2006a, 2006b; Wells, 2005).
5. (http://www.santander.com).
6. We emphasise the fact that the Spanish banking industry went through a strong deregulation process in the 1970s and 1980s, which ended up in banking crisis leading many banks to bankruptcy. The consolidation of banks by mergers and acquisitions was its outcome.
7. José Luis Leal, the former president of AEB (Asociación Española de Banca) points out that the efficiency ratio of Spanish banks is situated in the vicinity of 50 per cent, fourteen points better than the Eurozone banks' average estimated around 64 per cent (Foro de la Nueva Economía, 2006).
8. In the words of some IT specialists consulted by the authors. At any rate Banesto served as IT laboratory for Santander.
9. As mentioned in Table 4.4 regarding its vision (towards a global bank), 'Santander wants to consolidate itself as a large international financial group, which provides an increasingly high return to its shareholders and meets all the financial needs of its customers. In order to achieve this, it combines a strong presence in local markets with corporate policies and global capacities.'
10. According Wikipedia, 'a building society is a financial institution, owned by its members, that offers banking and other financial services, especially mortgage lending. The term building society first arose in the 19th century, in the United Kingdom, from working men's co-operative savings groups: by pooling savings, members could buy or build their own homes.

    In the UK today building societies actively compete with banks for most 'banking services' especially mortgage lending and deposit accounts. As of 2007 there are 60 building societies in the UK with total assets exceeding £305 billion.' (http://en.wikipedia.org/wiki/Building_society).

11. See Annex 1 Content Analysis for information on the 'belief system' expressed by the CEOs of Spanish banks compared with that of the CEOs of Japanese banks. The Annex also analyses the frequency of mentions of 'concepts' and their associations with other concepts.

12. On year end comparison the supercuenta increased Santander's market share by 50 per cent in 1989. It constituted a revolution in the Spanish banking where for the first time, deposits were remunerated. Competitors did not follow in the first six months, with the exception of Banesto which already had some serious financial difficulties. This initiative came at an opportune moment because it coincided with the merger of Banco Bilbao and Banco Vizcaya, who had the same customer portfolio for their strong implementation in the Basque country.

13. The success of the *superfondos* can be measured in terms of market share (+50 per cent) and turnover that increased eight-fold in three years.

14. The real estate balance increased by 42 per cent in the first year.

15. The *depósito supersatisfacción* was worth € 4.7 billon euros in 2002 in terms of deposits.

16. The *hipóteca superoportunidad* increased its balance by 33 per cent during the first year.

17. Also referred to as 'economic profit'. According to Investopiea 'A measure of a company's financial performance based on the residual wealth calculated by deducting cost of capital from its operating profit (adjusted for taxes on a cash basis). The formula for calculating EVA is Net Operating Profit After Taxes (NOPAT) – (Capital * Cost of Capital)' (http://www.investopedia.com/terms/e/eva.asp).

18. Berger and Mester (1997) argue that profit efficiency is not positively correlated with cost efficiency, and suggest that a bank with higher costs may compensate the cost inefficiency by higher revenues than its competitors. Maudos et al. (2002) conclude that 'market concentration is positively related to profit efficiency – the higher the concentration, the greater the market power, and therefore, higher profitability – and negatively with cost efficiency – banks operating in more concentrated markets are less pressured to control costs'; that 'higher risk – proxied by the standard deviation of return on assets – is positively related, as expected, to profit efficiency, and has no significant relationship with cost efficiency'; and that 'those banks that operate in markets with a higher network density – and therefore, have higher structural overheads – are less cost efficient.' Here cost and profit efficiencies relate to cost minimisation and profit maximisation.

19. *Investopedia* defines the efficiency ratio as 'a ratio used to calculate a bank's efficiency. Not all banks calculate the efficiency ratio the same way. We've seen the ratio calculated as all of the following:

    1. Non-interest expense divided by total revenue less interest expense
    2. Non-interest expense divided by net interest income before provision for loan losses
    3. Non-interest expense divided into revenue
    4. Operating expenses divided by fee income plus tax equivalent net interest income.

For all versions of the ratio, an increase means the company is losing a largerpercentage of its income to expenses. If it is getting lower, it is good for the bank and its shareholders.

However the ratio is calculated, its purpose is to evaluate the overhead structure of a financial institution. Banking is no different from any mature industry – the surviving companies are those that keep costs down. The efficiency ratio gives us a measure of how effectively a bank is operating. Efficiency is usually a decent measure of profitability. Also referred to as the 'overhead burden' or 'overhead efficiency ratio'. (http://www.investopedia.com/terms/e/efficiencyratio.asp).

20. See (Berger & Humphrey, 1994; Clark, 1996; Dermine, 1999; DeYoung & Whalen, 1994; Mitchell & Onvural, 1996; Odagiri, 1992; Tachibanaki & Haneda, 1999; Tachibanaki & Kitagawa, 1991; Tadesse, 2005; Tseng, 1999).
21. (Expansión, 2007b).
22. According to a piece of information to which we had access, Santander's top executives draw a line between mergers among equals and acquisitions. For them the mergers between equals in Europe are complicated since the merged banks need clear strategy and command line. They believe, however, in the feasibility of acquisitions in Europe, if the latter-mentioned condition is complied with.
23. The Center for International Development at Harvard University explains the 'Washington Consensus': 'John Williamson (an economist) originally coined the phrase in 1990 'to refer to the lowest common denominator of policy advice being addressed by the Washington-based institutions to Latin American countries as of 1989.' These policies were:

    - Fiscal discipline
    - A redirection of public expenditure priorities toward fields offering both high economic returns and the potential to improve income distribution, such as primary health care, primary education, and infrastructure
    - Tax reform (to lower marginal rates and broaden the tax base)
    - Interest rate liberalization
    - A competitive exchange rate
    - Trade liberalization
    - Liberalization of inflows of foreign direct investment
    - Privatization
    - Deregulation (to abolish barriers to entry and exit)
    - Secure property rights'

    (http://www.cid.harvard.edu/cidtrade/issues/washington.html).
24. http://es.wikipedia.org/wiki/Evo_Morales
    http://www.voltairenet.org/article132847.html
25. Spain, Portugal and UK also have their own Santander Consumer Division.
26. It has to be said that Santander has allocated some vast provisions in case of default of the Spanish consumers linked to a strong increase in the interest rates.
27. In an interview with the authors on 31st July 2006.
28. http://www.rinconcastellano.com/economia

29. 'An information silo is a management system incapable of reciprocal operation with other, related management systems. A bank's management system, for example, is considered a silo if it cannot exchange information with other related systems within its own organisation, or with the management systems of its customers, vendors or business partners. 'Information silo' is a pejorative expression that is useful for describing the absence of operational reciprocity.' (Wikipedia, http://en.wikipedia.org/wiki/Information_silo).
30. Interview held on 31st July 2006 at GS's office in Santander.

5   Business Model of BBVA – Banco Bilbao Vizcaya Argentaria

1. Much of the material, if not specifically cited, comes from (BBVA, 2005a, 2005b, 2005c, 2006; Caballero, 2004; Cacho, 1990; Goirigolzarri, 2006; Gómez Escorial, 2004; González, 2002; Nafría, 2004; Ontiveros & Valero, 2003; Pueyo, n.d.; Termes, 1991b, 1991a, 1995; Universia-Knowledge@ Wharton, ; Van Rooyen & Chiavarini, 2006; Zorrilla Salgador, 2006).
2. (http://www.bbva.com/TLBB/tlbb/jsp/ing/home/index.jsp).
3. (http://www.bbva.com/TLBB/tlbb/jsp/ing/conozca/areanego/index.jsp) accessed on May 20th 2007.
4. (http://www.bbva.com/TLBB/tlbb/jsp/ing/conozca/organi/index.jsp).
5. http://www.bbva.com/TLBB/tlbb/jsp/ing/conozca/areanego/index.jsp accessed on May 20th 2007.
6. BBVA's website (http://www.bbva.com/TLBB/tlbb/jsp/ing/conozca/expbbva/index.jsp) on corporate vision and culture highlights brand, corporate culture and reputation. '[T]hus consistency between what the group says (communication), how it behaves (corporate culture) and what it offers (products and services) helps to build and strengthen the corporate reputation.'
7. 'The value demonstrated by BBVA regarding Factor 1 (Growth and Earning) is far higher than Santander's and Sabadell's, while in Factor 2 (Internationalisation and Income) Santander showed more improvement than BBVA and Sabadell. This may mean that BBVA's focus is on growth and earning while Santander's is on internationalisation and income.'
8. See (Monden, 1983, 1985, 1998, 1999; Nagao, 1985; Shibakawa, 1985).
9. (Goirigolzarri, 2006).
10. Berger and Mester (1997) argues that profit efficiency is not positively correlated with cost efficiency and suggests that a bank with higher costs may compensate the cost inefficiency by higher revenues than its competitors. Maudos, Pastor, Pérez, and Quesada (2002) conclude that 'market concentration is positively related to profit efficiency – the higher the concentration, the greater the market power, and therefore, the higher profitability – and negatively with cost efficiency – banks operating in more concentrated markets are less pressured to control costs'; than 'higher risk – proxied by standard deviation of return on assets – is positively related, as expected, to profit efficiency, and has no significant relationship with cost efficiency,'; and that 'those banks operating in markets with a higher network

density – therefore, with higher structural overheads – are less cost efficient.' Here cost and profit efficiencies relate to cost minimisation and profit
maximisation.

11. Moody's and S&P's classification is as:

	Moody's	S&P
Investment Grade Ratings	Aaa	AAA
	Aa	AA
	A	A
	Baa	·BBB
Below Investment Grade ('Junk Bont')	Ba	BB
	B	B
	Caa	CCC
	Ca	C
	C	C
In Default		D

12. 'A coverage ratio encompasses many different types of financial ratios.
Typically, these kinds of ratios involve a comparison of assets and liabilities.
The better the assets cover the liabilities, the better off the company is.'
(Investopedia: http://www.investopedia.com/terms/c/coverageratio.asp).
13. (Administrative expenses + Amortisation) divided by (Ordinary revenues +
Net income from companies accounted for by the equity method) according to BBVA (BBVA, 2005b: 31).
14. 'This is the name of a group subsidiary in the immigrant segment that operates a chain of one-stop shops exclusively for such customers. It is designed
around an innovative value proposition with specific services associated
with the needs of new immigrants. These services cover all their financial
needs: money transfers, personal loans, insurance, performance bonds for
rental contracts, cards and mortgages. They also include non-financial services such as guidance, a job database, travel arrangements, available accom-
modation listings and grants, and so on. Dinero express is based on:

- specialisation and differentiation: a network exclusively for immigrants.
  The plan is to open 50 outlets in 2005 and have 100 by the end of 2006.
- convenience for immigrants: it provides a single place for satisfying
  basic financial and non-financial needs. Outlets are open from 10am to
  10pm including weekends and staff are all immigrants from different
  countries.
- accessible and fast: families in other countries can receive money in
  minutes and loan enquires are answered immediately.
- cost advantages: through promotions and product discounts.' (BBVA's
  website:http://www.bbva.com/TLBB/tlbb/jsp/ing/conozca/innova/dinexpr/
  index.jsp).

15. Due to the dearth of published information and data we principally make use of the information obtained through two survey interviews with industry specialists specifically conducted on the issue of IT systems at BBVA, but due to confidentiality reasons we are unable to disclose these sources.
16. (http://press.bbva.com/view_manager.html?root=25,27) accessed on May 29th 2007.
17. The advanced IT platform put in place by BBVA to centralise their operations across the world.

6 Conclusions and Discussions

1. They differ from mid-management change masters as conceived by Kanter (1983).
2. AEB, the Spanish Association of Banks.
3. 'Intermediate analytical profit and loss account item of banks and savings banks that is calculated by adding to the intermediation commission the net amount of other ordinary profits (coming mainly from the net commission for the rendering of financial services and the assumption of risks, as well as from the financial mediation and currency exchange differentials' according to Brokerhipotecario.com. (http://www.brokerhipotecario.com/html/glosariom-cen.php).
4. Our interview with Juan Arena, Bankinter's former CEO, in 2006 seems to point to an awareness of just such a choice, but he obviously prioritised profitability on the basis of selective products and customers.
5. An interview with the authors in April 16th 2007.
6. A notion expressed by executives including Santander's Alfredo Sáenz and BBVA's José Ignacio Goirigolzarri in interviews with the authors in 2006 and 2007.
7. 'The ability of a firm to alter the market price of a good or service. A firm with market power can raise price without losing all customers to competitors.' Wikipedia (http://en.wikipedia.org/wiki/Market_power).
8. For example, the authors' interview with Santander's Alfredo Sáenz in July 2006, in which the interviewee expressed his conviction that growth was inherent in the 'genes' of his bank.
9. See (Clark & Fujimoto, 1990; Fujimoto, 2003, 2004a, 2004b, 2005; Fujimoto & Nobeoka, 2004; Gulati & Eppinger, 1996; Nobeoka & Fujimoto, 2004; Okuno & Watanabe, 2006; Ulrich, 1995).
10. Investopedia (http://www.investopedia.com/terms/k/kpi.asp) defines term: A set of quantifiable measures that a company or industry uses to gauge or compare performance in terms of meeting their strategic and operational goals. KPIs vary between companies and industries, depending on their priorities or performance criteria. Also referred to as 'key success indicators (KSI)'.
11. As explained in Chapter 3, according to Webster's Third International Dictionary, 'an abstraction of features from empirical reality and their embodiment into a unified conceptual scheme of hypothetical validity.'
12. An appreciation expressed by the staff of both banking groups in our multiple survey interviews in 2005 and 2006.

Annex 1 – Content Analysis of Bank CEOs' Speeches

1. Leximancer Version 2.21 was used for the analysis.
2. A reproduction of Table 1.1.
3. For comparison, the speech summary of Mizuho Bank's CEO is also copied below. Words such as cost reduction, products, etc., stand out, while business model, growth, efficiency, etc., do not even appear.

Leximancer Document Summary

File: data/./mizuho ceo 2003.doc Document: S1 Summary Sample: Mizuho Bank is increasing its profitable assets by developing financial products and services according to customer segmentation, while other group companies are further strengthening their own expertise and strategic focuses as well as actively pursuing group synergies through stronger collaboration within the group. (TG_MIZUHO_CEO_2003_TG) Additionally, in order to accelerate cost structure reform through thoroughgoing corporate restructuring, we are implementing drastic management rationalization measures that include a significant decrease in the num- ber of employees and redundant offices ahead of schedule, as well as a reduction in the annual compensation of all senior executives and employees. (TG_MIZUHO_CEO_2003_TG) On another front, we achieved a dynamic rejuvenation of the organization by launching a job application system for branch general manager positions to encourage the development and advancement of young employees especially in their thirties, and by introducing an early retirement plan. (TG_ MIZUHO_CEO_2003_TG)

File: data/./mizuho ceo 2004.doc Document: S1 Summary Sample: The Mizuho Mileage Club, a new membership service, aims to expand and increase transactions with customers who have accounts with Mizuho Bank and encourage them to make Mizuho their main bank. (TG_MIZUHO_CEO_2004_TG) These initiatives will work to significantly strengthen the earning power of retail banking operations and fully realise the potential of our customer base, which is one of our most important resources. (TG_MIZUHO_CEO_2004_TG) In the corporate banking area, Mizuho Bank will improve its capability to provide financial solutions to meet the needs of SMEs and middle market cor- (TG_ MIZUHO_CEO_2004_TG)

File: data/./mizuho ceo 2005.doc Document: S1 Summary Sample: 3 Repayment of More Than Half of Public Funds With respect to the repayment of public funds, we have fully redeemed the outstanding Subordinated Bonds and repurchased part of the Preferred Stocks by steadily securing stable profits, enabling us to repay a total of •1,482.6 billion to date, which represents more than half of the initial amount of public funds. (TG_ MIZUHO_CEO_2005_TG) Even after making these repayments, our consolidated BIS Capital Adequacy Ratio as of March 31, 2005 was maintained at a high level of 11.91per cent, sufficient for securing our financial soundness. (TG_MIZUHO_CEO_2005_TG) Completion of Mizuho Bank's IT Systems Integration Along with these measures to enhance our financial strength, we have also moved forward with measures to reform our cost structure. (TG_MIZUHO_CEO_2005_TG)

4. Wikipedia explains Factor Analysis as follows:

   '**Factor analysis** is a statistical technique used to explain variability among observed random variables in terms of fewer unobserved random variables called **factors**. The observed variables are modelled as linear combinations of the factors, plus "error" terms.' (http://en.wikipedia.org/wiki/Factor_analysis)

5. Our interview with Alfredo Sáenz, the CEO of Santander on 31st July 2006.

Annex 2A – Japanese Banks: A Contrast to Spanish Banks

1. (Nihon Keizai Shimbun, 2007).

Annex 2B – Suruga Bank

1. Reproduced with the permission of Globis Corporation.
2. (Suruga Bank, 1995).
3. (Nihon Keizai Shimbun, 1987).
4. (Nihon Keizai Shimbun, 1987).
5. (Nihon Keizai Shimbun, 1984).
6. (Kodaira, 2003).
7. (Oya, 2001).
8. (Nikkie Kin'yu Shinbun, 2003).
9. (Oya, 2001).
10. (Furuki, 2003).
11. (Kodaira, 2003).
12. (Kodaira, 2003).
13. (Furuki, 2003).
14. (Kodaira, 2003).
15. (Furuki, 2003).
16. (Kodaira, 2003).
17. (Nomura Securities, 2004).
18. (Kodaira, 2003).
19. (Furuki, 2003).
20. (Kodaira, 2003).
21. (Nikkei Joho Strategy, 2000).
22. (Akiyama, 2002).
23. (Hanazawa, 1999).
24. (Hanazawa, 1999).
25. (Hanazawa, 1999).
26. (Hanazawa, 1999).
27. (Hanazawa, 1999).
28. (Hanazawa, 1999).
29. (Hanazawa, 1999).
30. (Hanazawa, 1999).
31. (Hanazawa, 1999).
32. (Kodaira, 2003).

33. (Oya, 2001).
34. (Nomura Securities, 2003).
35. (Nikkei Kin'yu Shinbun, 2003).
36. (Nikkei Kin'yu Shinbun, 2003).
37. (Tamura, Sasajima, & Kojima, 2003).
38. (Tamura et al., 2003).

Annex 3 – Banco Sabadell's Business Model

1. 'A concept, model, or schematic idea' (The American Heritage Dictionary, 3rd Edition).
2. 'In the social science, mental construct derived from observable reality although not conforming to it in detail because of deliberate simplification and exaggeration. It is not ideal in the sense that it is excellent, nor is it an average; it is rather a logical ideal used to order reality by selecting and accentuating certain elements.' (Encyclopaedia Britannica: http://web.archive.org/web/20001016212033/www.britannica.com/).
3. Investopedia (http://www.investopedia.com/terms/b/bancassurance.asp).
4. Basel II Loss Given Default (http://www.productprofitability.com/BaselIILoss GivenDefault.htm).

The Credit Risk Exposure Data requirements are:

Credit Exposure: represents the on or off balance sheet amount or market value of the underlying asset on the 'as at' date of the data extract in currency.

Gross Average Exposure (GAE): is the numeric average exposure (up to 1 year or maturity whichever is soonest) as calculated by the EAD Credit Risk Model.

Exposure At Default (EAD): a measure of forward exposure (in currency) as calculated by a Basel Credit Risk Model for the period of 1 year or until maturity whichever is soonest. This value is calculated taking account of the underlying asset, forward valuation, facility type and commitment details. This value does not take account of guarantees, collateral or security (i.e. ignores Credit Risk Mitigation Techniques with the exception of on-balance sheet netting where the effect of netting is included in EAD).

Effective Maturity: Is the contractual maturity of the facility/transaction which will be either:
> The maximum remaining time over which the Obligor could take to fully discharge its contractual obligation (principal, interest and fees) under a loan; or A weighted maturity taking account of any pre-determined amortisation schedule. The effective maturity will be used in the IRB Advanced approach therefore is only applicable to the 'Corporate' segment.

Loss Given Default (LGD): is a weighting that represents the proportion of EAD that will be lost if default occurs. It is derived within a Credit Risk Model by taking account of any collateral or security that applies to the transaction/facility and the degree of Subordination of a facility.

Probability of Default (PD) for the Corporate segment: the Probability of Default is calculated using the following steps:

Analyse the credit risk aspects of the counterparty; Map the counterparty to an internal risk grade which has an associated PD: and Determine the facility specific PD. This last step will gives a weighted Probability of Default for facilities that are subject to a guarantee or protected by a credit derivative. The weighting takes account of the PD of the guarantor or seller of the credit derivative.

Probability of Default (PD) for the 'Other' segment: is derived from a credit scoring process for a new customer and behavioral scoring for existing business. The resulting PD is mapped to an internal risk grade.

5. A technique used to estimate the probability of portfolio losses based on the statistical analysis of historical price trends and volatilities. (http://en.wikipedia.org/wiki/Loss_function).
6. a function that maps an event (technically an element of a sample space) onto a real number representing the economic cost or regret associated with the event.

Bibliography

Abdelal R, Bruner CM. 2005. European financial integration. Harvard Business School: Boston, MA

Aiken CB, Keller SP. 2007. The CEO's role in leading transformation. The McKinsey Quarterly www.mckinseyquarterly.com/article

Akiyama T. 2002. 2002 strategy: 43 CIOs interviewed (2002 nen senryaku: CIO 43 interview), *Nikkei Joho Strategy*: 26–37: Tokyo

Ansoff HI. 1991. Critique of Henry Mintzberg's 'The Design School: Reconsidering the basic premises of strategic management'. *Strategic Management Journal* **12**: 449–461

Anthony RN, Dearden J, Bedford NM. 1989. *Management Control Systems* (6th ed.). Irwin: Homewood, IL

Banco de España. 2005. Annual Report 2004: Madrid

Bankecon. 2002. Rethinking bank efficiency: when the cost/income efficiency ratio is inherently flawed: London

Barney J. 1991. Firm resources and sustained competitive advantage. *Journal of Management* **17**(1): 99–120

Barney JB. 2001. Resource-based theories of competitive advantage: A ten-year retrospective on the resource-based view. *Journal of Management*(27): 643–650

Barr PS, Stimpert JL, Huff AS. 1992. Cognitive change, strategic action, and organizational renewal. *smj*(13): 15–36

BBVA. 2005a. BBVA: a coherent strategy focussed on growth, *Merrill Lynch Banking & Insurance Conference, October 6th*: London

BBVA. 2005b. Growth, strategy and execution, *Goldman Sachs European Financials Conference, June 10th*: Marbella, Spain

BBVA. 2005c. Implementing a strategy to deliver profitable growth, *Morgan Stanley European Banks Conference, April 8th*

BBVA. 2006. Actividad y resultados 2005: Madrid

Beaujean M, Reiche D, Roxburgh C. 2005. How Europe's banks can win in tougher times. McKinsey Quarterly (http://www.mckinseyquarterly.com/article_page.aspx? ar=1620&L2=10&L3=51)

Berger AN, Humphrey DB. 1994. Bank scale economies, mergers, concentration, and efficiency: the US experience. The Wharton Financial Institutions Center: Philadelphia

Berger AN, Mester LJ. 1997. Inside the black box: what explains differences in the efficiencies of financial institutions?, *The Working Paper Series*. The Wharton Financial Institutions Center: Philadelphia, PA

Botín E. 2002. La experiencia internacional de Santander Central Hispano. *ICE*(April-May): 119–125

Brealey RA, Myers SC. 2000. *Principles of Corporate Finance* (Sixth ed.). McGraw-Hill: New York

Caballero G. 2004. De la jerarquía al mercado: la reforma financiera española desde la nueva economía institucional. *Papeles de Economía Española* **101**: 64–89

Cacho J. 1990. *Pedro Toledo: el Desafío*. Ediciones Temas de Hoy: Madrid

Canals J. 1990. *Estrategias del sector bancario en Europa : el reto de 1993* (1a. ed.). Editorial Ariel: Barcelona

Canals J. 1991. El sector bancario en Europa. IESE Technical note #0–392-015

Canals J. 1993. Banco Santander – Banco Popular 1993. IESE Case #0–394-062

Canals J. 1993. *Competitive Strategies in European Banking*. Oxford University Press: Oxford

Canals J. 1996. Bancos universales y bancos especializados: Los límites de la diversificación bancaria. IESE: Barcelona

Canals J. 1996a. Bancos universales y bancos especializados: Los límites de la diversificación bancaria. IESE: Barcelona

Canals J. 1996b. *Estrategias Financieras de la Empresa Española ante la Intergración Financiera Europea*. Instituto de Estudios Superiores de la Empresa, Universidad de Navarra: Barcelona, España

Canals J. 1996c. Universal banks: the need for corporate renewal, *Research Paper No. 321*: 26. IESE: Barcelona

Canals J. 1997. *Universal Banking: International Comparison and Theoretical Perspectives*. Oxford University Press: Oxford

Canals J. 2000. *Managing Corporate Growth*. Oxford University Press: New York

Caruana J. 2004. Antecedentes y perspectivas de la construcción del Mercad Único Europeo, *Estudios sobre la reforma de los mercados financieros europeos*: 43–53. La Fundación de Estudios Financieros: Madrid

Clapham SE, Schwenk CR. 1991. Self-serving attributions, managerial cognition, and company performance. *Strategic Management Journal* 12: 219–229

Clark JA. 1996. Economic cost, scale efficiency and competitive viability in banking. *Journal of Money, Credit & Banking* 28: 342–364

Clark KB, Chew WB, Fujimoto T. 1987. Product development in the world auto industry. *Brookings Papers on Economic Activity* 3: 729–781

Clark KB, Fujimoto T. 1990. The power of product integrity. *Harvard Business Review*(November-December): 107–118

Clark KB, Fujimoto T. 1991a. *Product Development Performance: Strategy, Organization, and Management in the World Auto Industry*. Harvard Business School Press: Boston, MA

Clark KB, Fujimoto T. 1991b. World-class manufacturing: Heavyweight product managers. *McKinsey Quarterly*(1): 42–60

Clark KB, Fujimoto T. 1992. Product development and competitiveness. *Journal of the Japanese and International Economies*(6): 101–143

Cocheo S. 2005. The efficiency ratio: how good a tool? *ABA Banking Journal* 97(6)

Collis DJ, Montgomery CA. 1997. *Corporate Strategy: Resources and the Scope of the Firm*. Irwin: Chicago

Collis DJ, Montgomery CA. 1998. *Corporate Strategy: A Resource-Based Approach*. Irwin McGraw-Hill: Boston, MA

Daft RL, Weick KE. 1984. Toward a model of organization as interpretation systems. *Academy of Management Review* 9(2): 284–295

Datamonitor. 2002. Core Systems in European Retail Banking:

Dermine J. 1999. The economics of bank mergers in the European Union: a review of the public policy, *INSEAD Working Paper No. 99/35/FIN*: Fontainebleau

Dermine J. 2002. Banking in Europe: past, present and future. In EC Bank (Ed.), *The Second ECB Central Banking Conference*: 31–118

DeYoung R, Whalen G. 1994. Banking industry consolidaiton: efficiency issues, *Conference of the Jerome Levy Economics Institute April 14th-16th* Office of the Comptroller of the Currency Bank Research Division: Washington, DC

Drucker PF. 1994. The theory of the business. *Harvard Business Review*(September-October): 95–107

Eisenhardt KM. 1989a. Building theories from case study research. *Academy of Management Review* **14**(4): 532–550

Eisenhardt KM. 1989b. Making fast strategic decisions in high-velocity environments. *Academy of Management Journal*

ESADE Business School. 2006. Caso Santander. Servicio de Estudios: Barcelona

Euromoney. 2005. The banks that got it right..: and how Citi got it wrong, *Awards for Excellence 2005*. Separata on Santander

European Commission. 2004. Commission sets priorities for catching up with Lisbon Agenda:

Expansión. 2007a. Más de 700 bancos europeos pueden desaparecer por la consolidación, *April 25th*: 30: Madrid

Expansión. 2007a. Más de 700 bancos europeos pueden desaparecer por la consolidación, *April 25th*: 30: Madrid

Expansión. 2007b. Santander se lanza a la mayor operación de compra de su historia, *April 26th*: 22: Madrid

Fernández de Guevara J, Maudos J, Pérez F. 2002. La evolución de la estructura de ingresos en el sector bancario español. Papeles de Economía Española (http://www.uv.es/~maudosj/publicaciones/PEE2002.pdf)

Fernández P, Carabias JM. 2007. Creación de valor para los accionistas de bancos españoles 1991–2006, http://ssrn.com/author=12696 IESE Business School: Madrid

Fernández P, Carabrias JM. 2006. Creación de valor para los accionistas del Banco Santander. IESE Business School: Madrid

Fernández P, Carabrias JM. 2006a. Creación de valor para los accionistas de BBVA. IESE Business School: Madrid

Fernández P, Carabrias JM. 2006b. Creación de valor para los accionistas del Banco Santander. IESE Business School: Madrid

Fernández P. 2002. *Valuation Methods and Shareholder Value Creation*. Academic Press: Amsterdam

Foro de la Nueva Economía. 2006. Leal Maldonado destaca que la banca española es notablemente más eficiente que la de la zona euro. In EdS Financiero (Ed.). www.foronuevaeconomia.com: Madrid

Franzosi R. 1998. Narrative analysis – or why (and how) sociologists should be interested in narrative. *Annual Review of Sociology* **24**(1): 517–555

Fujimoto T, Nobeoka K. 2004. At which industries is Japan good? Fit of architecture and organizational capability (Nihon no tokui sangyo towa nanika: architecure to soshiki noryoku no aisho), *RIETI Discussion Paper Series 04-J-040*. RIETI: Tokyo

Fujimoto T. 2003. *Capability-Building Competition: Why is Japan's Automotive Industry Competitive? (Noryoku kochiku kyoso: nihon no jidosha sangyo wa naze tsuyoinoka)*. Chuo Koron: Tokyo

Fujimoto T. 2004a. Brush up the manufacturing industry's integrating skills: Strengthen its strategy-designing capability (Seizogyo suriawaseryoku wo migake: senryaku kosoryoku mo kyoka), *Nihon Keizai Shimbun*: 16: January 12th: Tokyo

Fujimoto T. 2004b. *Japan's Manufacturing Philosophy (Nihon no mono zukuri tetsugaku)*. Nihon Keizai Shimbun: Tokyo

Fujimoto T. 2005. A notes on comparative advantage of architectures (Architecture no hikaku yui ni kansuru ichi kosatsu), *RIETI Discussion Paper Series*: 05-J-013. RIETI: Tokyo

Furuki K. 2003. Suruga Bank: the structural problem in Japan's banks highlighted thanks to the success of a regional bank in the lendings to private individuals over the competition with megabanks (Suruga Ginko: ote ginko kaomake no kojin senryaku ga shisa suru ginkogyo no kozo mondai), *Diamond*, 29 ed.: 46–47: Tokyo

Gallifa AM, Pérez J. 2002. La globalización del conflicto sindical BSCH-Banespa, *DP-146 0–402-020*. IESE Business School: Barcelona

García-Lombardía P, Kase K, Pin JR. 2006. Presidentes transformadores: claves del éxito de la banca española. *Harvard Deusto*(October): 44–54

Ghemawat P, Ballarín E, Campa JM. 2005. Santander's acquisition of Abbey: banking across borders. Harvard Business School: Boston, MA

Glasser BG, Strauss AL. 1967. *The Discovery of Grounded Theory: Strategies for Qualitative Research*. Aldine de Gruyter: New York

Goirigolzarri JI. 2006. Risk, return and growth: getting the balance right, *Merrill Lynch Euorpean Banking & Insurance Conference, October 5th*: London

Gómez Escorial A. 2004. Banca 15: los secretos de las fusiones (capítulos I to XVI), Cuadernos de Historia http://www.banca15.com/historia: Madrid

Gómez Muñoz CF. 2007. Los sistemas IT en el sector bancario. Unpublished paper: Madrid

González F. 2002. Las Empresas Multinacionales Españolas: El caso de BBVA en Latinoamérica. *ICE*(April-May): 127–132

González F. n.d. Determinants of bank market structure: efficiency and political economy variables, *Documento de Trabajo No. 219/2005*. Fundación de las Cajas de Ahorros

Goold M, Campbell A, Alexander M. 1994. *Corporate-Level Strategy: Creating Value in the Multibusiness Company*. John Wiley: New York

Goold M, Campbell A. 1987. *Strategies and Styles: The Role of the Centre in Managing Diversified Corporations*. Basil Blackwell: Oxford

Goold M. 1996. Design, learning and planning: A further observation on the design school debate. *CMR* **38**(4): 94–95

Grant RM. 2004. *Contemporary Strategy Analysis: Concepts, Techniques, Applications* (Fifth ed.). Blackwell Publishers: Oxford

Gual J. n.d. *La Competencia en el Sector Bancario Español*. Fundación BBVA: Bilbao

Guillen MF. 2006. *The Rise of Spanish Multinationals: European Business in the Global Economy*. Cambridge University Press: Cambridge

Gulati R, Eppinger SD. 1996. The coupling of product architecture and organizational structure decisions, *Massachusetts Institute of Technology Sloan School of Management Working Paper*. Massachusetts Institute of Technology: Boston, MA

Hamel G, Prahalad CK. 1989. Strategic intent. *Harvard Business Review* (May-June): 63–76

Hanazawa Y. 1999. Suruga Bank: on its way to become an ideal, low cost bank – part-time staff can cope with client relationships thanks to CRM (Suruga Ginko: kyukyoku no low cost ginko e – CRM de part shain demo eigyo kano na taisei wo jitsugen), *Nikkei Joho Strategy*: 186–191: Tokyo

Härle P. 2005. Negotiating better cross-border banking mergers in Europe: for those who take a tough stance, such mergers can be lucrative. McKinsey Quarterly(http://www.mckinseyquarterly.com/article_page.aspx?ar=1704& L2=10&L3=51)

Hart S, Banbury C. 1994. How strategy-making processes can make a difference. *smj* **15**: 251–269

Ishimura S. 2001. *The Steps for Multivariate Analysis with SPSS (SPSS ni yoru tahenryo data kaiseki no tejun)* (2nd ed.). Tokyo Tosho: Tokyo

Jameson DA. 2000. Telling the investment story: a narrative analysis of shareholder reports. *THe Journal of Business Communication* **37**(1): 7–38

Kagono T. 1988. *Soshiki Ninshikiron – Kigyo ni okeru Sozo to Kakushin no Kenyu (Organisational Cognition Theory – Research into the Creativity and Innovation in Enterprises)*. Chikura Shobo: Tokyo

Kametani S. 2007. The securitisation and the indirect financing – two strategic schemes for financial institutions, *Japan Academy of Management EU–Japan Comparative Study Group*: Tokyo

Kanter RM. 1983. *The Change Masters: Corporate Entrepreneurs at Work*. Unwin Hyman: London

Kase K, Kinoshita T. 2001. Development patterns of Spanish MNCs. In T Hara (Ed.), *EU Management (EU Keieishi)*: 245–275. Zeimu Keiri Kyokai: Tokyo

Kase K, Sáez F, Riquelme H. 2005. *Transformational CEOs: Leadership and Management Success in Japan*. Edward Elgar Publishing: Cheltenham, UK

Kawamoto Y. 2000. *The Profitability Revolution in the Banking Industry (Ginko shueki kakumei)*. Toyo Keizai Shimposha: Tokyo

Kawamoto Y. 2004. Fixing Japan's banking system. *The McKinsey Quarterly*(3): Ebsco

Kodaira K. 2003. Suruga Bank: a theme park of money (Suruga Ginko: okane no tema park), *Nikkkei Business*: 54–59: Tokyo

Krippendorff K. 1980. *Content Analysis: an Introduction to its Methodology*. Sage Publications: London

Kumbhakar SC, Lozano-Vivas A, Knox Lovell CA, Hasan I. 2001. The effects of deregulation on the performance of financial institution: the case of Spanish savings banks. *Journal of Money, Credit and Banking* **33**(1): 101–120

Kumbhakar SC, Lozano-Vivas A. 2005. Deregulation and productivity: the case of Spanish banks. *Journal of Regulatory Economics* **27**(3): 331–351

Lamfalussy A. 2001. The Chairman of the Committee of Wise Men opening comments to the Press on the release of the Committee's final report on the regulation of European securities markets, *February 15th*. European Commission: Brussels

Leximancer. 2005. Leximancer Manual (Version 2.2). http://www.leximancer.com/services.html

Llewellyn DT. 2003. Technology and the new economies of banking: a UK perspective. In M Balling, F Lierman, A Mullineux (Eds.), *Technology and Finance:*

Challenge for Financial Markets, Business Strategies and Policy Makers. Routledge: London

Lucas JL, Palacios JA. 2006. Telefónica. Instituto Internacional San Telmo: Seville

Lucas JL. 2006. El contenido de la política de empresa, *El Perfeccionamiento de la Alta Dirección*: 15–44. Instituto Internacional San Telmo: Sevilla

Mann L, Ball C. 1992. Information processing and decision making. The University of Melbourne, the Graduate School of Management

March JG, Simon HA. 1958. *Organizations*. Wiley: New York

March JG. 1978. Bounded Rationality, Ambiguity, and the Engineering of Choice. *The Bell Journal of Economics* 9(2): 587–608

Maudos J, Pastor JM, Pérez F, Quesada J. 2002. Cost and profit efficiency in European banks. *Journal of International Financial Markets, Institutions and Money* 12: 33–58

Maudos J, Pérez F. 2003. Competencia versus poder de mercado en la banca española. Instituto Valenciano de Investigaciones Económicas (Ivie)

McCune J. 2005. Efficiency ratios – what do they tell you? *ABA Banking Journal* 97(5): 8

McKinsey & Company, Copeland T, Koller T, Murrin J. 2000. *Valuation: Measuring and Managing the Value of Companies* (Third ed.). John Wiley & Sons

McKinsey & Company, Koller T, Goedhart M, Wessei D. 2005. *Valuation: Measuring and Managing the Value of Companies*. John Wiley & Sons: Hoboken, NJ

Meyer GE. 1993. *SPSS: A Minimalist Approach*. Harcourt Brace Jovanovich College Publishers: Fort Worth

Mintzberg H, Pascale RT, Goold M, Rumelt RP. 1996. The 'Honda Effect' revisted. *California Management Review* 38(4): 78–91

Mintzberg H, Quinn JB, Ghoshal S (Eds.). 1995. *The Strategy Process* (Revised European Edition ed.). Prentice Hall: London

Mintzberg H, Waters JA. 1985. Of strategies, deliberate and emergent. *Strategic Management Journal* 6: 257–272

Mintzberg H. 1973. Strategy making in three modes. *California Management Review* 16(4): 44–58

Mintzberg H. 1990a. Strategy formation: Schools of thoughts. In JW Fredrickson (Ed.), *Perspectives on Strategic Management*: 105–236. Harper & Row: New York

Mintzberg H. 1990b. The design school: Reconsidering the basic premises of strategic management. *Strategic Management Journal* 11: 171–195

Mintzberg H. 1990c. The manager's job: folklore and fact. *Harvard Business Review*(March-April): 17–29

Mintzberg H. 1991. Learning 1, planning 0: Reply to Igor Ansoff. *Strategic Management Journal* 12: 463–466

Mintzberg H. 1994. The fall and rise of strategic planning. *Harvard Business Review*(January-February): 107–114

Mintzberg H. 1996. Reply to Michael Goold. *CMR* 38(4): 96–99

Mirón D. 2006. La tecnología en el sector bancario español:

Mitchell K, Onvural NM. 1996. Economies of scale and scope at large commercial banks: evidence from the Fourier flexible function form. *Journal of Money, Credit & Banking* 28(2): 178–199

Monden Y. 1983. *Toyota Production System*. Industrial Engineering and Management Press, Institute of Industrial Engineers: Atlanta, GA

Monden Y. 1985. Japanese management control systems. In Y Monden, R Shibakawa, S Takayanagi, T Nagao (Eds.), *Innovations in Management: The Japanese Corporation*: 41–58. Industrial Engineering and Management Press: Atlanta, GA

Monden Y. 1998. *Toyota Production System* (Third ed.). Industrial Engineering & Management Press: Atlanta, GA

Monden Y. 1999. *Toyota Management System: Linking the Seven Key Function Areas*. Productivity Press, Incorporated

Moreno JP, Avendaño E. 2006. Situación Competitiva de la Banca Española en el Marco Internacional. Accenture

Nafría VM. 2004. La estrategia geográfica: más allá de Europa, *III Encuentro del Sector Bancario, IESE Business School*. BBVA: Madrid

Nagao T. 1985. Japanese organizational behavior. In Y Monden, R Shibakawa, S Takayanagi, T Nagao (Eds.), *Innovations in Management: The Japanese Corporation*: 23–40. Industrial Engineering and Management Press: Altanta, GA

Nakao M. n.d. Large-scale systems failure at Mizuho Financial Group – April 1st to the beginning of May 2005 (Mizuho Finacial Group dai kibo system shogai), http://shippai.jst.go.jp/: Tokyo

Nihon Keizai Shimbun. 1984. New situations in the financial industry (1) – new financial products (kin'yu shin jijo (jo) shin shohin kyosoryoku), *February 22nd*: 6: Tokyo

Nihon Keizai Shimbun. 2007. *Industry Maps (Gyokai chizu)*. Nihon Keizai Shimbun: Tokyo

Nikkei Joho Strategy. 2000. Suruga Bank: the president himself visits branches to stress the use of CRM system – the knowhow is shared by video (Shacho mizukara ga CRM teichaku ni eigyoten o homon – knowhow o video de kyoyu), *Nikkei Joho Strategy*: 30–31: Tokyo

Nikkei Kin'yu Shinbun. 2003. Suruga Bank's Mr Mitsuyoshi Okano – Lending to individuals to be increased to 70 per cent (Suruga ginko shacho Okano Mitsuyoshi-shi – kojin loan hiritsu 7 wari ni). http://telcom21.nikkei.co.jp/ nt21/service/CMN1000. Nihon Keizai Shimbun 1984, New situation in the financial industry (1). (Kinyu shin jijo): February 22nd: 6: Tokyo

Nihon Keizai Shimbun. 1987. Money chronicle of Shizuoka (Okane Fudoki Shizuoka), *February 19th*: 9: Tokyo

Nikkie Kin'yu Shinbun. 2003. Suruga Bank president Mr Mitsuyoshi Okano – lending to all the individual loan applicants (Suruga ginko shacho Okano Mitsuyoshi-shi – zen kojin kokyaku ni yoshin waku). http://telecom21.nikkei. co.jp/nt21/service/CMN1000: Tokyo

Nobeoka K, Fujimoto T. 2004. The organizational capability for the product development: the competitiveness of Japan's automobile industry (Seihin kaihatsu no soshiki noryoku: nihon jidosha kigyo no kokusai kyosoryoku), *RIETI Discussion Paper Series 04-J-039*. RIETI: Tokyo

Nomura Securities. 2003. Suruga Bank (8358), *Japanese Equity Research*: June 5th

Nomura Securities. 2004. Nomura Equity Research: Regional banks (chiho ginko gyokai). Nomura Securities: Tokyo

Nozaki H. 2006. *Banks: Study of Industry Series (Gyokai kenkyu series: ginko)*. Nihon Keizai Shimbun: Tokyo

Observatorio de Corporaciones Transnacionales. 2006. El sector de la banca, *Boletín*, Vol. 12: Cordoba/Madrid

Odagiri H. 1992. *Growth through Competition, Competition through Growth: Strategic Management and the Economy in Japan*. Oxford University Press: Oxford

Okuno M, Watanabe Y. 2006. The product architecture as a co-ordination system (Co-ordination system to shiteno seihin architecture), *RIETI Discussion Paper Series 06-J-007*. RIETI: Tokyo

Oliu J. 2006. Banco Sabadell, carácter emprendedor, *Encuentro del Sector Financiero*. Foro de la Nueva Economía: Madrid

Ontiveros E, Valero FJ. 2003. El sistema financiero español desde la Constitución. *Economía Industrial*(349–350): 111–126

Oya N. 2001. The top runner in the bank renewal: Mitsuyoshi Okano, Suruga Bank's president – continually providing unique, unimagined services, specialising in retail business, and sending new breath to the banking industry (Ginko kaikaku no top runner: Okano Mitsuyoshi, Suruga Ginko shacho – kiso tengai service wo yatsugibaya ni tenkai, retail ni tokka, kyutai izen no gyokai ni shinpu), *Nikkei Business*: 146–148: Tokyo

Palacios J. 2004. El sistema financiero y la Unión Europea, *VI Encuentro Internacional de Profesores de Política de Empresa*. Instituto Internacional San Telmo: Sevilla

Palacios JA, Alvarez L. 2003. Resultados de los fondos de inversión españoles: 1992–2001. *Análisis Financiero* **91**(Second Quarter)

Palacios JA. 2006. The leap of Spanish banks: 1987–2005. Unpublished manuscript: Madrid

Palacios JA. 2007. El Sistema Financiero y la Unión Europea. In JL Lucas (Ed.), *La Iniciativa y las Personas en la Empresa*. Instituto Internacional San Telmo: Seville

Pascale RT. 1988. The Honda effect. In JB Quinn, H Mintzberg, RM James (Eds.), *The Strategy Process: Concepts, Contexts, and Cases*: 105–113. Prentice-Hall International: Englewood Cliffs, NJ

Pascale RT. 1996. Reflections on Honda. *California Management Review* **38**(4): 112–117

Peek J, Rosengren ES. 2003. Unnatural selection: perverse incentives and the misallocation of credit in Japan, *NBER Working Paper No. 9643*. National Bureau of Economic Research

Picoult E. 2006. Basel II and economic risk, *IAFE Annual Meeting*: New York

Pita Barros P, Berglöf E, Fulghieri P, Gual J, Mayer C, Vives X. n.d. *Integration of European Banking: the Way Forward*. Fundación BBVA: Bilbao

Planellas M. 2006. Caso Santander, *Presentation*. ESADE Business School: Barcelona

Planellas M. 2006a. Caso Santander, *Presentation*. ESADE Business School: Barcelona

Planellas M. 2006b. Santander. ESADE Business School: Barcelona

Porter ME. 1987. From competitive advantage to corporate strategy. *Harvard Business Review*(May-June): 43–59

Porter ME. 1996. What is strategy. *Harvard Business Review*(November-December): 61–78

Pueyo J. n.d. Interlocking directorates in Spanish banking in the twentieth century. Universitat Pompeu Fabra: Barceloa

Rodríguez Inciarte M. 2006. Santander: Productos pan-europeos, banca minorista en Europa, *IESE Encuentro Sector Bancario*: Madrid

Sáenz A. 2005. Convención de Directivos, *March 1st* Santander: Madrid

Sáenz A. 2006. Santander: Developing sources of structural growth, *Merril Lynch Conference*: Madrid

Salas V, Saurina J. 2003. Deregulation, market power and risk behaviour in Spanish banks. *European Economic Review* **47**(6): 1061–1076

Santander. 2003. Informe anual 2002:

Santander. 2004a. A leading multi-local retail bank. Santander

Santander. 2004b. Informe anual 2003:

Santander. 2005a. Informe anual 2004:

Santander. 2005b. La tecnología en América: un modelo innovador: Barcelona

Santander. 2006a. Informe anual 2005:

Santander. 2006b. Modelo de negocio e internacionalización, *Foro de la Nueva Economía*: Madrid

Santander. 2007. Informe Anual 2006: Madrid

Saracho E. 2006. El panorama bancario europeo, *Encuentro del Sector Financiero. Foro de la Nueva Economía*: Madrid

Shibakawa R. 1985. Management strategies of Japanese companies. In Y Monden, R Shibakawa, S Takayanagi, T Nagao (Eds.), *Innovations in Management*: 13–22. Industrial Engineering and Management Press: Atlanta, GA

Smith A, Grech M, Horberry T. 2002. Application of the Leximancer text analysis systems to human factors research. Key Center for Human Factors and Applied Cognitive Psychology, The University of Queensland: Queensland, Australia

Suruga Bank. 1995. A Hundred Years' Navigation: 1895–1995 (Hyakunen kokai): Mishima

Tachibanaki T, Haneda A. 1999. Merger effects of city banks (Toshi ginko no gappei koka). *Financial Review*(52): 139–176

Tachibanaki T, Kitagawa H. 1991. Economies of scope and shareholding of banks in Japan. *Journal of the Japanese and International Economies* 5(3): 261–281

Tadesse S. 2005. Consolidation, scale economies and technological change in Japanese banking, *William Davidson Institute Working Paper Number 747*. The University of Michigan Business School

Tamura S, Sasajima K, Kojima R. 2003. UBS Investment Research: review of regional banks' performance in March-September semester 2003 (2003nen 9 gatsu chukanki chigin kessan review). UBS: Tokyo

Termes R. 1991a. *Desde la Banca: Tres Décadas de Vida Económica Española*. Rialp: Madrid

Termes R. 1991b. *Desde la Banca: Tres Décadas de Vida Económica Española*. Rialp: Madrid

Termes R. 1995. Los últimos años del sistema bancario español, *Sistema Financiero y Economía Española: 1984–1994*: 186–220. Asesores Bursátiles: Madrid

The Basel Committee on Banking Supervision. 2004. Basel II: International Convergence of Capital Measurement and Capital Standards: a Revised Framework. http://www.bis.org/publ/bcbs107.htm

The Economist. 2006. Capital city: London as a financial centre, *October 21st*: 85–88: London

Tikkanen H, Lamberg J-A, Parvinen P, Kallunki J-P. 2005. Managerial cognition, action and the business model of the firm. *Management Decision* **43**(6): 789–809

Tseng KC. 1999. Bank scale and scope economies in California. *American Business Review* **17**(1): 79–85

Ulrich D, Barney JB. 1984. Perspectives in organizations: Resource, dependence, efficiency, and population. *Academy of Management Review* **9**(3): 471–481

Ulrich D, Smallwood N. 2004. Capitalizing on capabilities. *Harvard Business Review*(June): 119–204

Ulrich K. 1995. The role of product architecture in the manufacturing firm. *Research Policy* **24**: 419–440

Universia-Knowledge@Wharton. 2005. Spain's banking armada: http://wharton.universia.net/index.cfm?fa=viewArticle&id=958&language=english&specialId= Wharton School

Uriarte PL. 1994. Las fuerzas del cambio en la banca. *Boletín de Estudios Económicos* **XLIX**(152): 303–322

Valero y Vicente A, Lucas Tomás JL. 2005. *Política de Empresa: El Gobierno de la Empresa de Negocios* (Sixth ed.). Ediciones Universidad de Navarra: Pamplona

Van Rooyen G, Chiavarini S. 2006. Spanish Banks, *Q-Series, July 11th*. UBS

Van Rooyen G, Chiavarini S. 2006a. Santander, *Global Equity Research, Feb. 8th*. UBS

Van Rooyen G, Chiavarini S. 2006b. Santander, *Global Equity Research, July 27th*. UBS

Vilar P. 1977. *Brief History of Spain* (RB Tate, Trans.). Elsevier: Amsterdam

Walter I. 2004. *Mergers and Acquisitions in Banking and Finance*. Oxford University Press: Oxford

Weick KE. 1979. Cognitive process in organization. In BM Staw (Ed.), *Research in Organizational Behavior*, Vol. 1: 41–74. JAI Press: Greenwich, Conn.

Wells T. 2005. Santander is coming to town: the acquisition of Abbey National by Santander, *305–512-1*. Cass Business School: London

Yasuda R. 2006. *Future Evolution of Japanese Banks (Nihon no ginko shinka eno kyoso senryaku)*. Toyo Keizai Shimposha: Tokyo

Zorrilla Salgador JP. 2006. El desarrollo y expansionismo de la banca española en el mundo actual. *Entelequia*(1): 39–46

Zúñiga-Vicente JA, de la Fuente-Sabaté JM, Rodríguez-Puerta J. 2004. Study of industry evolution in the face of major environmental disturbances: group and firm strategies behaviour of Spanish banks, 1983–1997. *British Journal of Management* **15**: 219–245

Index